MIDNIGHT SUN

by Ben Towle

First Printing: December 2007
ISBN 978-1-59362-088-2

Midnight Sun, Published by SLG Publishing, P.O. Box 26427, San Jose, CA 95159. *Midnight Sun* is ™ and © Ben Towle, all rights reserved. No part of this publication may be reproduced without permission of Ben Towle and SLG Publishing, except for purposes of review. Printed in Canada.

Photographs: Library of Congress, Prints and Photographs Division, LC-USZ62-20262 & LC-USZ62-121520

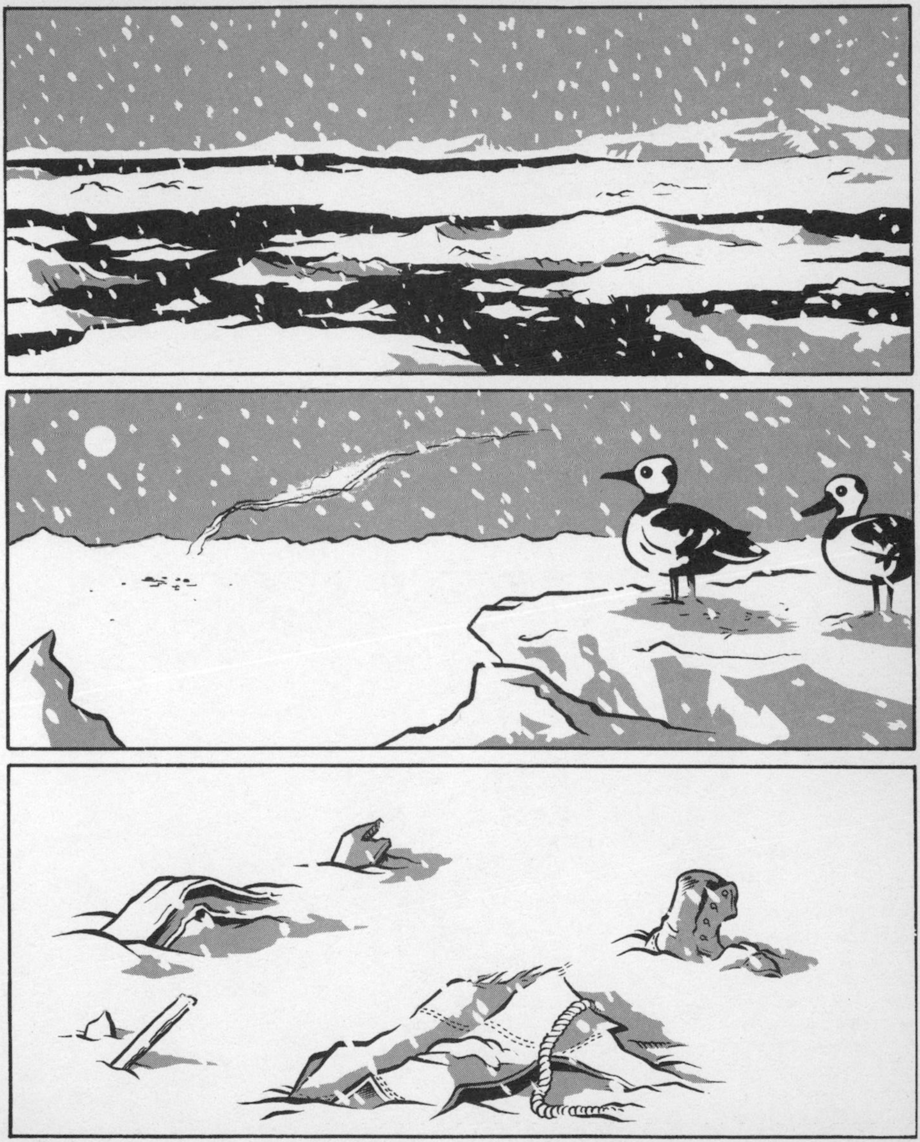

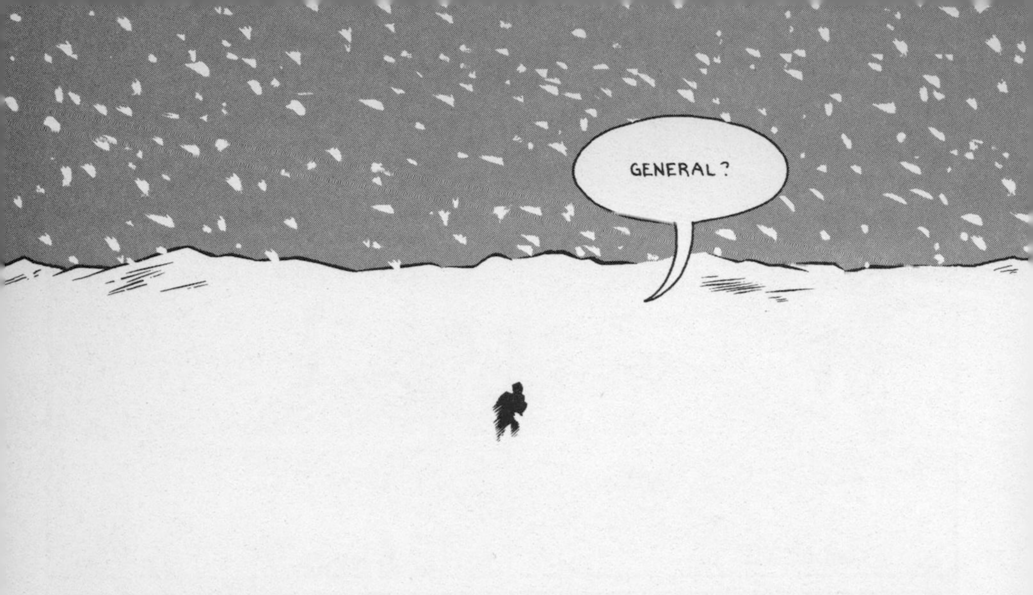
GENERAL?

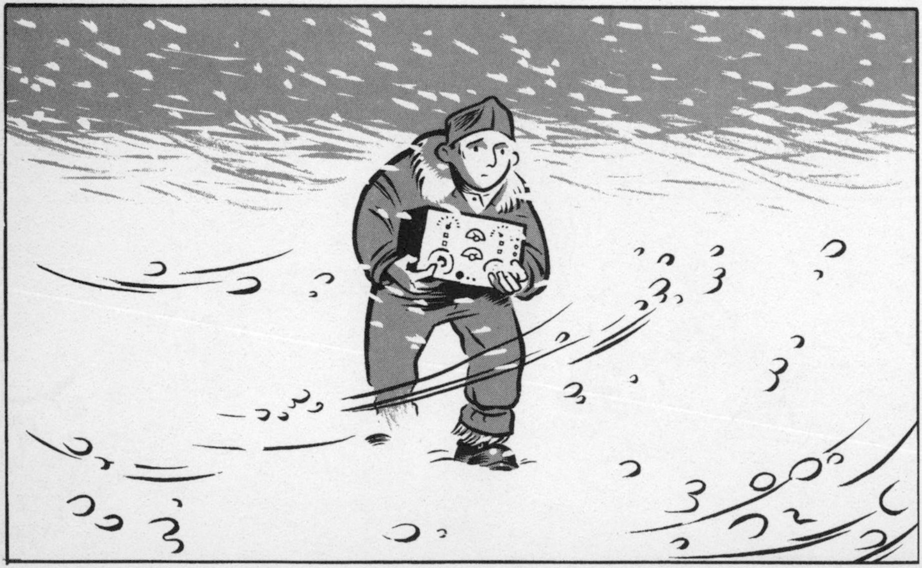

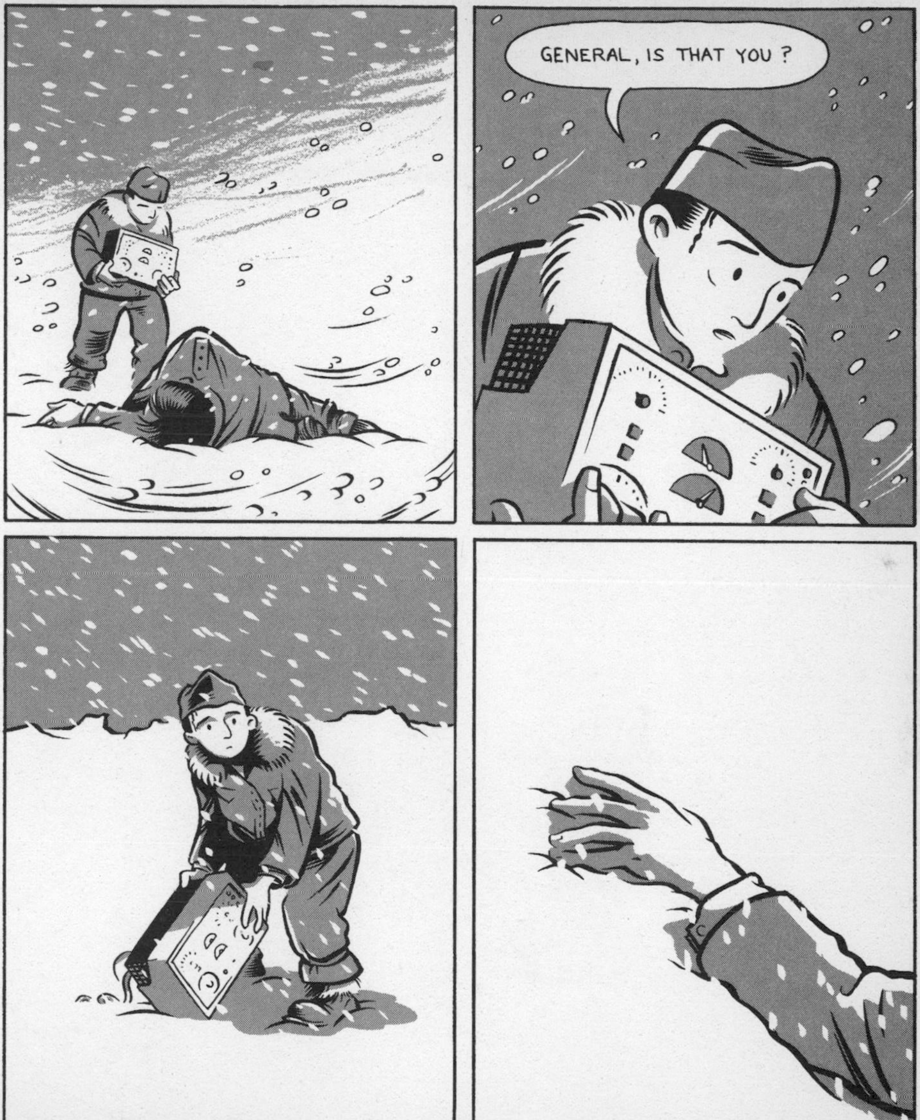
GENERAL, IS THAT YOU ?

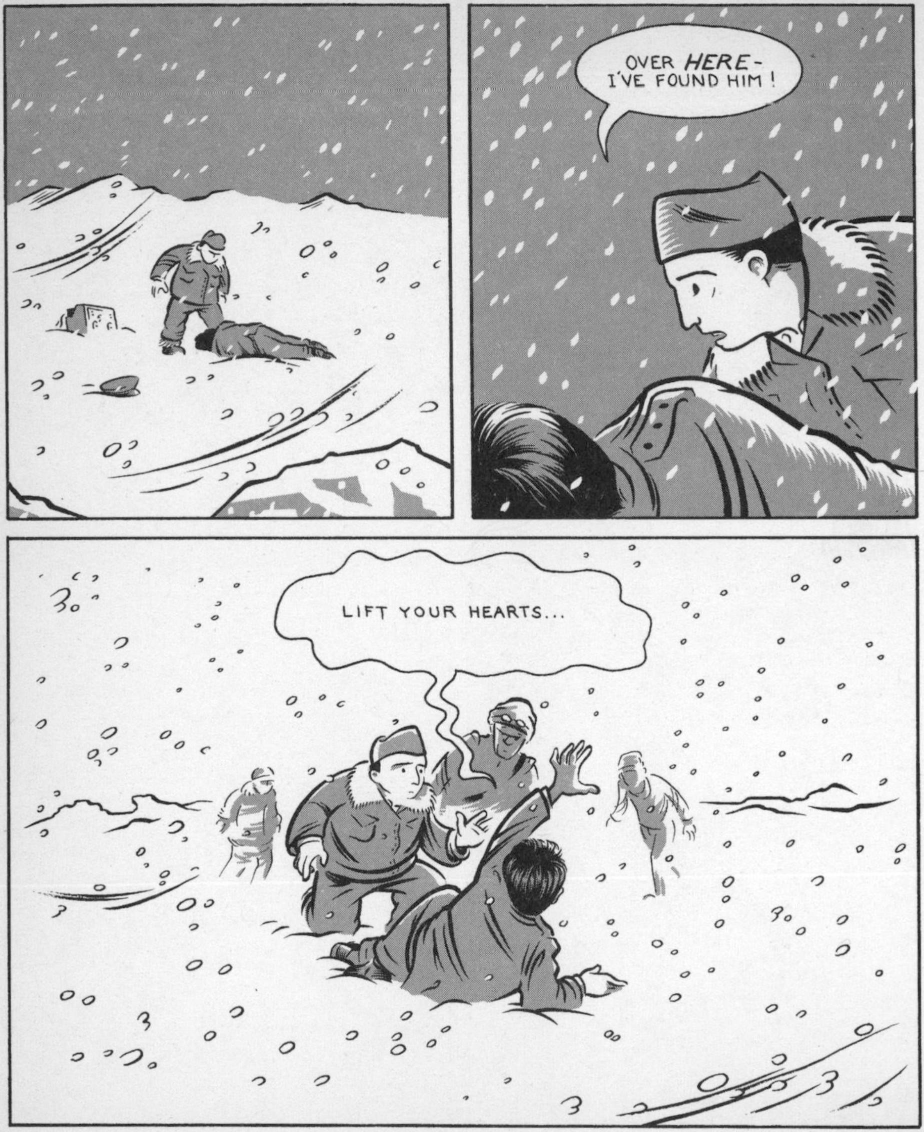
OVER HERE-
I'VE FOUND HIM!
LIFT YOUR HEARTS...

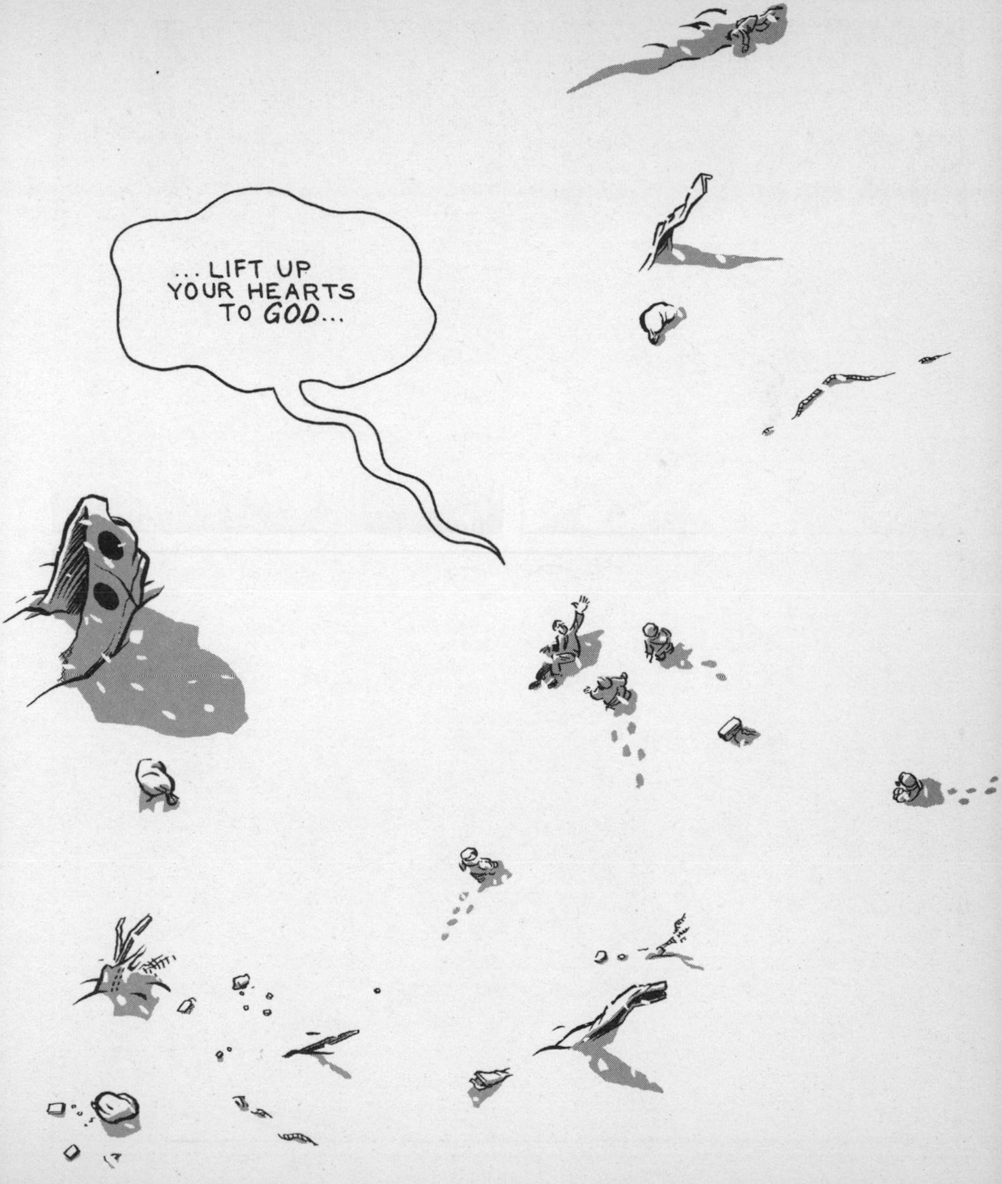
...LIFT UP YOUR HEARTS TO GOD...

I

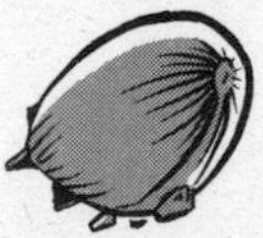

Stranded

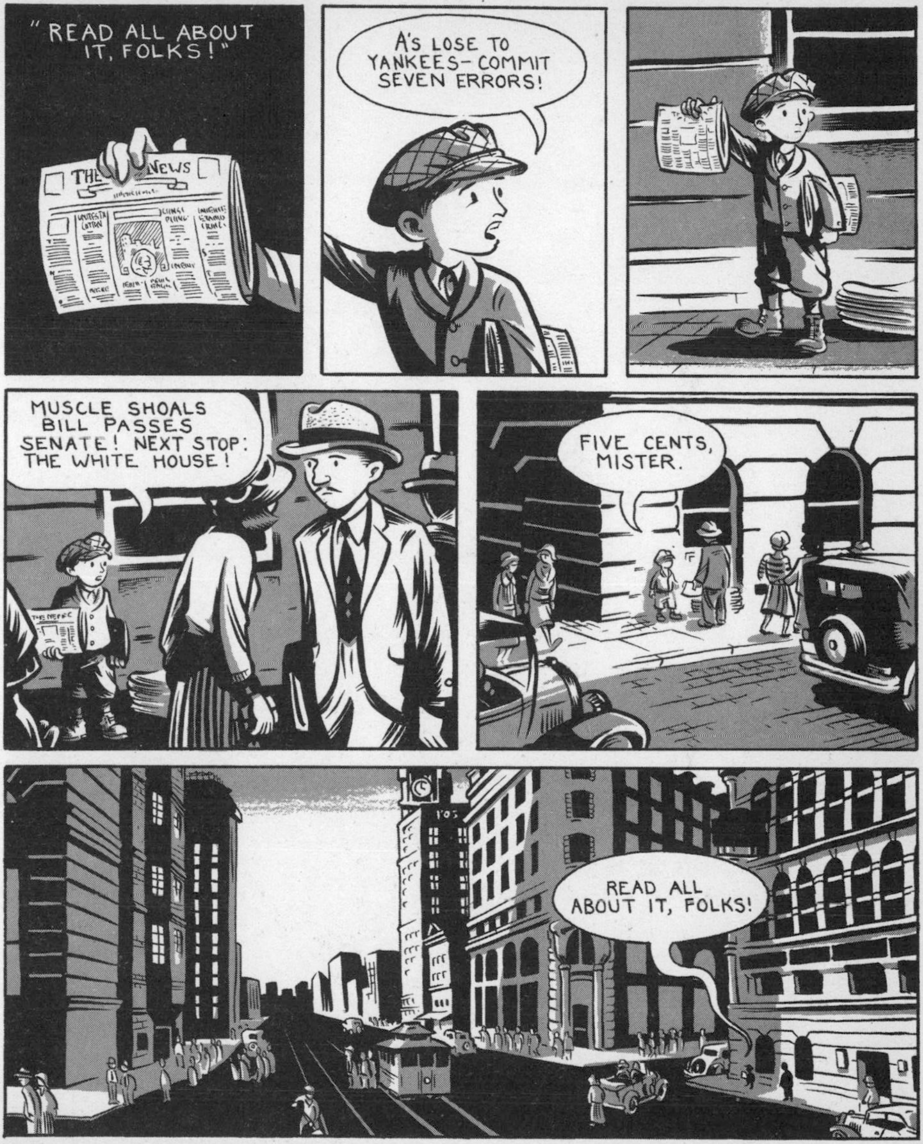
"READ ALL ABOUT IT, FOLKS!"
A'S LOSE TO YANKEES— COMMIT SEVEN ERRORS!
MUSCLE SHOALS BILL PASSES SENATE! NEXT STOP: THE WHITE HOUSE!
FIVE CENTS, MISTER.
READ ALL ABOUT IT, FOLKS!

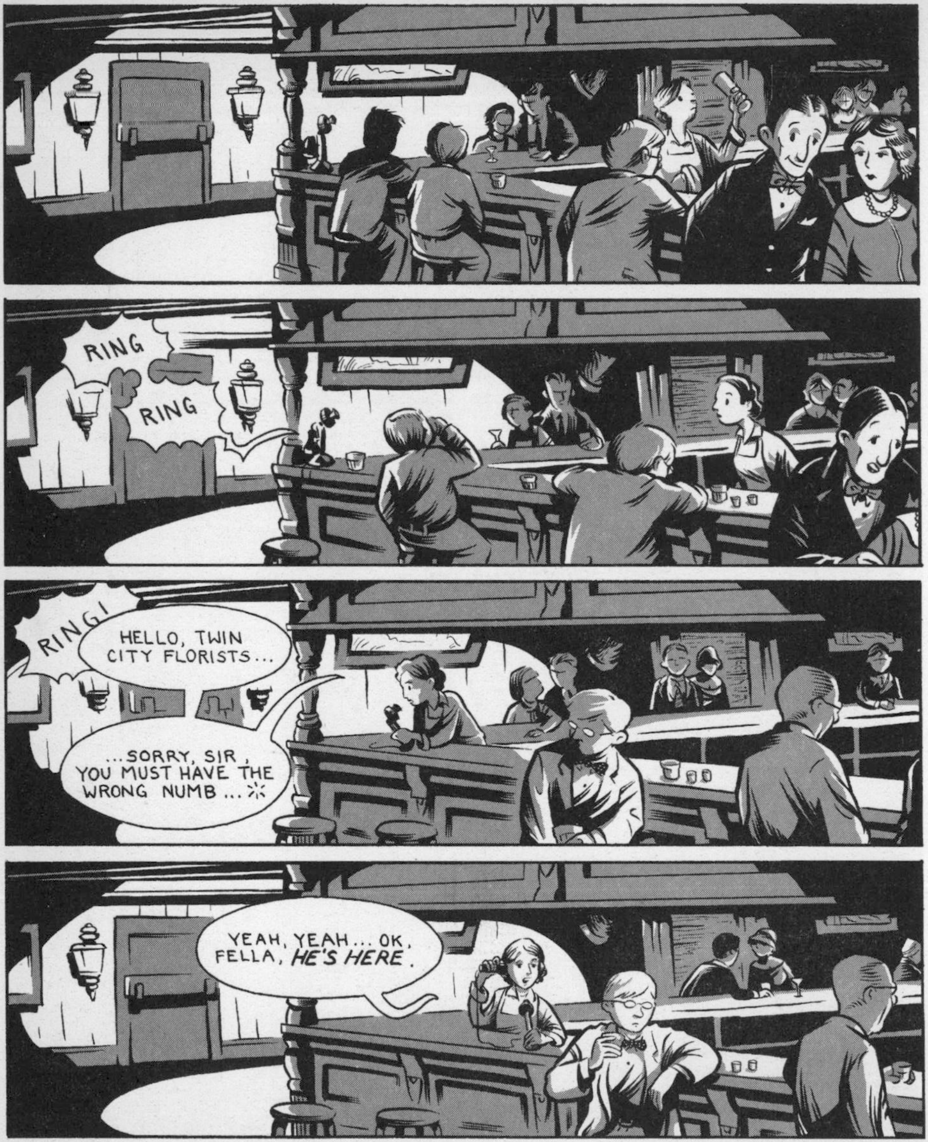
RING
RING
RING!
HELLO, TWIN CITY FLORISTS...
...SORRY, SIR, YOU MUST HAVE THE WRONG NUMB...
YEAH, YEAH... OK, FELLA, *HE'S HERE*.

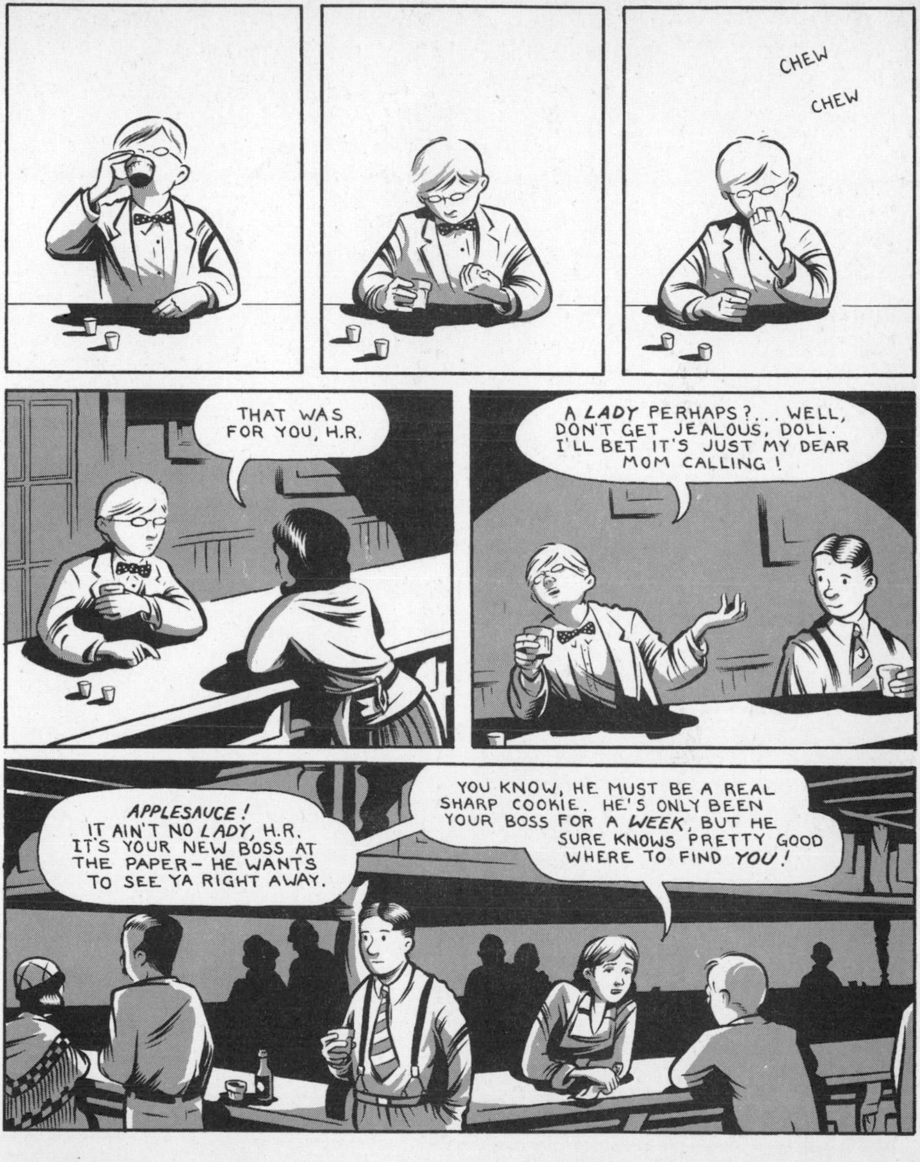
CHEW
CHEW
THAT WAS FOR YOU, H.R.
A *LADY* PERHAPS?... WELL, DON'T GET JEALOUS, DOLL. I'LL BET IT'S JUST MY DEAR MOM CALLING!
APPLESAUCE! IT AIN'T NO *LADY*, H.R. IT'S YOUR NEW BOSS AT THE PAPER– HE WANTS TO SEE YA RIGHT AWAY.
YOU KNOW, HE MUST BE A REAL SHARP COOKIE. HE'S ONLY BEEN YOUR BOSS FOR A *WEEK*, BUT HE SURE KNOWS PRETTY GOOD WHERE TO FIND *YOU*!

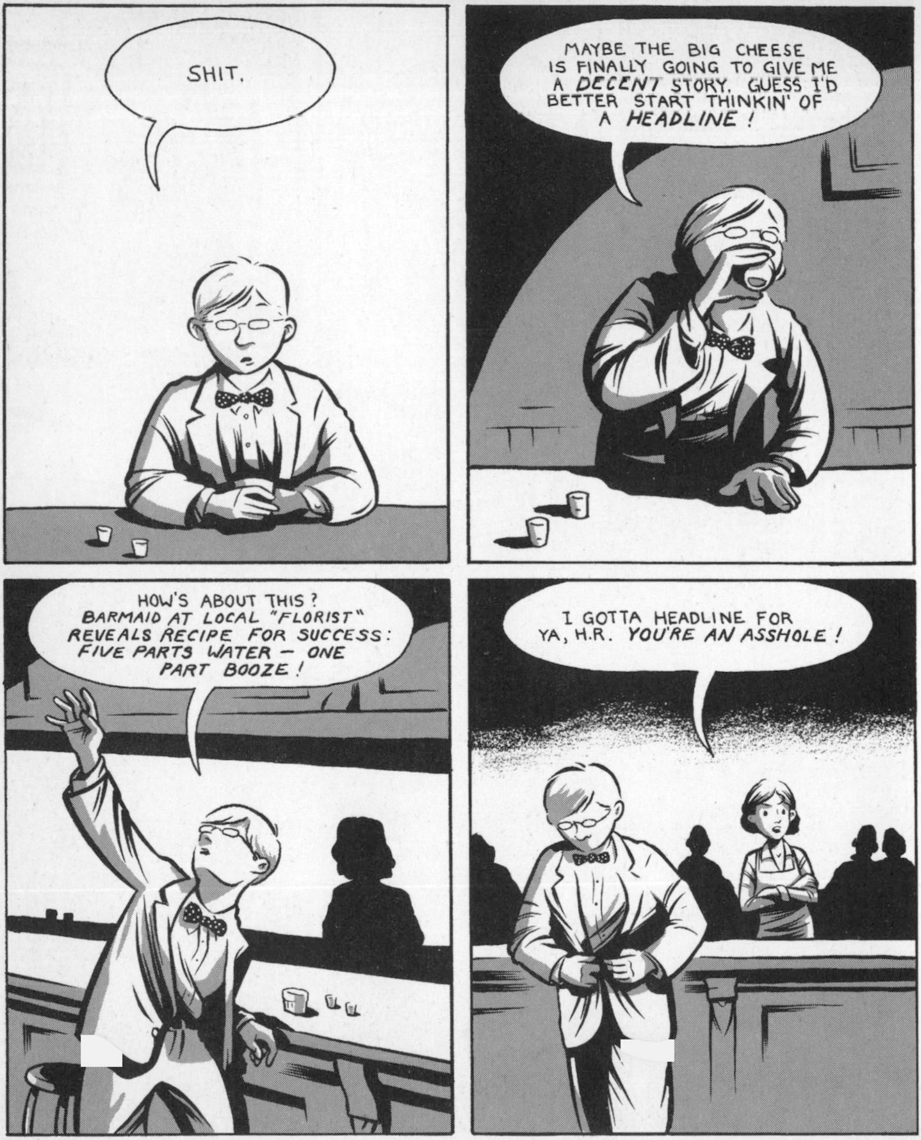
SHIT.
MAYBE THE BIG CHEESE IS FINALLY GOING TO GIVE ME A DECENT STORY. GUESS I'D BETTER START THINKIN' OF A HEADLINE !
HOW'S ABOUT THIS ? BARMAID AT LOCAL "FLORIST" REVEALS RECIPE FOR SUCCESS: FIVE PARTS WATER – ONE PART BOOZE !
I GOTTA HEADLINE FOR YA, H.R. YOU'RE AN ASSHOLE !

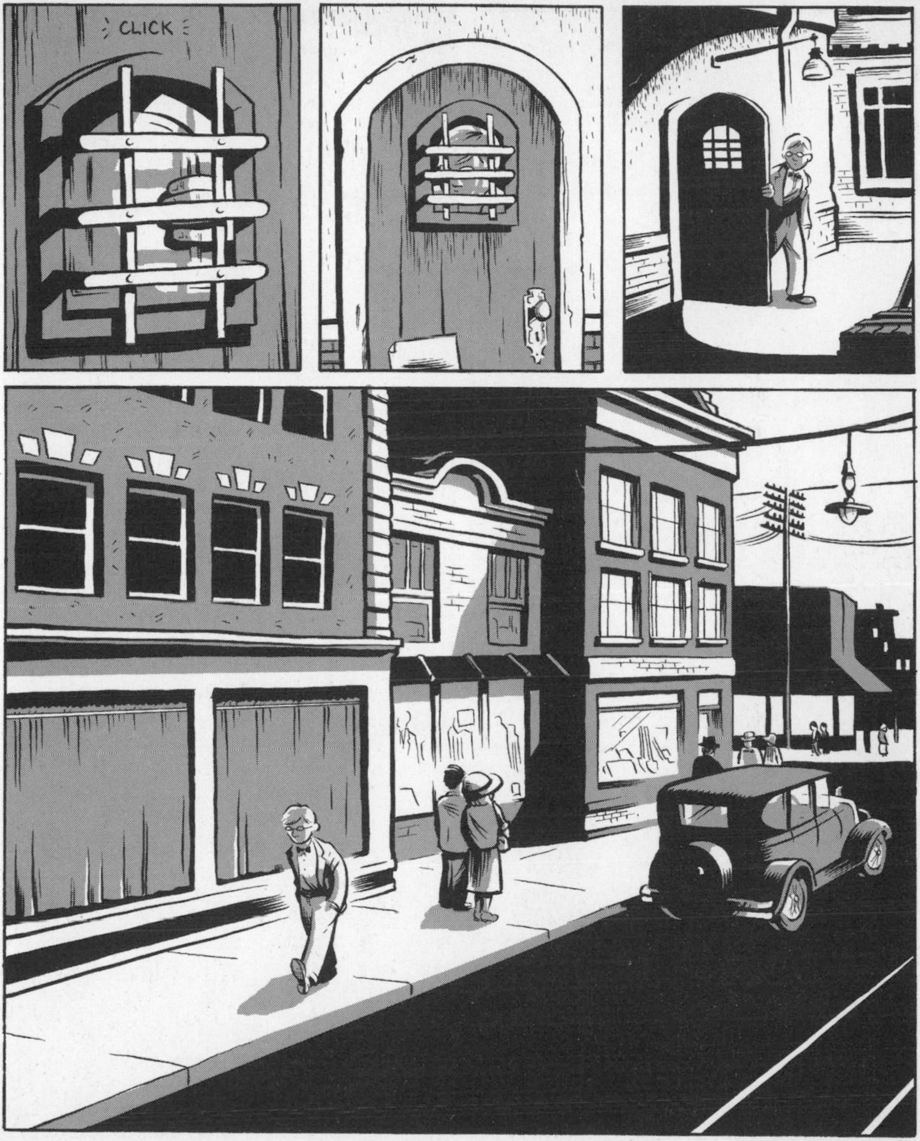
CLICK

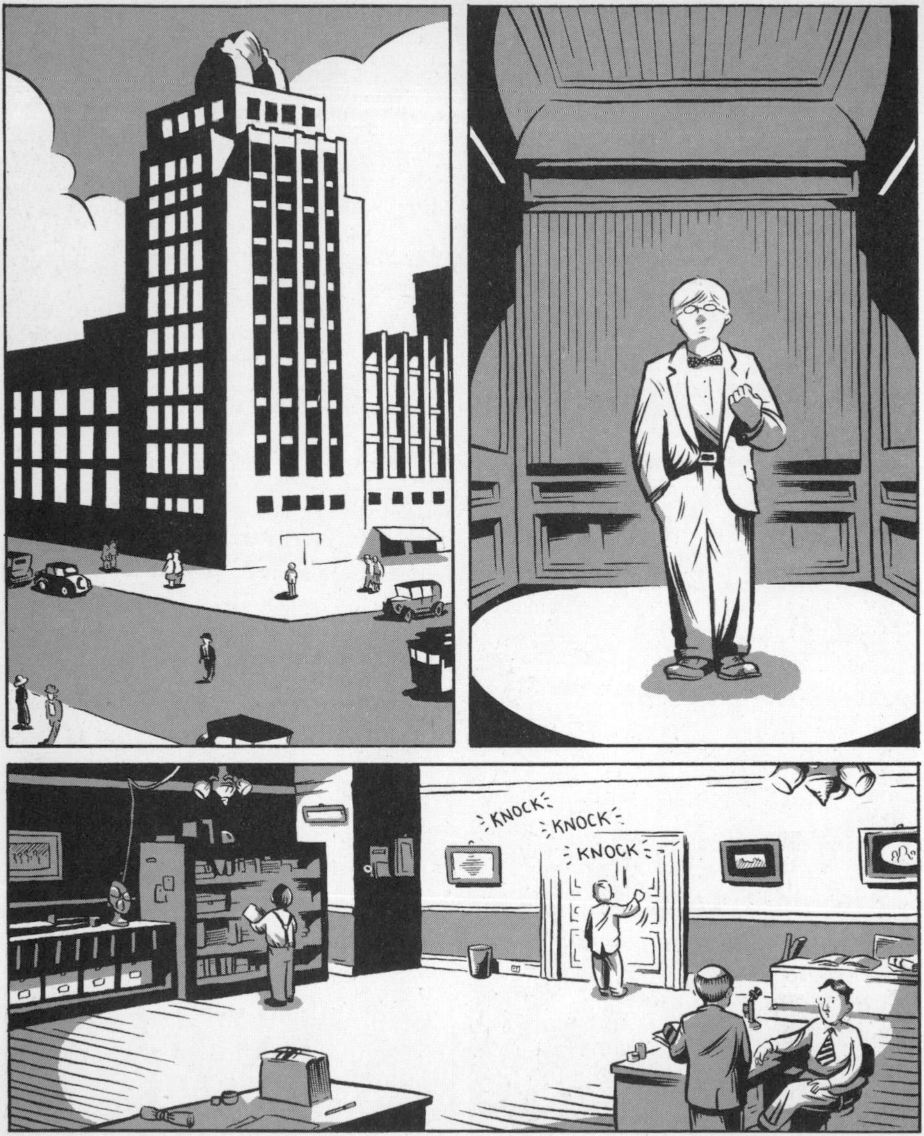
KNOCK
KNOCK
KNOCK

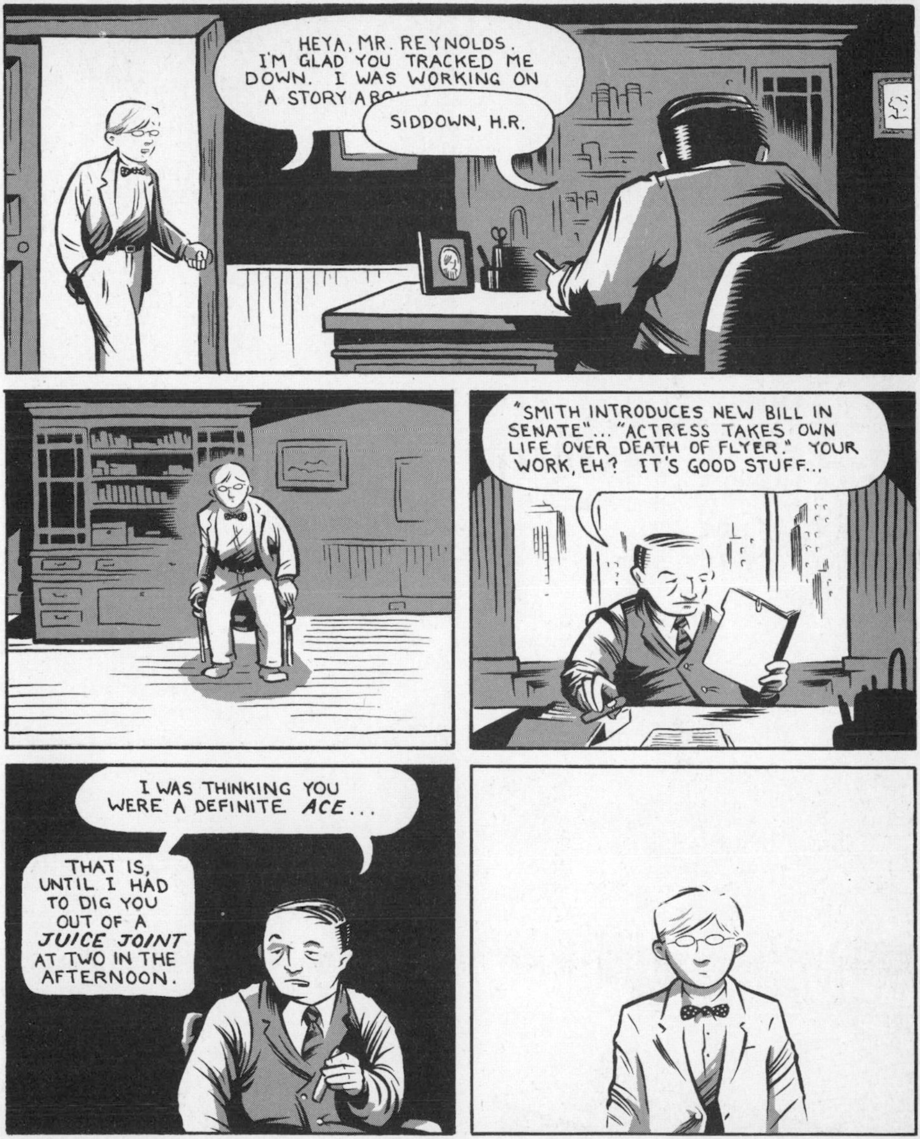
HEYA, MR. REYNOLDS. I'M GLAD YOU TRACKED ME DOWN. I WAS WORKING ON A STORY ABO
SIDDOWN, H.R.
"SMITH INTRODUCES NEW BILL IN SENATE"... "ACTRESS TAKES OWN LIFE OVER DEATH OF FLYER." YOUR WORK, EH? IT'S GOOD STUFF...
I WAS THINKING YOU WERE A DEFINITE *ACE*...
THAT IS, UNTIL I HAD TO DIG YOU OUT OF A ***JUICE JOINT*** AT TWO IN THE AFTERNOON.

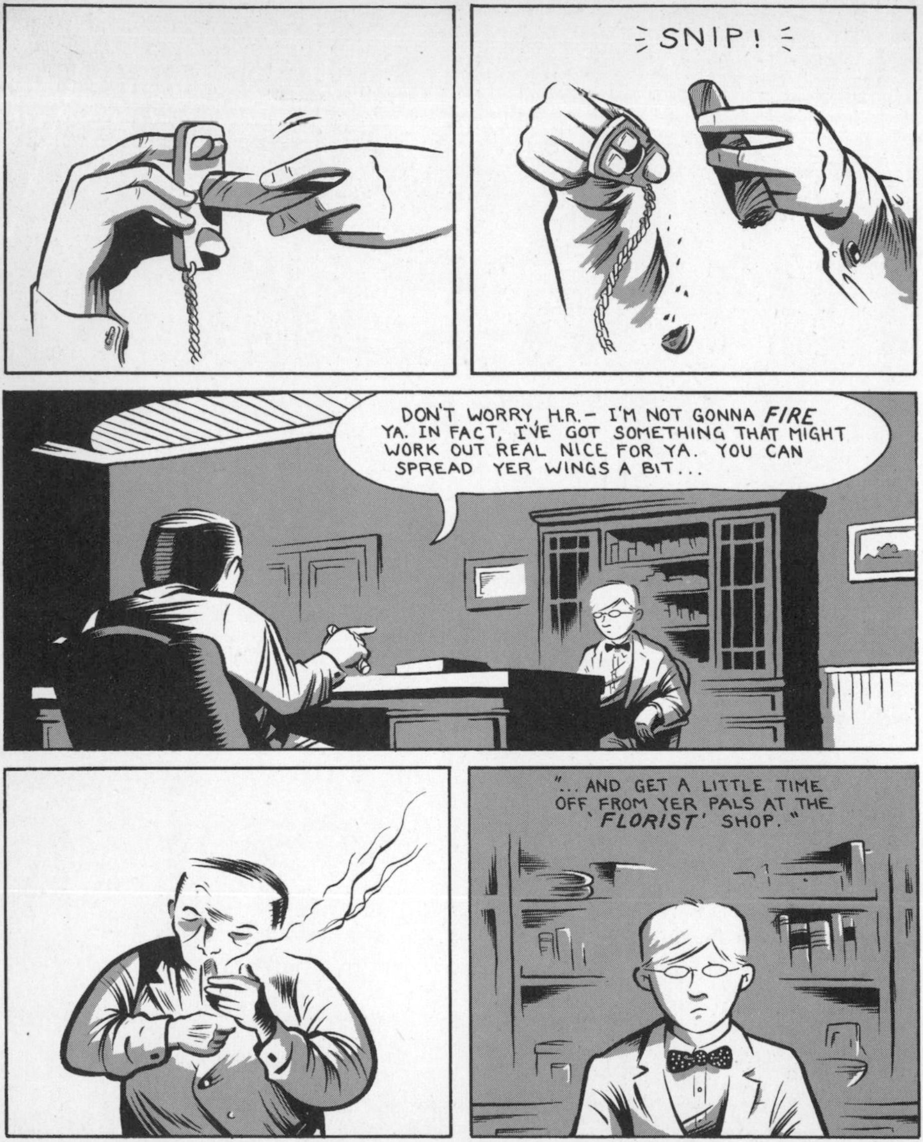
SNIP!
DON'T WORRY, H.R.– I'M NOT GONNA FIRE YA. IN FACT, I'VE GOT SOMETHING THAT MIGHT WORK OUT REAL NICE FOR YA. YOU CAN SPREAD YER WINGS A BIT...
"... AND GET A LITTLE TIME OFF FROM YER PALS AT THE 'FLORIST' SHOP."

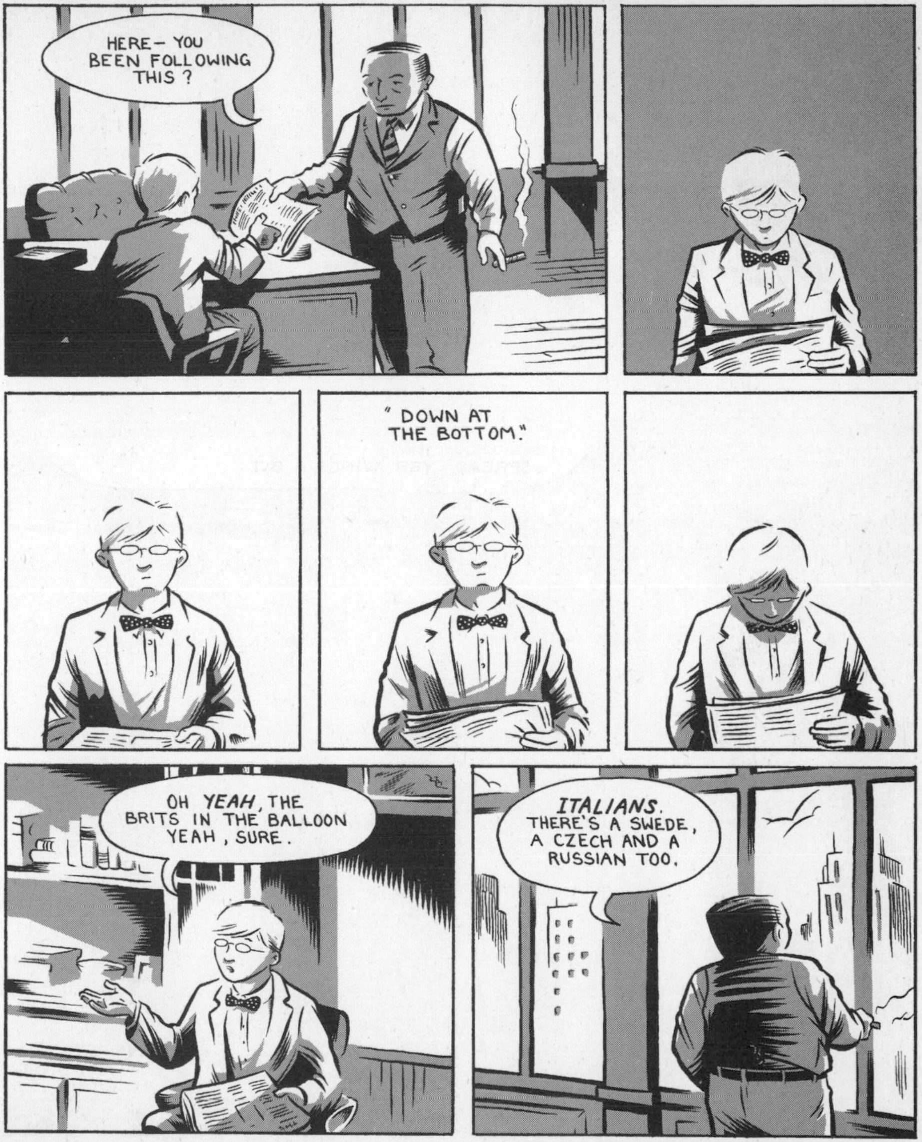
HERE— YOU BEEN FOLLOWING THIS ?
" DOWN AT THE BOTTOM."
OH *YEAH*, THE BRITS IN THE BALLOON YEAH , SURE .
ITALIANS. THERE'S A SWEDE, A CZECH AND A RUSSIAN TOO.

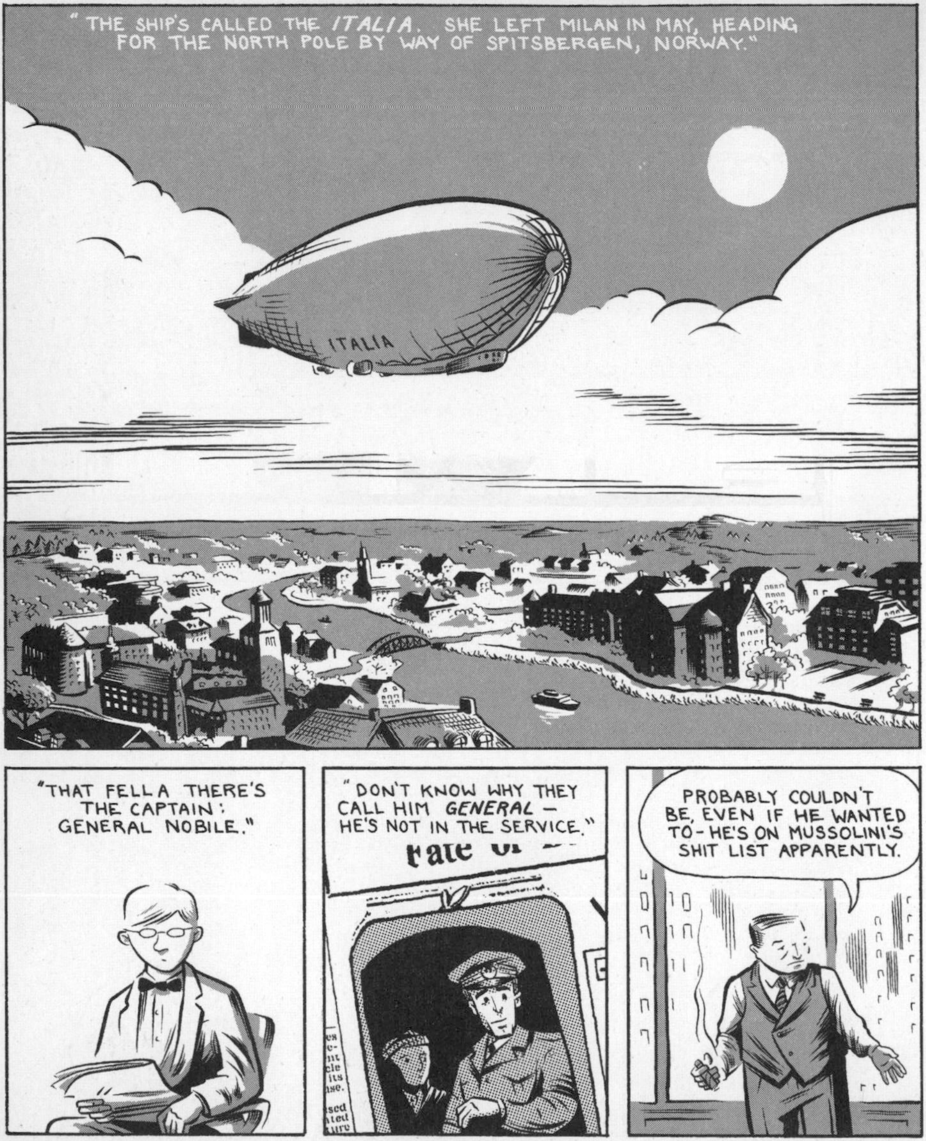
"THE SHIP'S CALLED THE *ITALIA*. SHE LEFT MILAN IN MAY, HEADING FOR THE NORTH POLE BY WAY OF SPITSBERGEN, NORWAY."
ITALIA
"THAT FELLA THERE'S THE CAPTAIN: GENERAL NOBILE."
"DON'T KNOW WHY THEY CALL HIM *GENERAL* — HE'S NOT IN THE SERVICE."
PROBABLY COULDN'T BE, EVEN IF HE WANTED TO – HE'S ON MUSSOLINI'S SHIT LIST APPARENTLY.

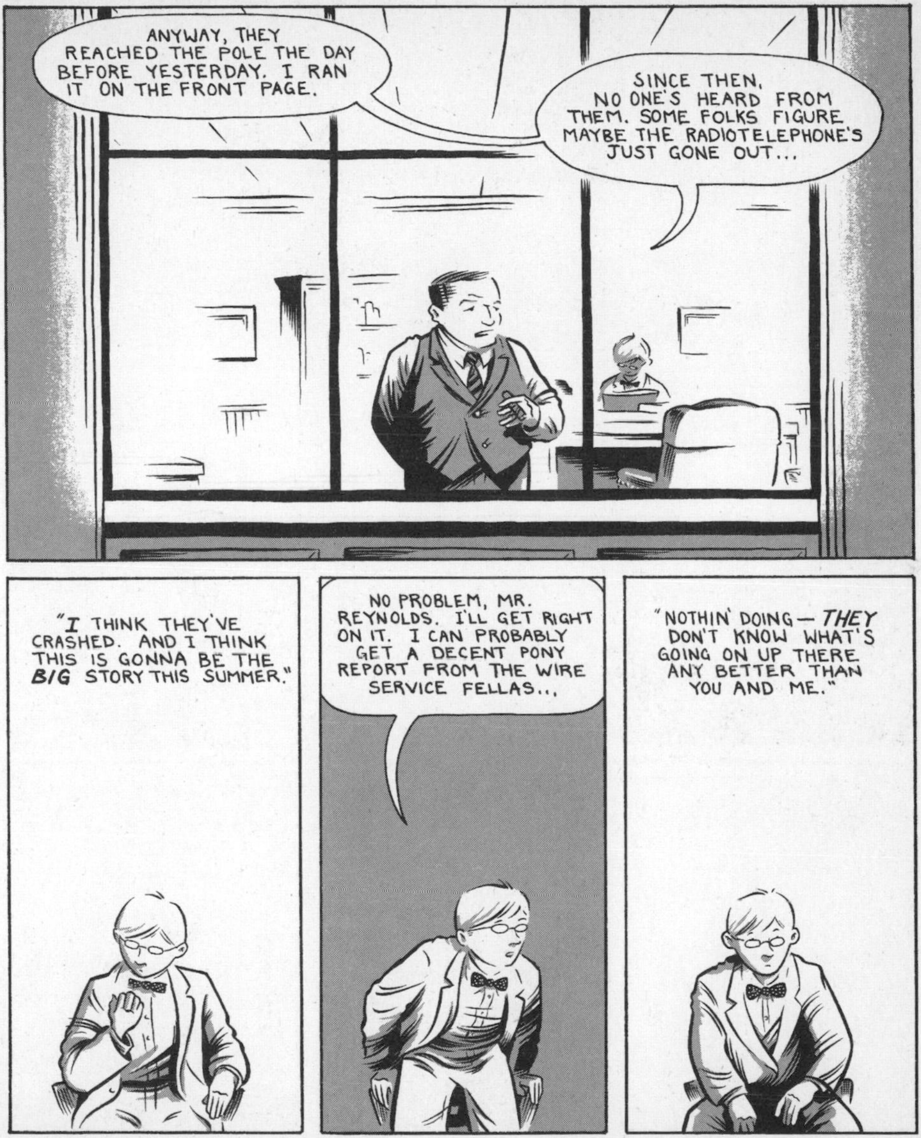
ANYWAY, THEY REACHED THE POLE THE DAY BEFORE YESTERDAY. I RAN IT ON THE FRONT PAGE.
SINCE THEN, NO ONE'S HEARD FROM THEM. SOME FOLKS FIGURE MAYBE THE RADIOTELEPHONE'S JUST GONE OUT...
"I THINK THEY'VE CRASHED. AND I THINK THIS IS GONNA BE THE BIG STORY THIS SUMMER."
NO PROBLEM, MR. REYNOLDS. I'LL GET RIGHT ON IT. I CAN PROBABLY GET A DECENT PONY REPORT FROM THE WIRE SERVICE FELLAS...
"NOTHIN' DOING—THEY DON'T KNOW WHAT'S GOING ON UP THERE ANY BETTER THAN YOU AND ME."

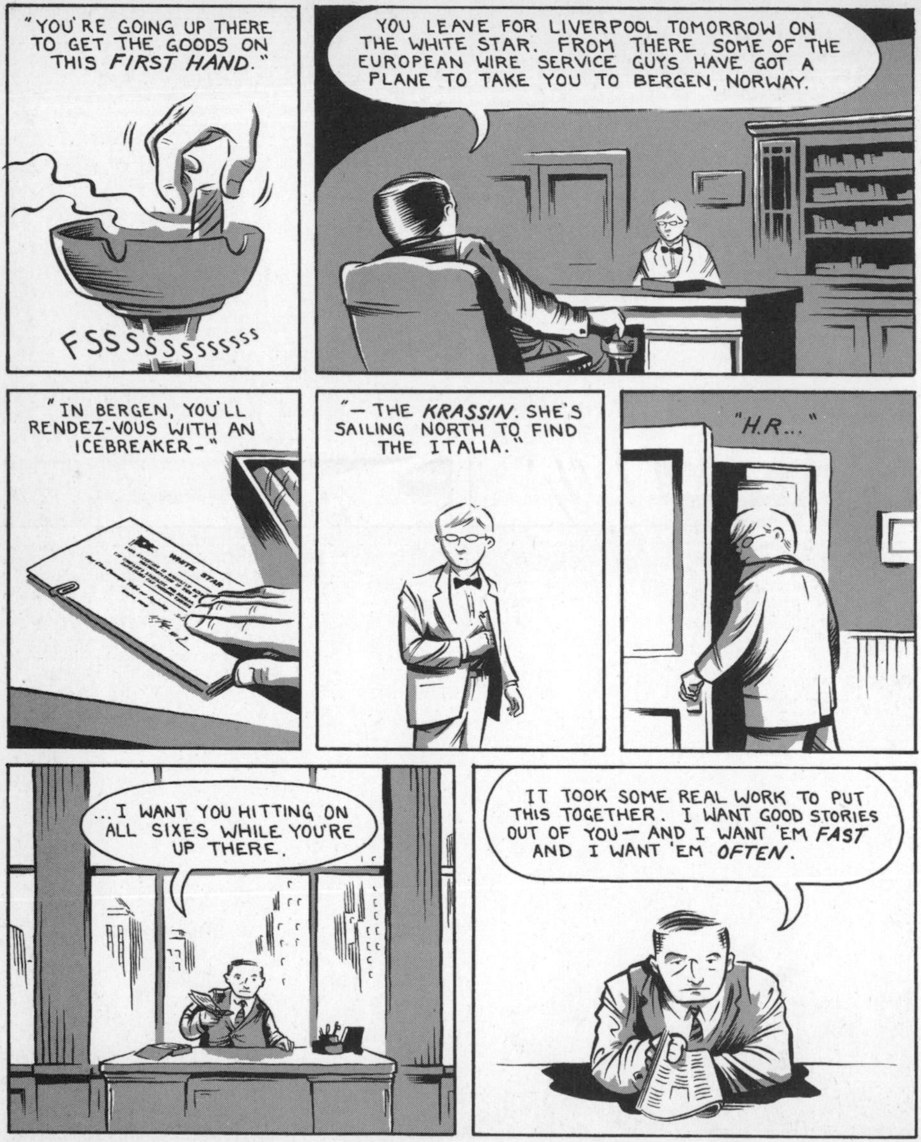
"YOU'RE GOING UP THERE TO GET THE GOODS ON THIS *FIRST HAND*."
FSSSSSSSSSSSS
YOU LEAVE FOR LIVERPOOL TOMORROW ON THE WHITE STAR. FROM THERE SOME OF THE EUROPEAN WIRE SERVICE GUYS HAVE GOT A PLANE TO TAKE YOU TO BERGEN, NORWAY.
"IN BERGEN, YOU'LL RENDEZ-VOUS WITH AN ICEBREAKER–"
WHITE STAR
"—THE *KRASSIN*. SHE'S SAILING NORTH TO FIND THE ITALIA."
"H.R..."
...I WANT YOU HITTING ON ALL SIXES WHILE YOU'RE UP THERE.
IT TOOK SOME REAL WORK TO PUT THIS TOGETHER. I WANT GOOD STORIES OUT OF YOU— AND I WANT 'EM *FAST* AND I WANT 'EM *OFTEN*.

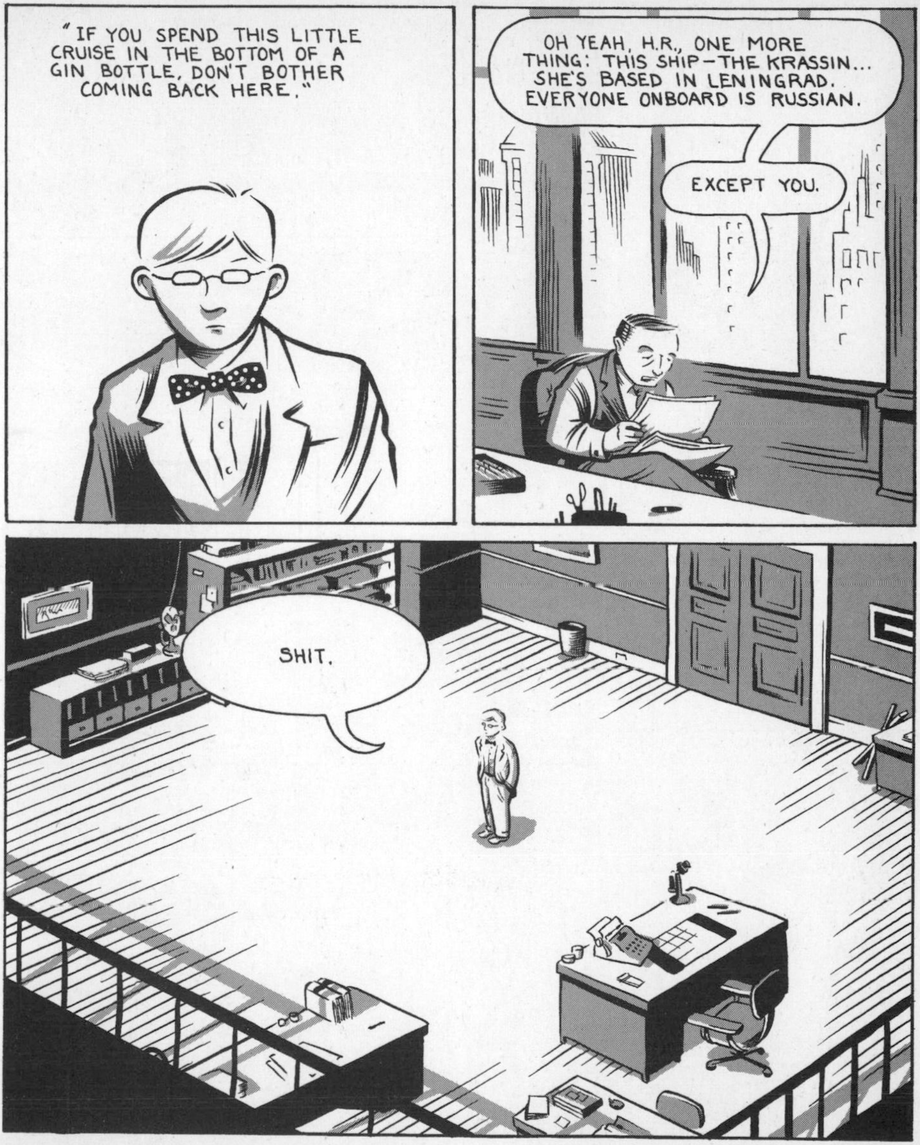
"IF YOU SPEND THIS LITTLE CRUISE IN THE BOTTOM OF A GIN BOTTLE, DON'T BOTHER COMING BACK HERE."
OH YEAH, H.R., ONE MORE THING: THIS SHIP—THE KRASSIN... SHE'S BASED IN LENINGRAD. EVERYONE ONBOARD IS RUSSIAN.
EXCEPT YOU.
SHIT.

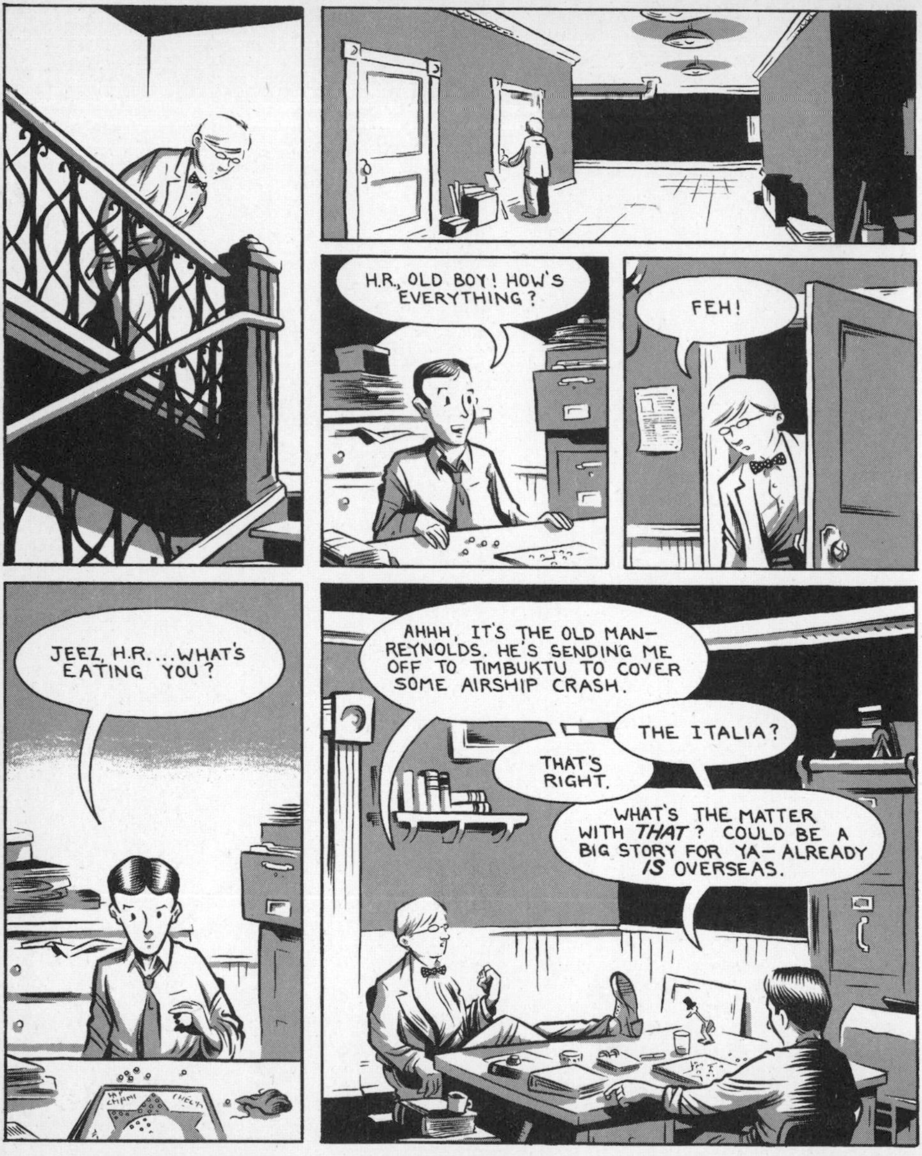
H.R., OLD BOY! HOW'S EVERYTHING?
FEH!
JEEZ, H.R.... WHAT'S EATING YOU?
AHHH, IT'S THE OLD MAN— REYNOLDS. HE'S SENDING ME OFF TO TIMBUKTU TO COVER SOME AIRSHIP CRASH.
THE ITALIA?
THAT'S RIGHT.
WHAT'S THE MATTER WITH *THAT*? COULD BE A BIG STORY FOR YA— ALREADY *IS* OVERSEAS.

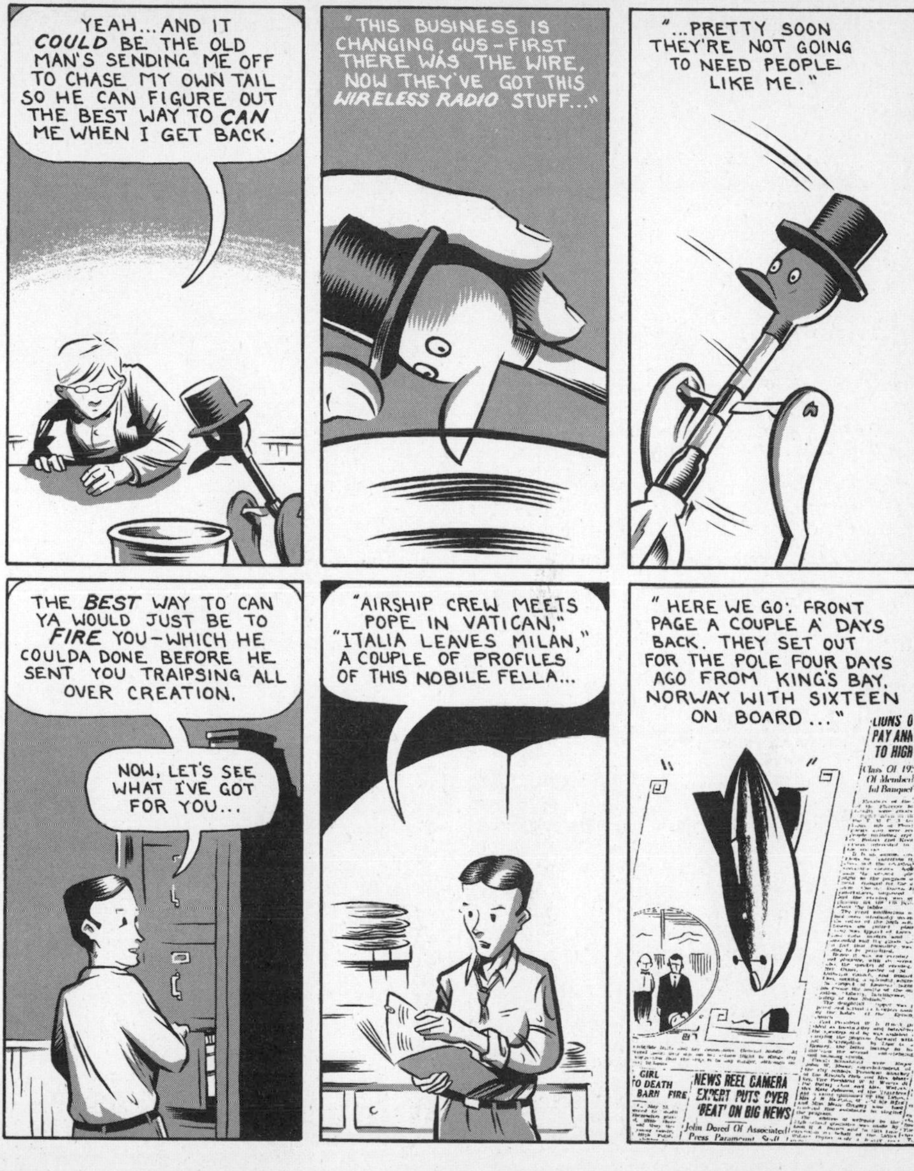
YEAH... AND IT *COULD* BE THE OLD MAN'S SENDING ME OFF TO CHASE MY OWN TAIL SO HE CAN FIGURE OUT THE BEST WAY TO *CAN* ME WHEN I GET BACK.
"THIS BUSINESS IS CHANGING, GUS - FIRST THERE WAS THE WIRE, NOW THEY'VE GOT THIS *WIRELESS RADIO* STUFF..."
"...PRETTY SOON THEY'RE NOT GOING TO NEED PEOPLE LIKE ME."
THE *BEST* WAY TO CAN YA WOULD JUST BE TO *FIRE* YOU - WHICH HE COULDA DONE BEFORE HE SENT YOU TRAIPSING ALL OVER CREATION.
NOW, LET'S SEE WHAT I'VE GOT FOR YOU...
"AIRSHIP CREW MEETS POPE IN VATICAN," "ITALIA LEAVES MILAN," A COUPLE OF PROFILES OF THIS NOBILE FELLA...
"HERE WE GO: FRONT PAGE A COUPLE A' DAYS BACK. THEY SET OUT FOR THE POLE FOUR DAYS AGO FROM KING'S BAY, NORWAY WITH SIXTEEN ON BOARD..."
NEWS REEL CAMERA EXPERT PUTS OVER 'BEAT' ON BIG NEWS
John Dored Of Associated Press Paramount Staff

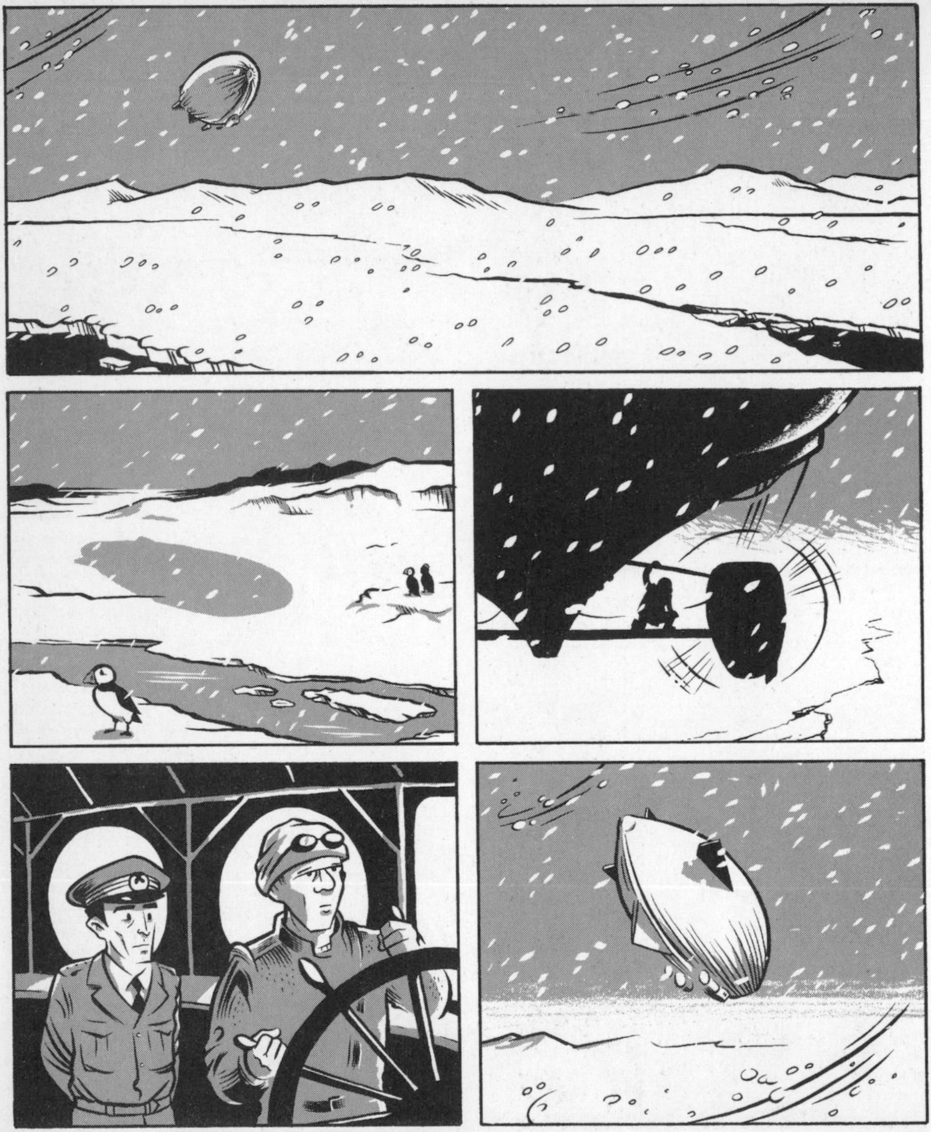

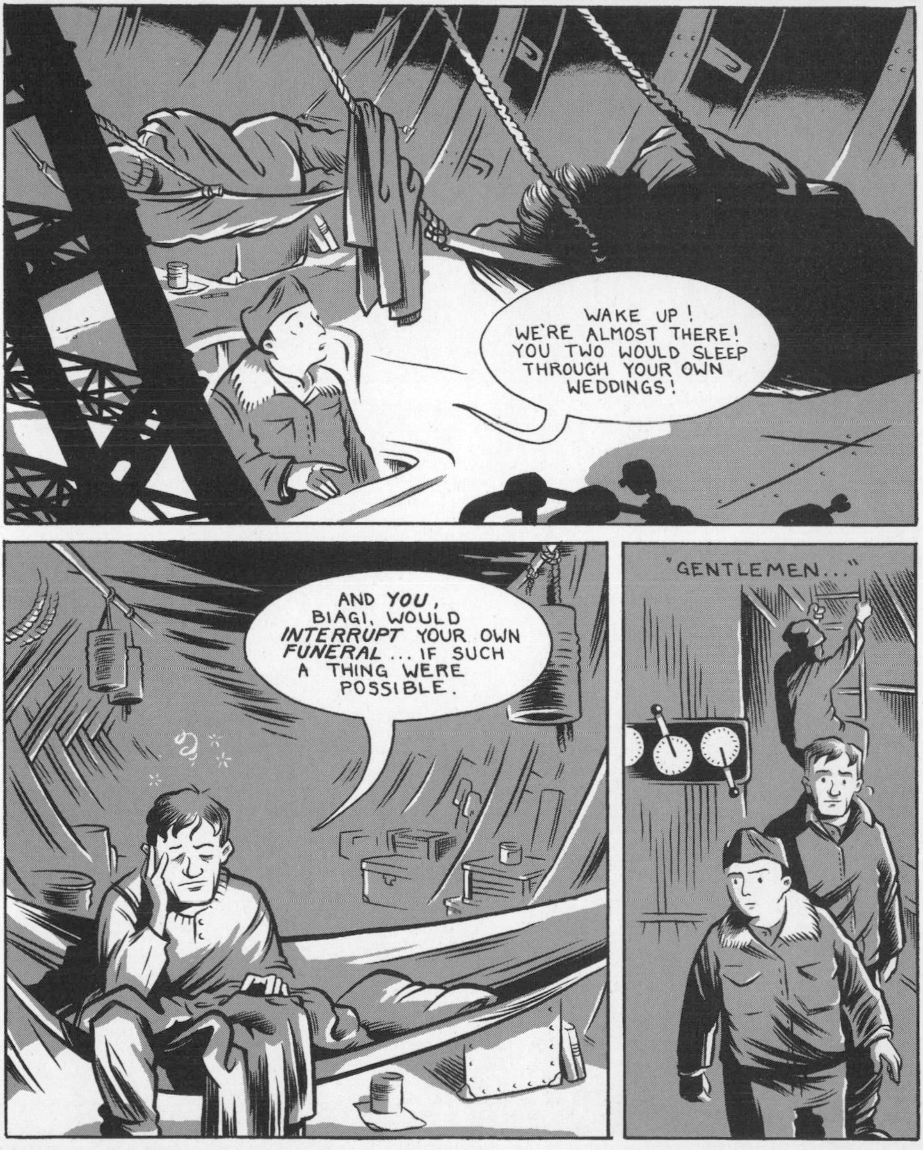
WAKE UP! WE'RE ALMOST THERE! YOU TWO WOULD SLEEP THROUGH YOUR OWN WEDDINGS!
AND YOU, BIAGI, WOULD INTERRUPT YOUR OWN FUNERAL... IF SUCH A THING WERE POSSIBLE.
"GENTLEMEN..."

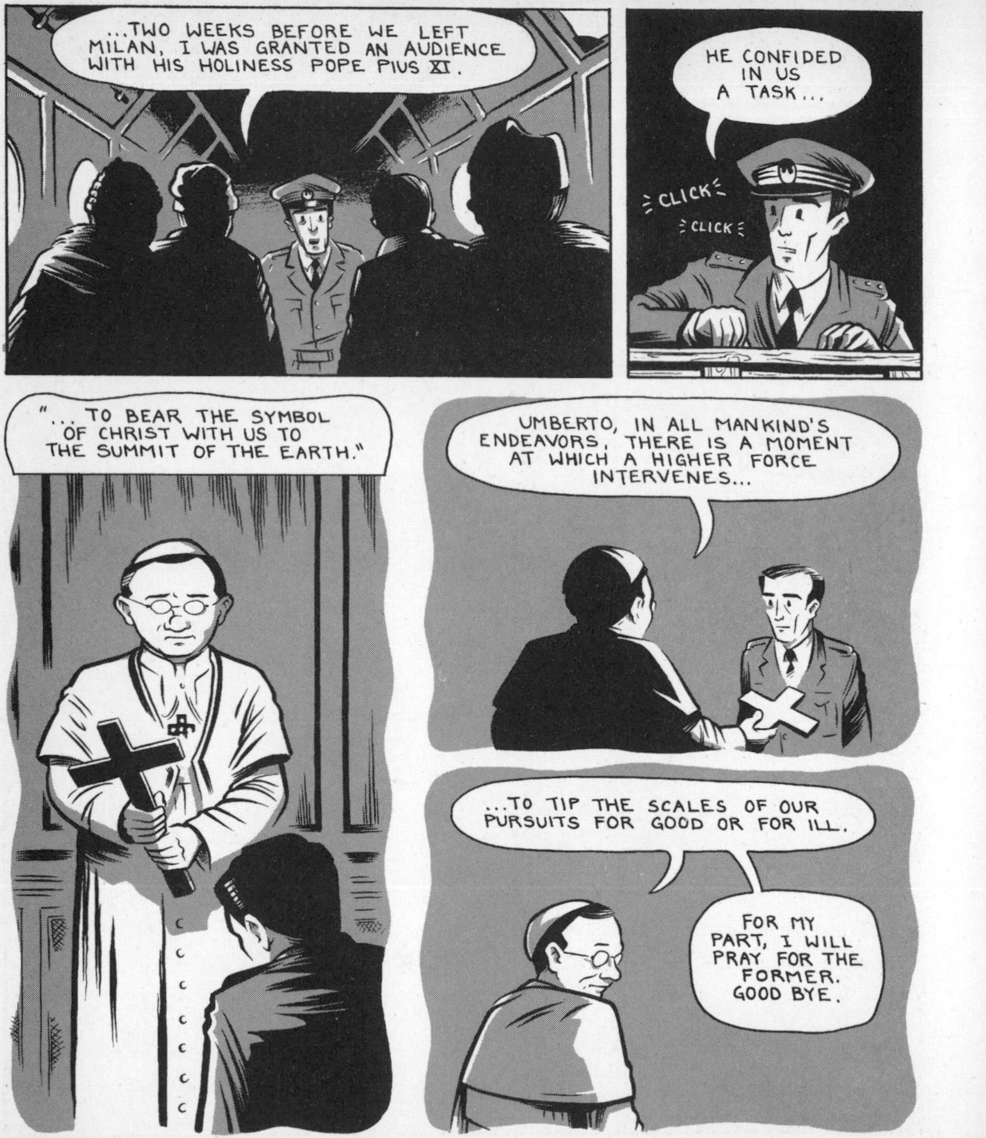
...TWO WEEKS BEFORE WE LEFT MILAN, I WAS GRANTED AN AUDIENCE WITH HIS HOLINESS POPE PIUS XI.
HE CONFIDED IN US A TASK...
CLICK
CLICK
"... TO BEAR THE SYMBOL OF CHRIST WITH US TO THE SUMMIT OF THE EARTH."
UMBERTO, IN ALL MANKIND'S ENDEAVORS, THERE IS A MOMENT AT WHICH A HIGHER FORCE INTERVENES...
...TO TIP THE SCALES OF OUR PURSUITS FOR GOOD OR FOR ILL.
FOR MY PART, I WILL PRAY FOR THE FORMER. GOOD BYE.

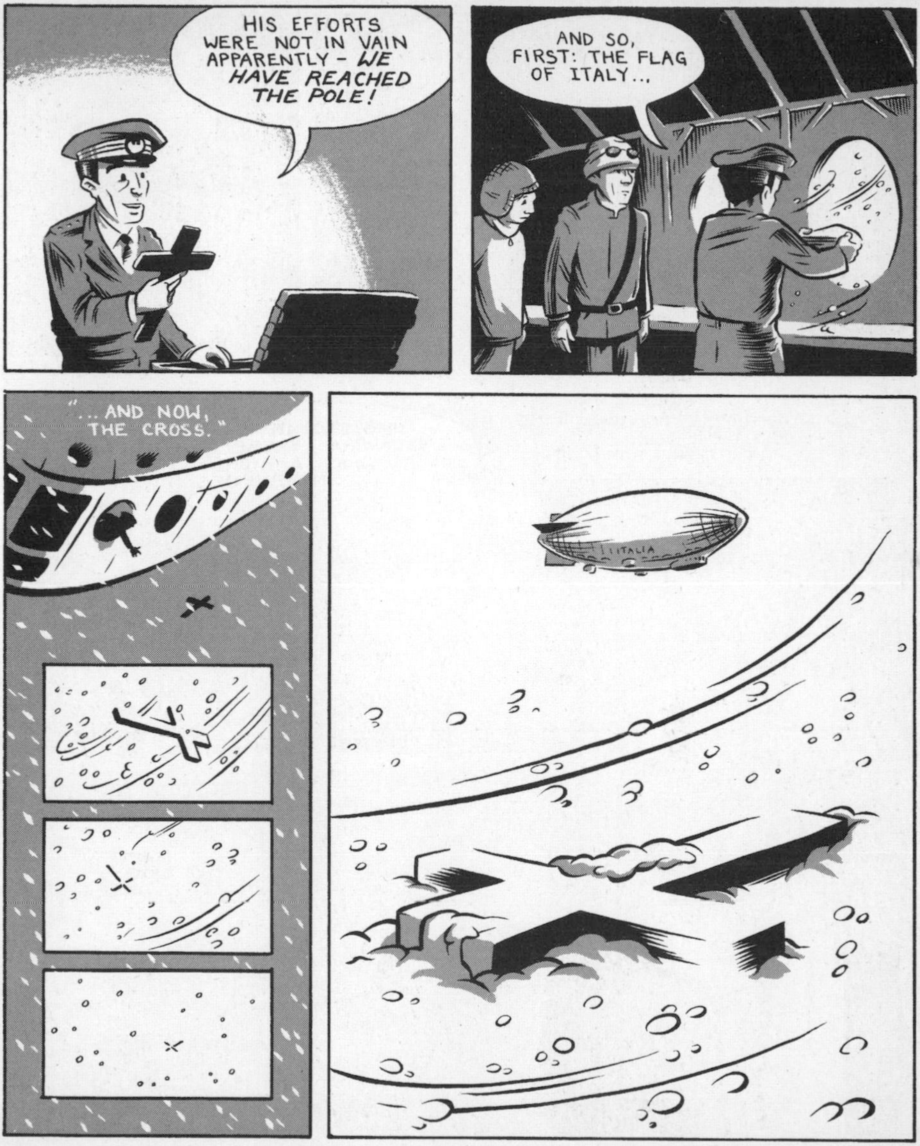
HIS EFFORTS WERE NOT IN VAIN APPARENTLY - WE HAVE REACHED THE POLE!
AND SO, FIRST: THE FLAG OF ITALY...
"...AND NOW, THE CROSS."
ITALIA

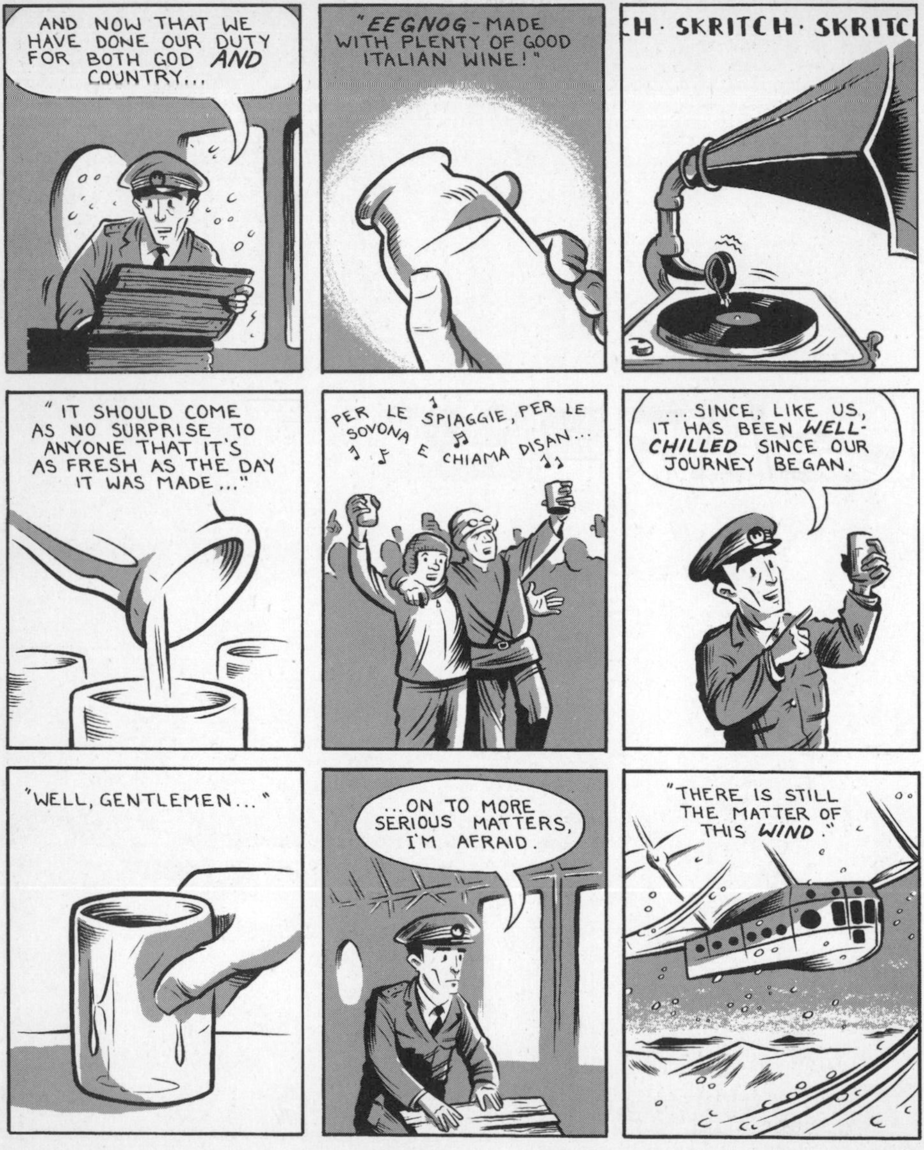
AND NOW THAT WE HAVE DONE OUR DUTY FOR BOTH GOD AND COUNTRY...
"EEGNOG - MADE WITH PLENTY OF GOOD ITALIAN WINE!"
CH · SKRITCH · SKRITCH
" IT SHOULD COME AS NO SURPRISE TO ANYONE THAT IT'S AS FRESH AS THE DAY IT WAS MADE..."
PER LE SPIAGGIE, PER LE SOVONA E CHIAMA DISAN...
... SINCE, LIKE US, IT HAS BEEN WELL-CHILLED SINCE OUR JOURNEY BEGAN.
"WELL, GENTLEMEN..."
...ON TO MORE SERIOUS MATTERS, I'M AFRAID.
"THERE IS STILL THE MATTER OF THIS WIND."

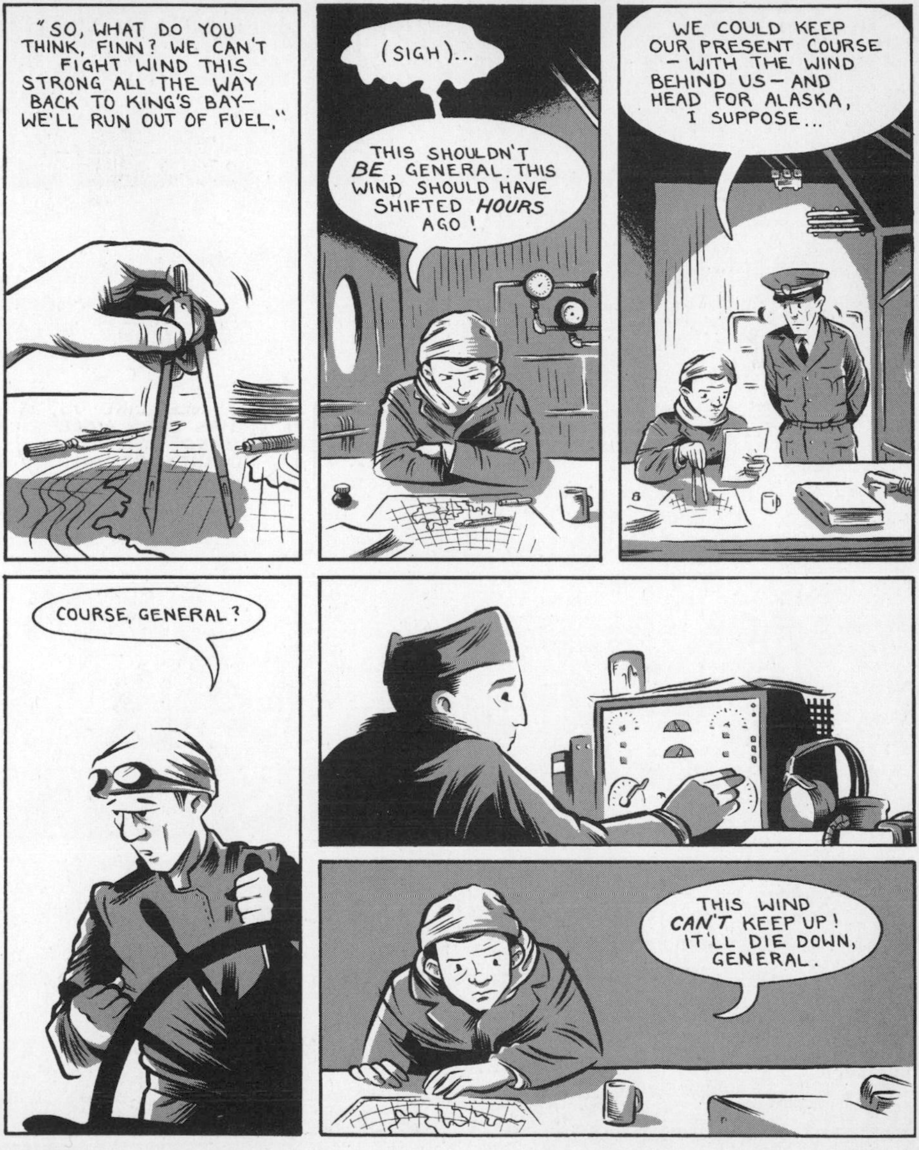
"SO, WHAT DO YOU THINK, FINN? WE CAN'T FIGHT WIND THIS STRONG ALL THE WAY BACK TO KING'S BAY— WE'LL RUN OUT OF FUEL."
(SIGH)...
THIS SHOULDN'T *BE*, GENERAL. THIS WIND SHOULD HAVE SHIFTED *HOURS* AGO!
WE COULD KEEP OUR PRESENT COURSE — WITH THE WIND BEHIND US — AND HEAD FOR ALASKA, I SUPPOSE...
COURSE, GENERAL?
THIS WIND *CAN'T* KEEP UP! IT'LL DIE DOWN, GENERAL.

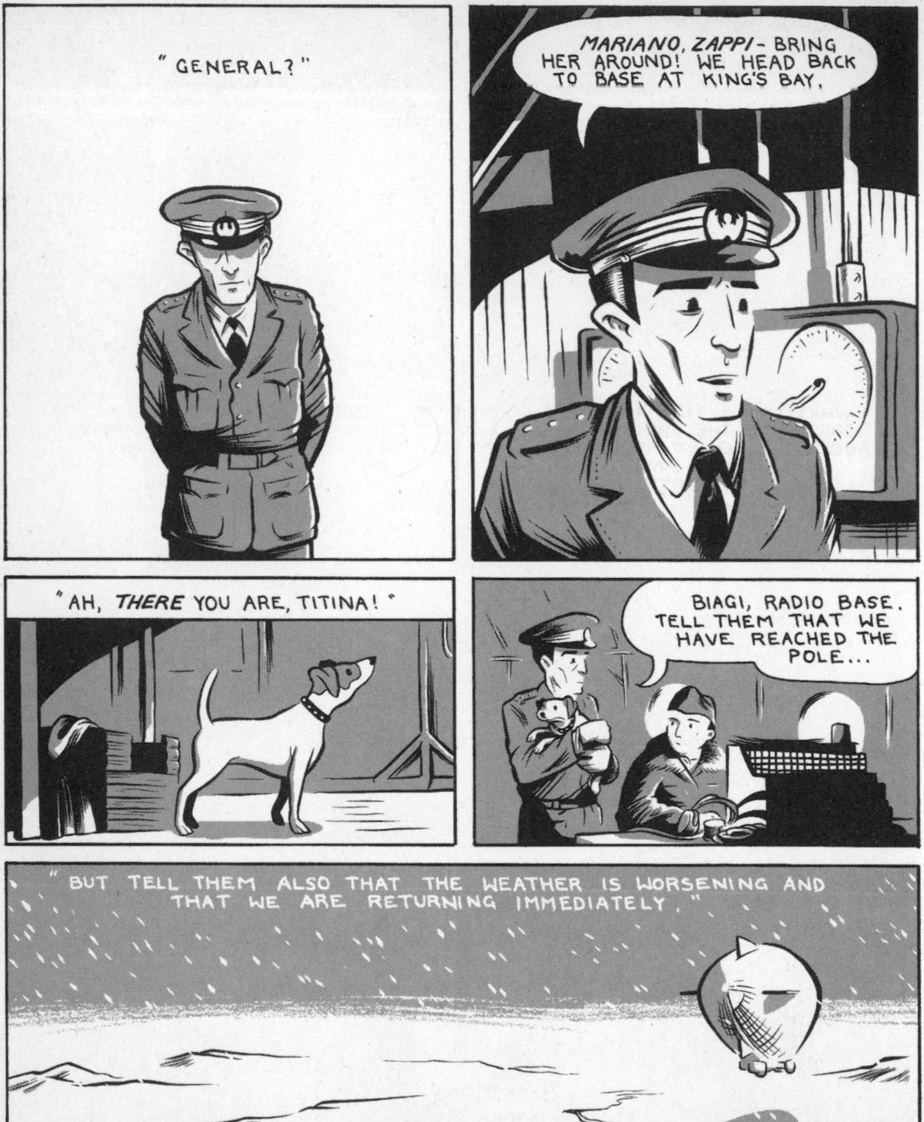

"GENERAL?"
MARIANO, ZAPPI - BRING HER AROUND! WE HEAD BACK TO BASE AT KING'S BAY.
"AH, THERE YOU ARE, TITINA!"
BIAGI, RADIO BASE. TELL THEM THAT WE HAVE REACHED THE POLE...
"BUT TELL THEM ALSO THAT THE WEATHER IS WORSENING AND THAT WE ARE RETURNING IMMEDIATELY."

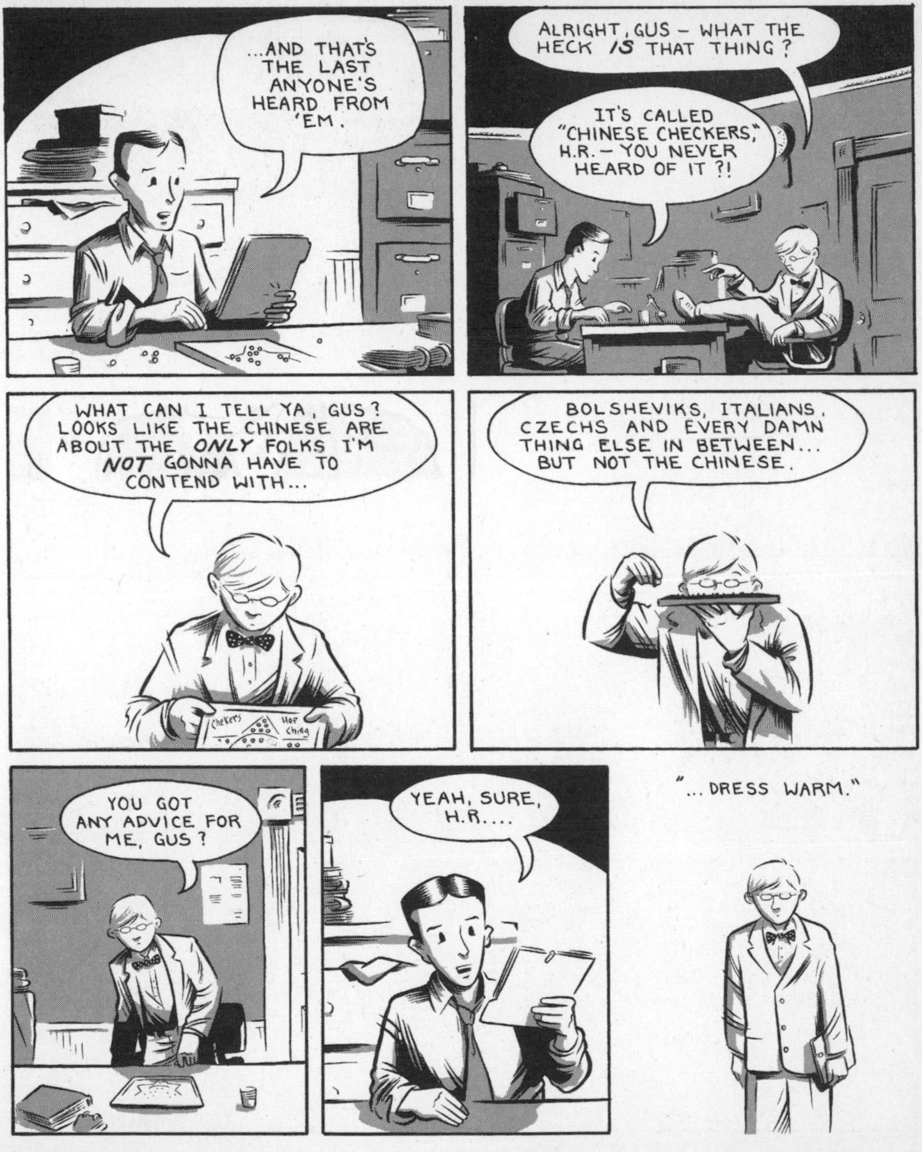
...AND THAT'S THE LAST ANYONE'S HEARD FROM 'EM.
ALRIGHT, GUS – WHAT THE HECK IS THAT THING?
IT'S CALLED "CHINESE CHECKERS," H.R. – YOU NEVER HEARD OF IT ?!
WHAT CAN I TELL YA, GUS? LOOKS LIKE THE CHINESE ARE ABOUT THE ONLY FOLKS I'M NOT GONNA HAVE TO CONTEND WITH...
Chekers
Hop Ching
BOLSHEVIKS, ITALIANS, CZECHS AND EVERY DAMN THING ELSE IN BETWEEN... BUT NOT THE CHINESE.
YOU GOT ANY ADVICE FOR ME, GUS?
YEAH, SURE, H.R....
"... DRESS WARM."

II

Fissure

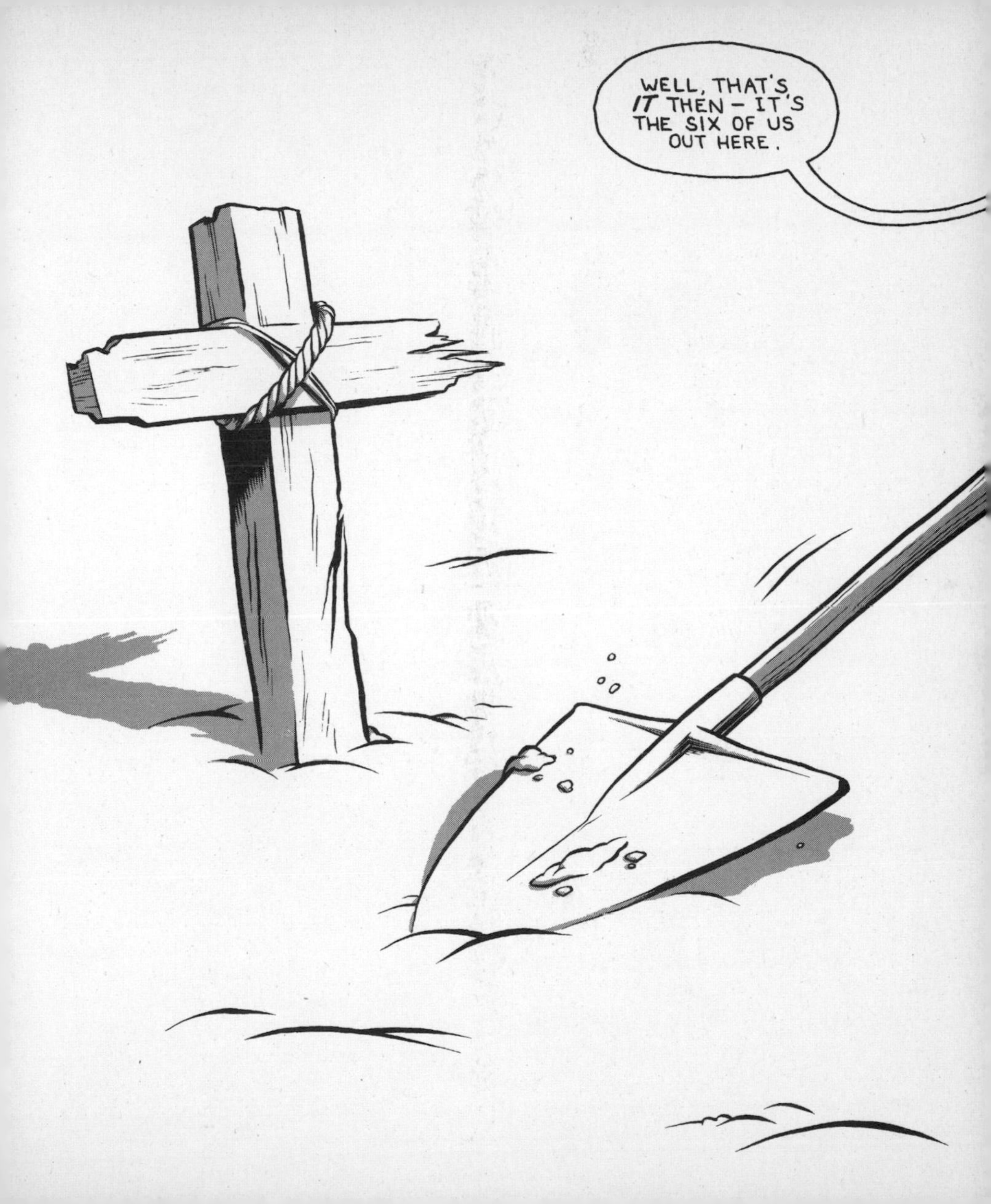
WELL, THAT'S *IT* THEN – IT'S THE SIX OF US OUT HERE.

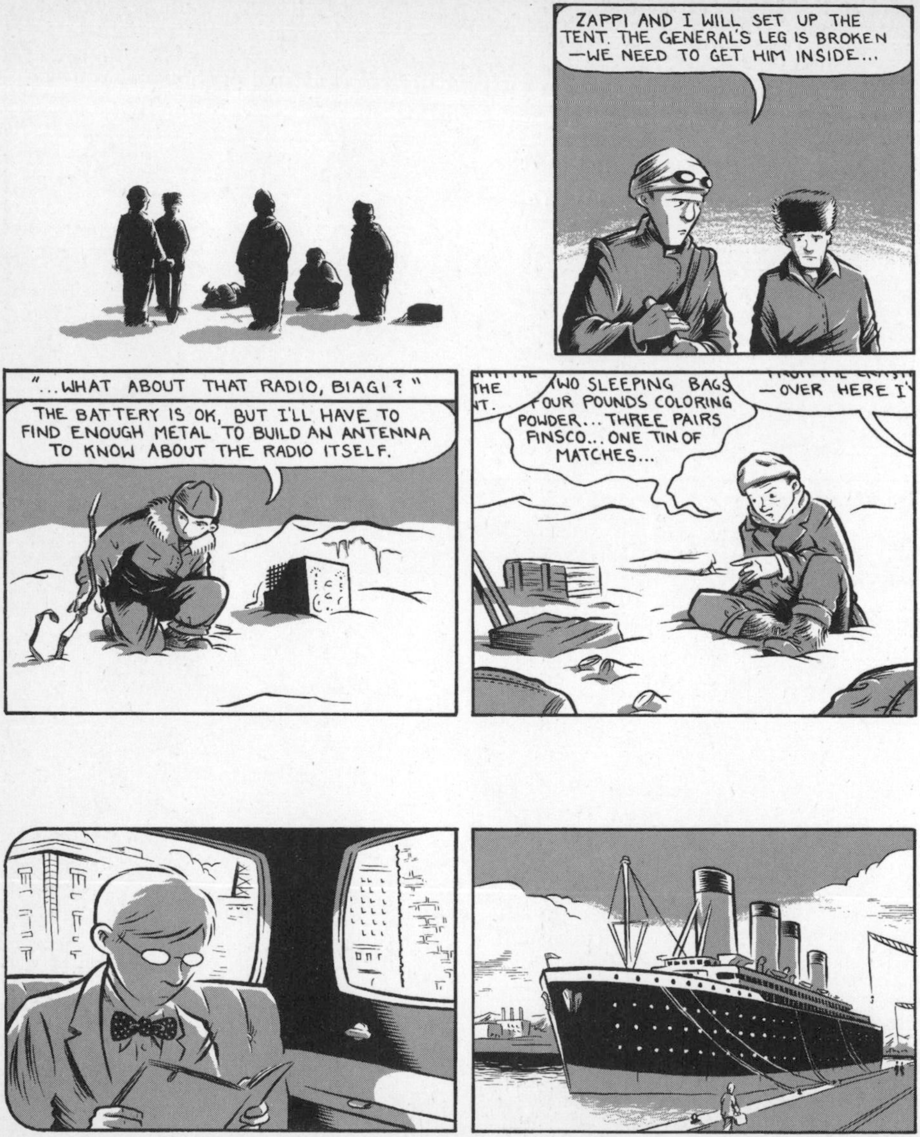

ZAPPI AND I WILL SET UP THE TENT. THE GENERAL'S LEG IS BROKEN —WE NEED TO GET HIM INSIDE...
"...WHAT ABOUT THAT RADIO, BIAGI?"
THE BATTERY IS OK, BUT I'LL HAVE TO FIND ENOUGH METAL TO BUILD AN ANTENNA TO KNOW ABOUT THE RADIO ITSELF.
TWO SLEEPING BAGS FOUR POUNDS COLORING POWDER... THREE PAIRS FINSCO... ONE TIN OF MATCHES...
—OVER HERE I'

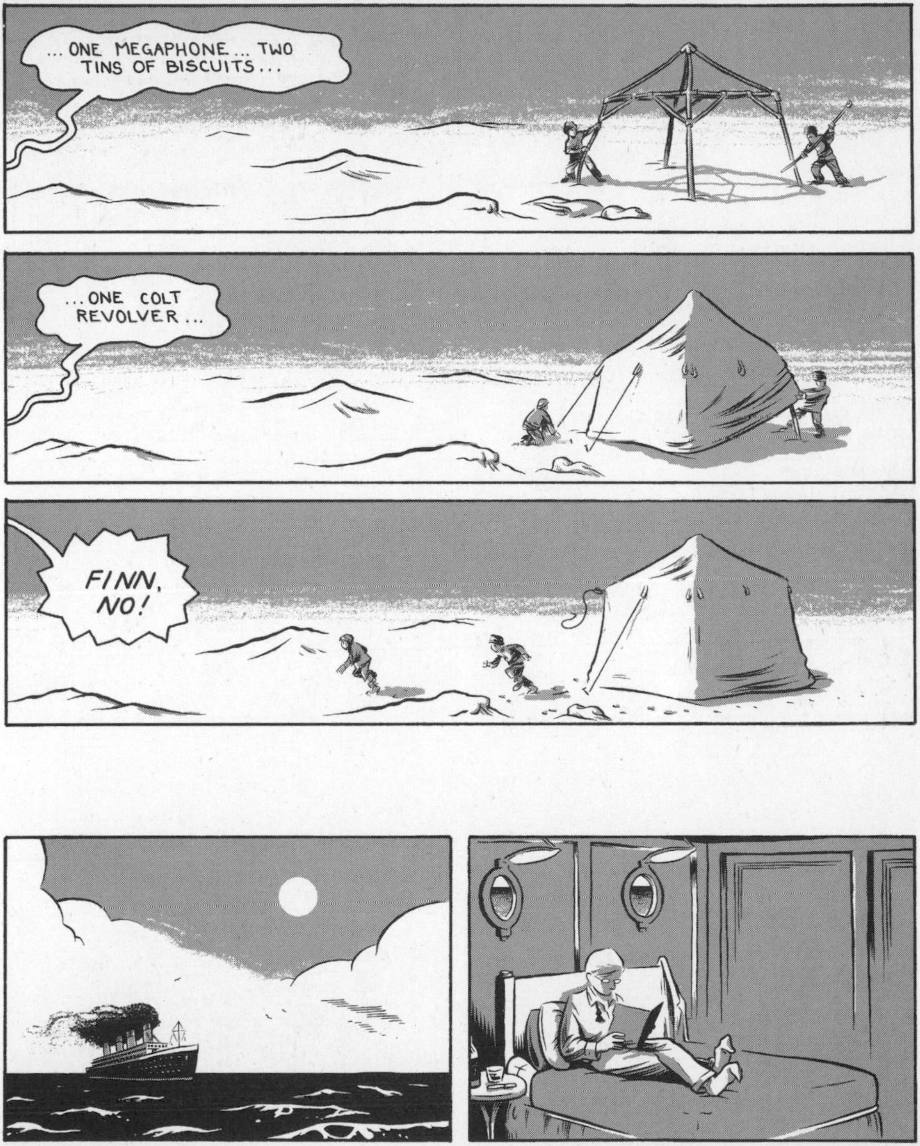
... ONE MEGAPHONE ... TWO TINS OF BISCUITS ...
... ONE COLT REVOLVER ...
FINN, NO!

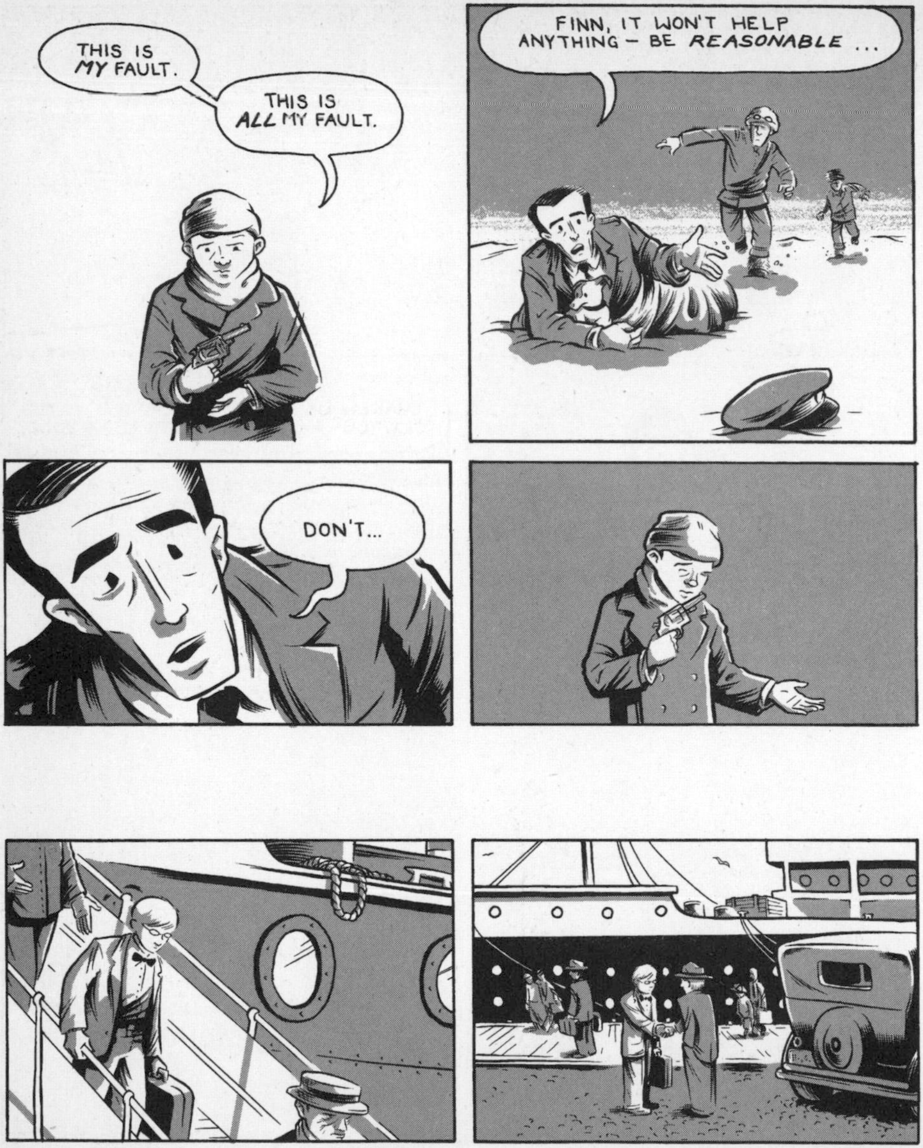
THIS IS MY FAULT.
THIS IS ALL MY FAULT.
FINN, IT WON'T HELP ANYTHING – BE REASONABLE ...
DON'T...

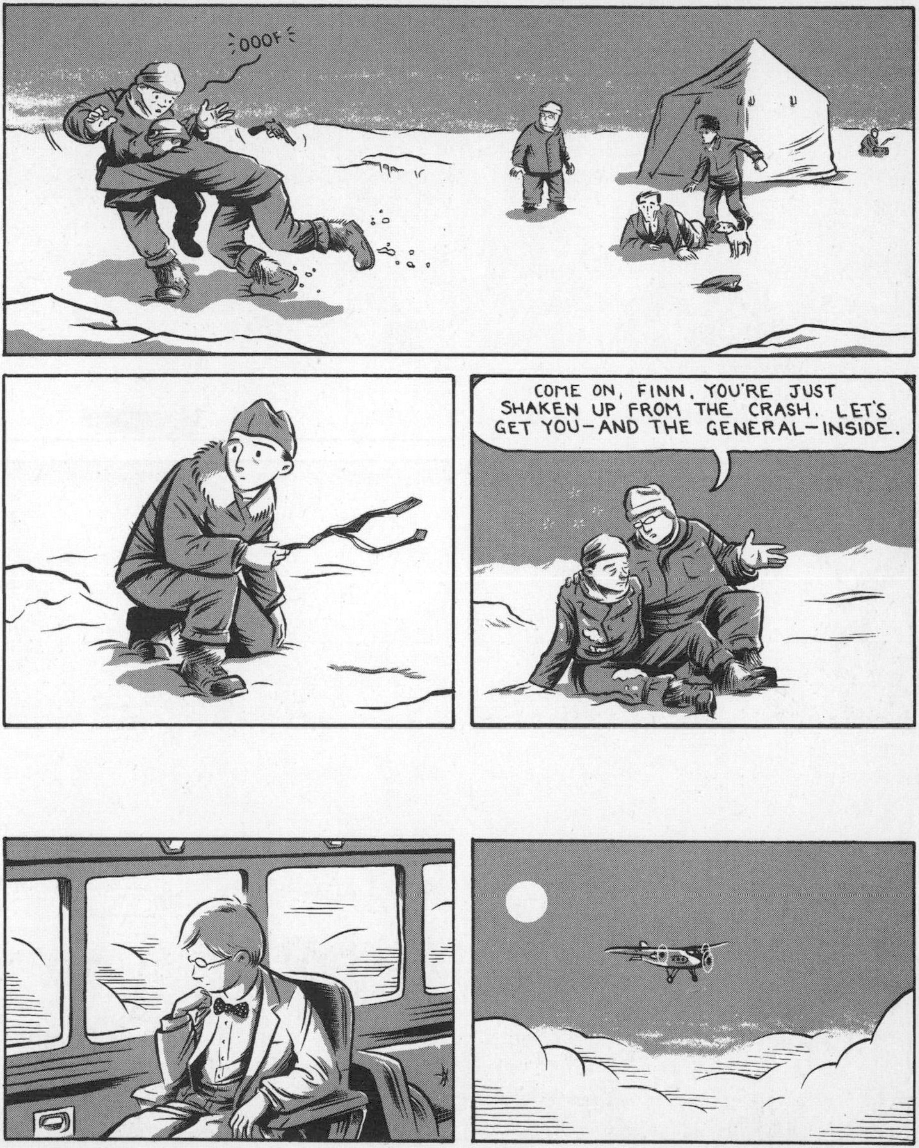
OOOF
COME ON, FINN. YOU'RE JUST SHAKEN UP FROM THE CRASH. LET'S GET YOU—AND THE GENERAL—INSIDE.

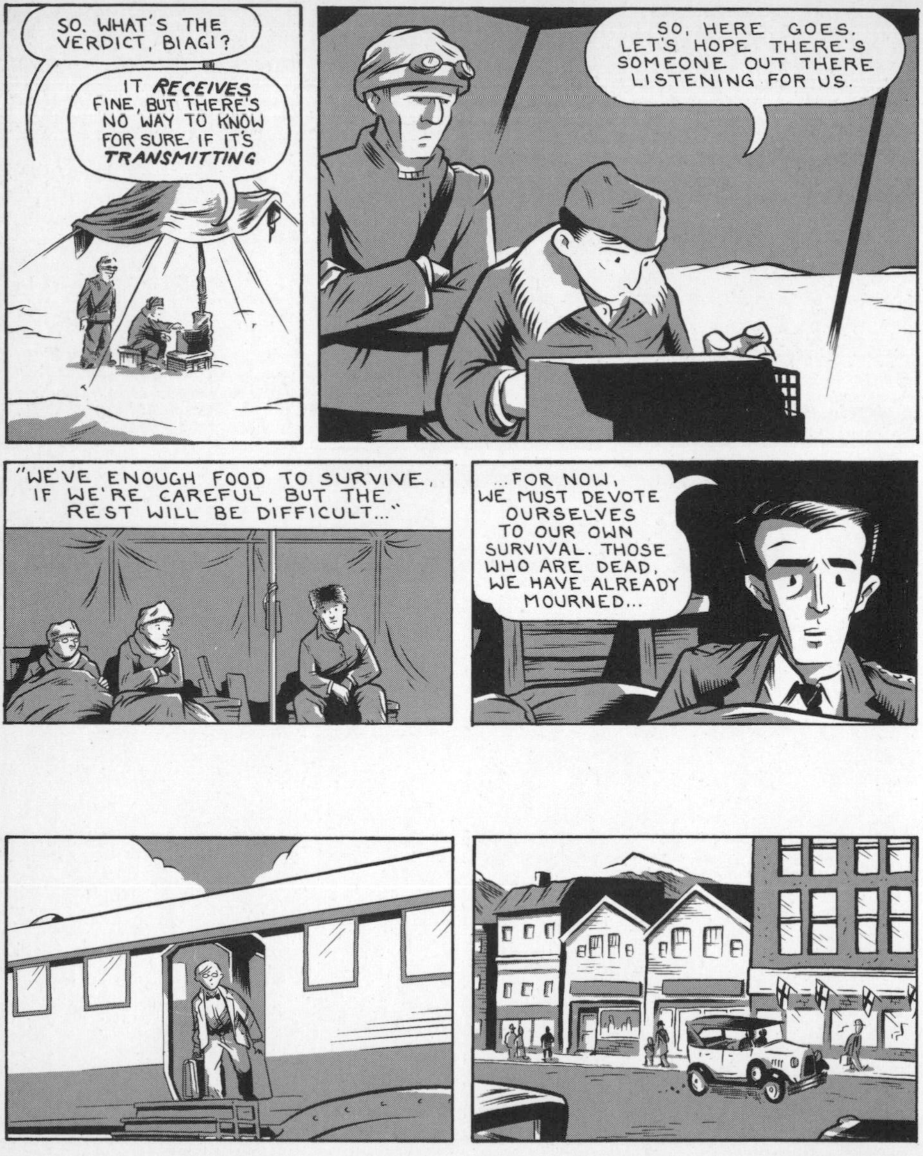
SO. WHAT'S THE VERDICT, BIAGI?
IT RECEIVES FINE, BUT THERE'S NO WAY TO KNOW FOR SURE IF IT'S TRANSMITTING
SO, HERE GOES. LET'S HOPE THERE'S SOMEONE OUT THERE LISTENING FOR US.
"WE'VE ENOUGH FOOD TO SURVIVE, IF WE'RE CAREFUL, BUT THE REST WILL BE DIFFICULT..."
...FOR NOW, WE MUST DEVOTE OURSELVES TO OUR OWN SURVIVAL. THOSE WHO ARE DEAD, WE HAVE ALREADY MOURNED...

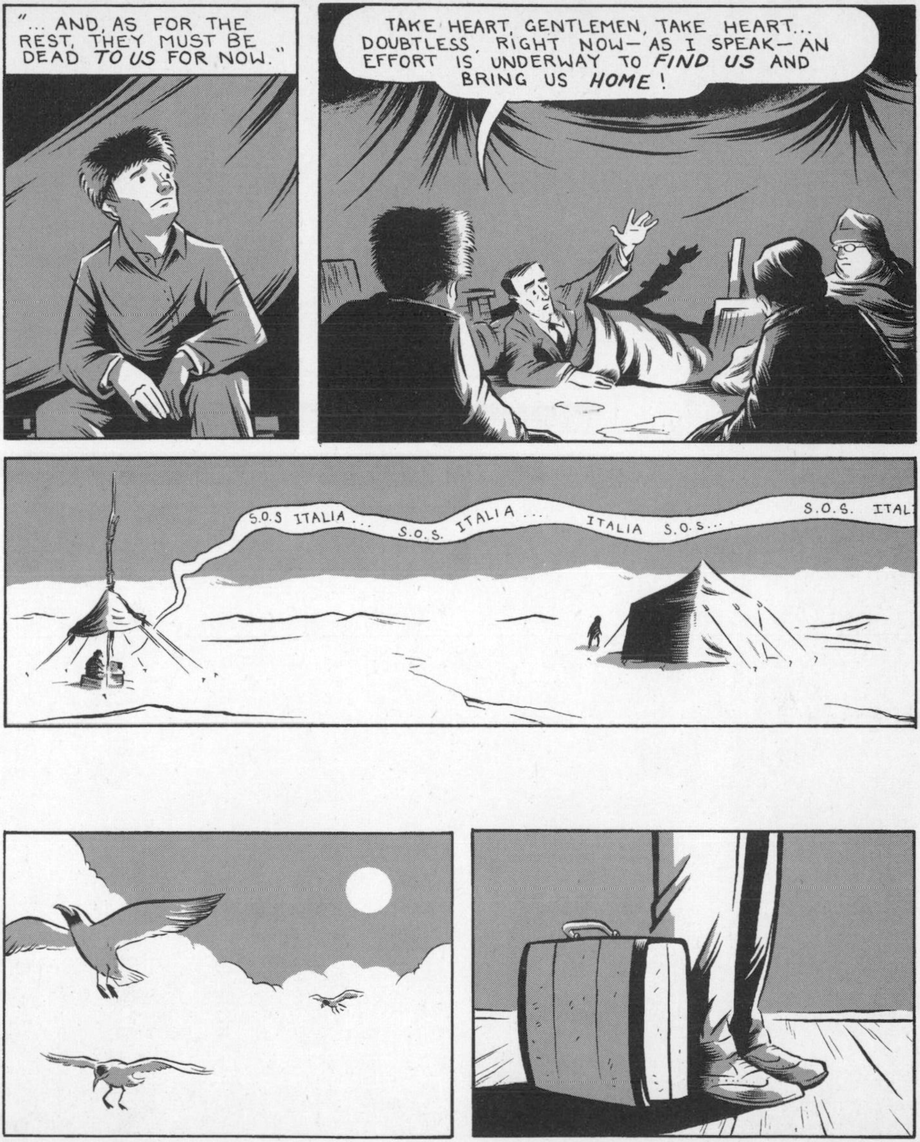
"... AND, AS FOR THE REST, THEY MUST BE DEAD TO US FOR NOW."
TAKE HEART, GENTLEMEN, TAKE HEART... DOUBTLESS, RIGHT NOW— AS I SPEAK— AN EFFORT IS UNDERWAY TO FIND US AND BRING US HOME!
S.O.S ITALIA... S.O.S. ITALIA... ITALIA S.O.S... S.O.S.

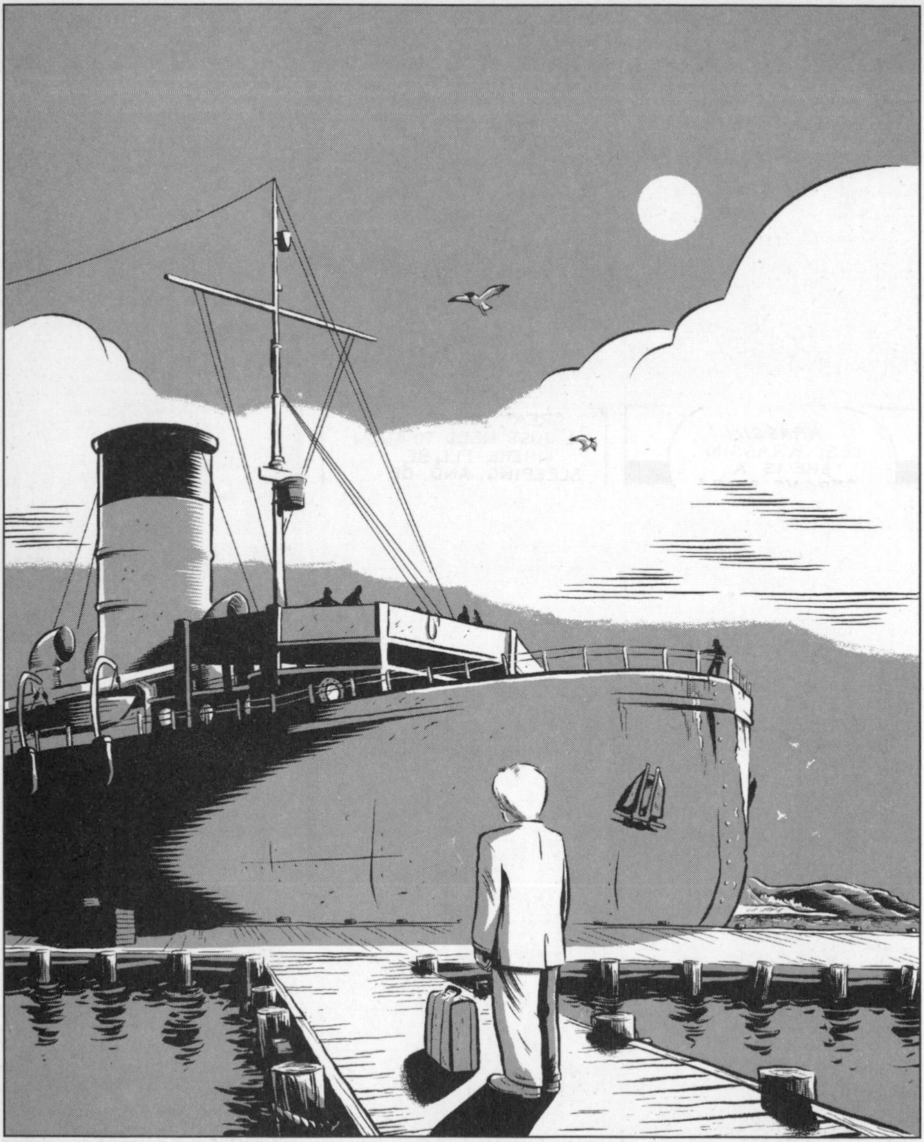

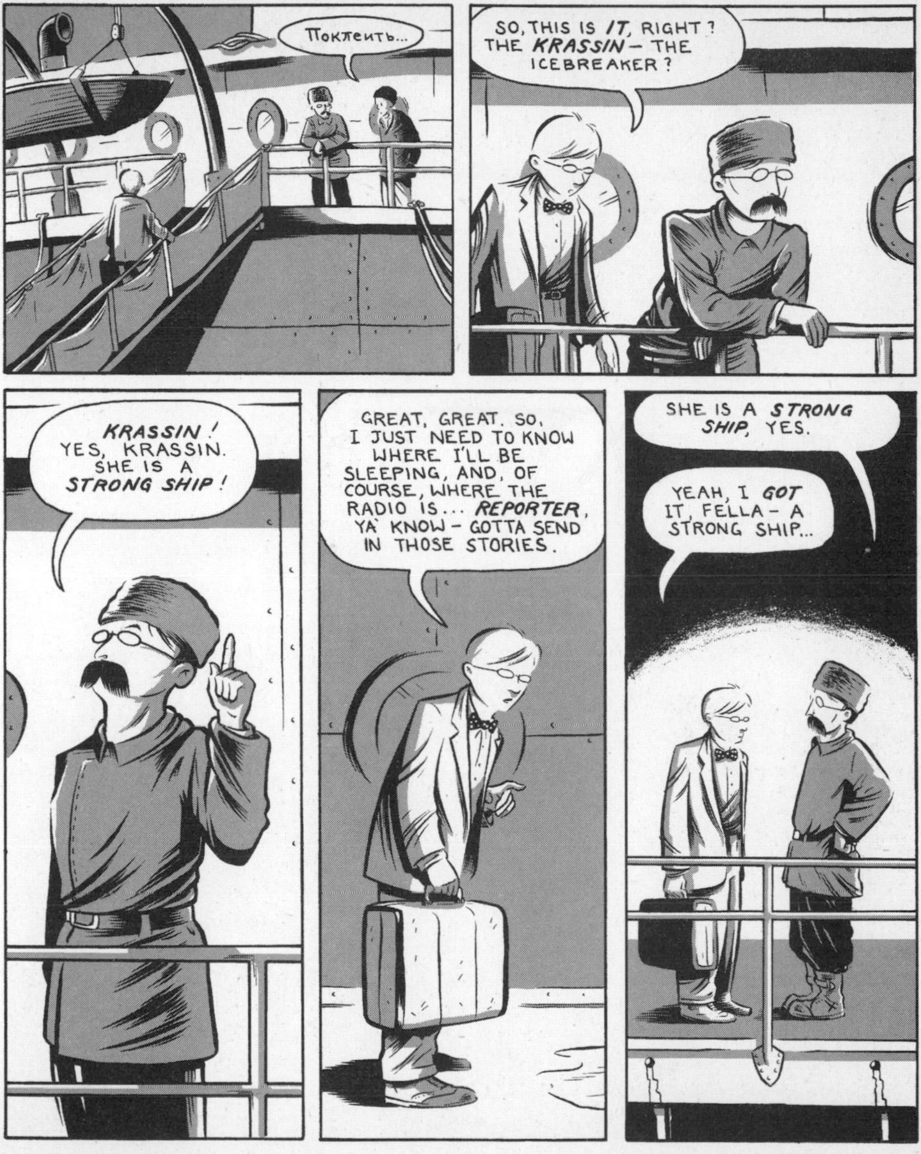
Покпеить...
SO, THIS IS *IT*, RIGHT? THE *KRASSIN* – THE ICEBREAKER?
KRASSIN! YES, KRASSIN. SHE IS A *STRONG SHIP*!
GREAT, GREAT. SO, I JUST NEED TO KNOW WHERE I'LL BE SLEEPING, AND, OF COURSE, WHERE THE RADIO IS... *REPORTER*, YA' KNOW – GOTTA SEND IN THOSE STORIES.
SHE IS A *STRONG SHIP*, YES.
YEAH, I *GOT* IT, FELLA – A STRONG SHIP...

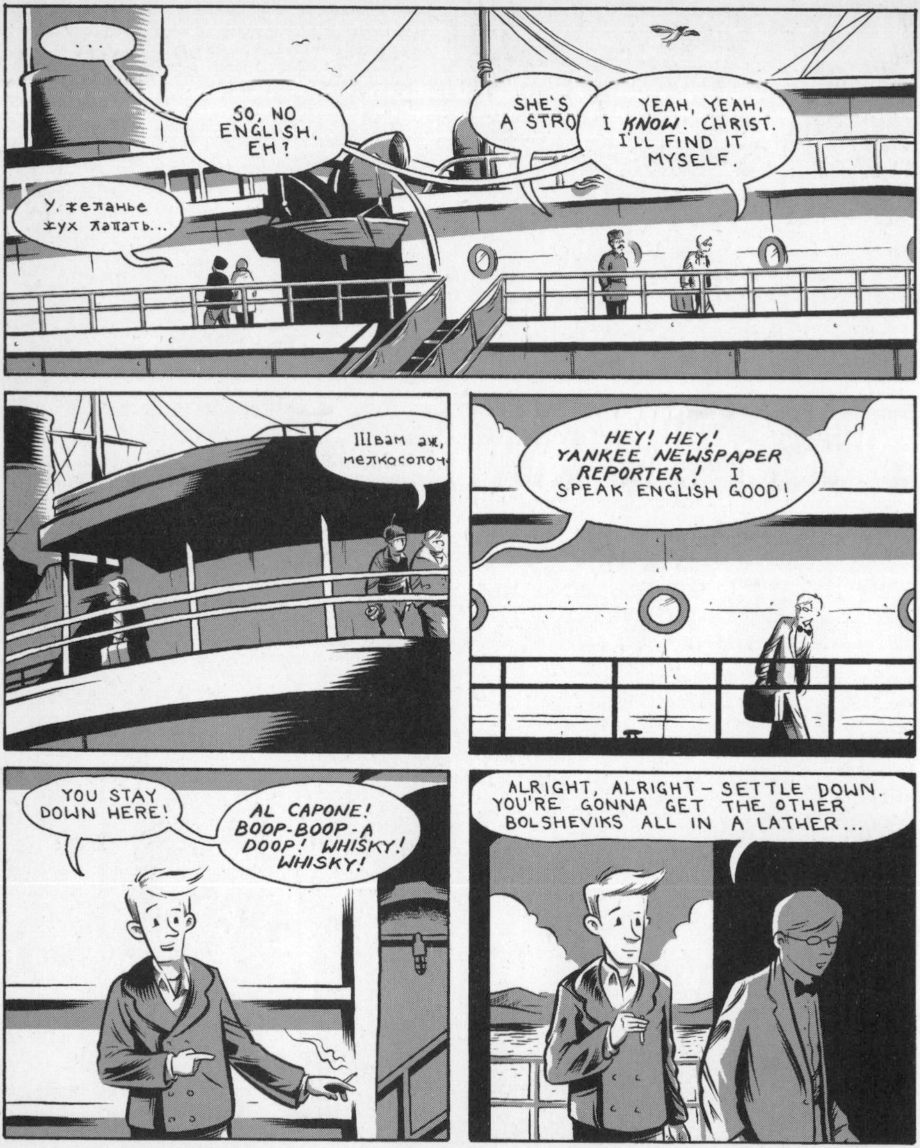

...
SO, NO ENGLISH, EH?
У. желанье жух лапать...
SHE'S A STRO
YEAH, YEAH, I KNOW. CHRIST. I'LL FIND IT MYSELF.
Швам аж, мелкосопоч
HEY! HEY! YANKEE NEWSPAPER REPORTER! I SPEAK ENGLISH GOOD!
YOU STAY DOWN HERE!
AL CAPONE! BOOP-BOOP-A DOOP! WHISKY! WHISKY!
ALRIGHT, ALRIGHT - SETTLE DOWN. YOU'RE GONNA GET THE OTHER BOLSHEVIKS ALL IN A LATHER...

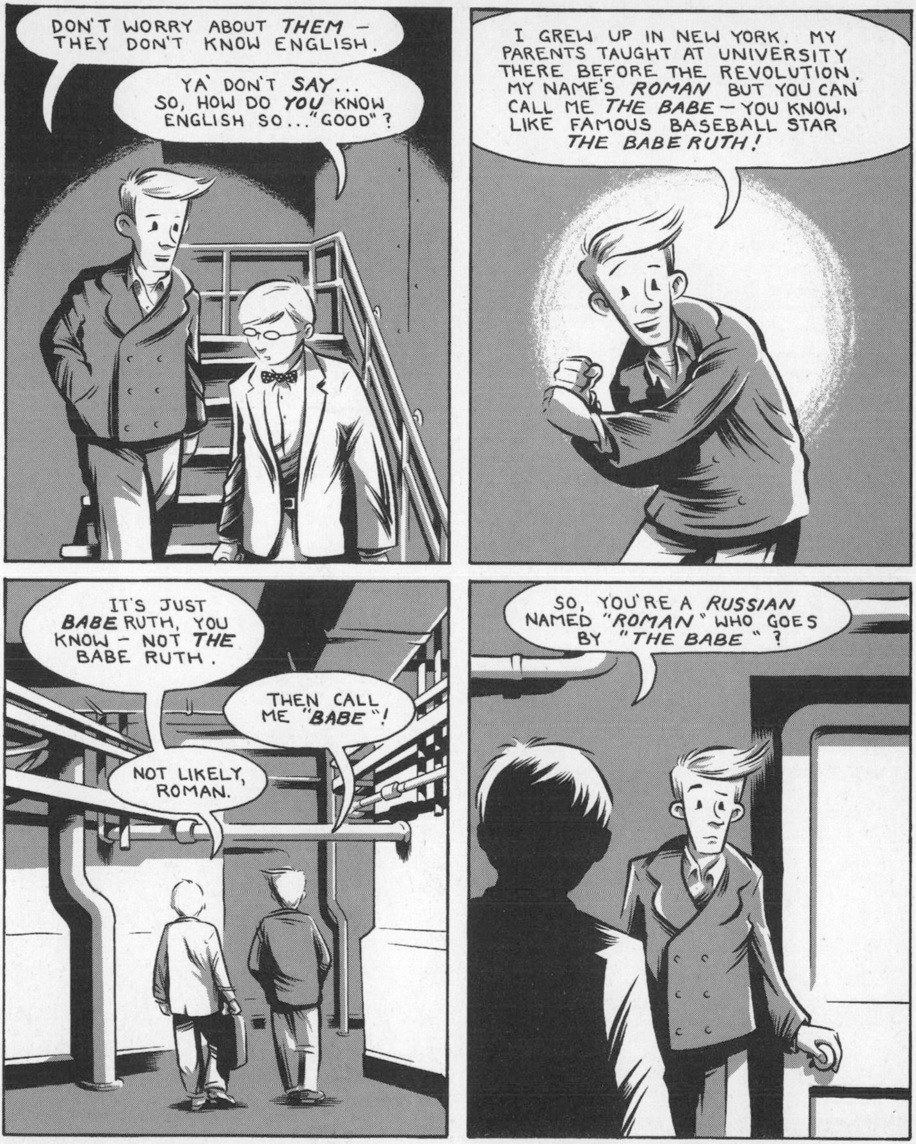

DON'T WORRY ABOUT THEM — THEY DON'T KNOW ENGLISH.
YA' DON'T SAY... SO, HOW DO YOU KNOW ENGLISH SO..."GOOD"?
I GREW UP IN NEW YORK. MY PARENTS TAUGHT AT UNIVERSITY THERE BEFORE THE REVOLUTION. MY NAME'S ROMAN BUT YOU CAN CALL ME THE BABE — YOU KNOW, LIKE FAMOUS BASEBALL STAR THE BABE RUTH!
IT'S JUST BABE RUTH, YOU KNOW — NOT THE BABE RUTH.
THEN CALL ME "BABE"!
NOT LIKELY, ROMAN.
SO, YOU'RE A RUSSIAN NAMED "ROMAN" WHO GOES BY "THE BABE"?

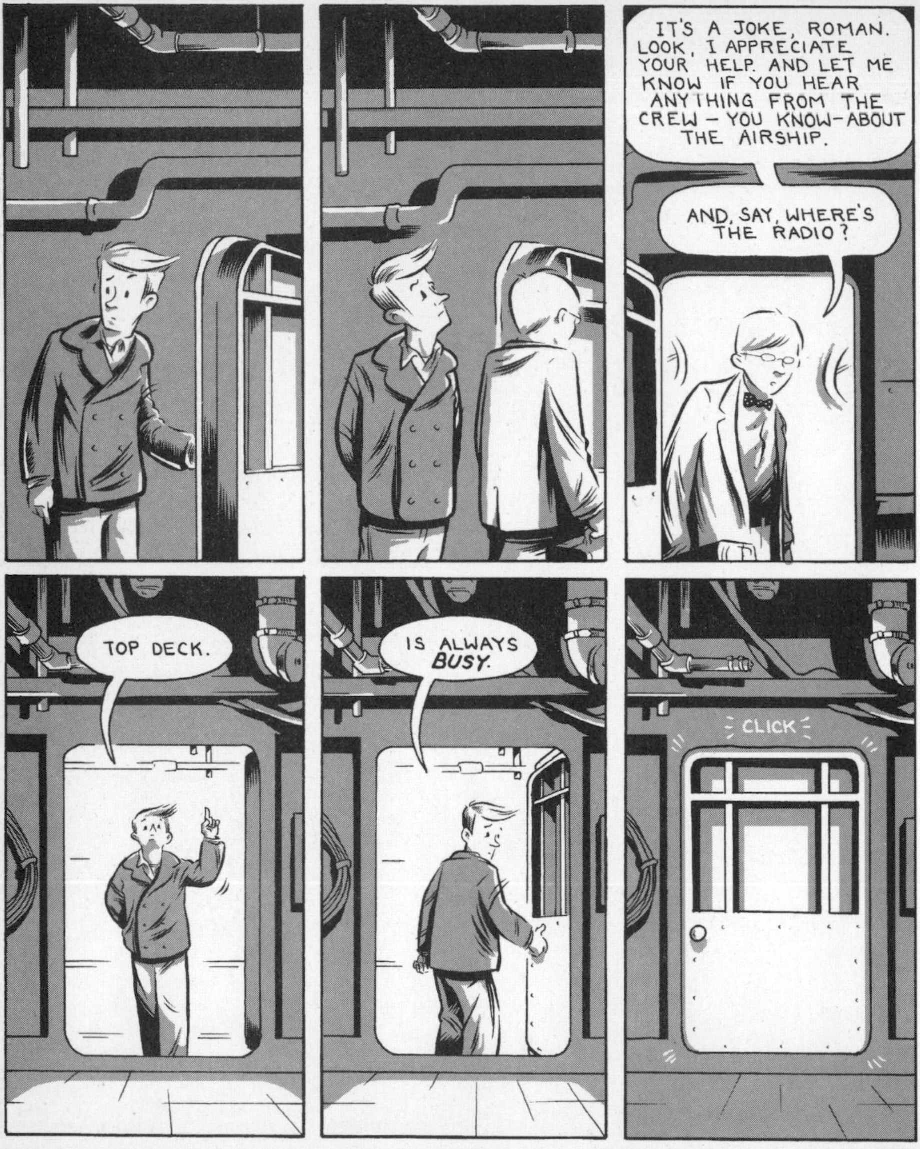
IT'S A JOKE, ROMAN. LOOK, I APPRECIATE YOUR HELP. AND LET ME KNOW IF YOU HEAR ANYTHING FROM THE CREW – YOU KNOW – ABOUT THE AIRSHIP.
AND, SAY, WHERE'S THE RADIO?
TOP DECK.
IS ALWAYS *BUSY*.
CLICK

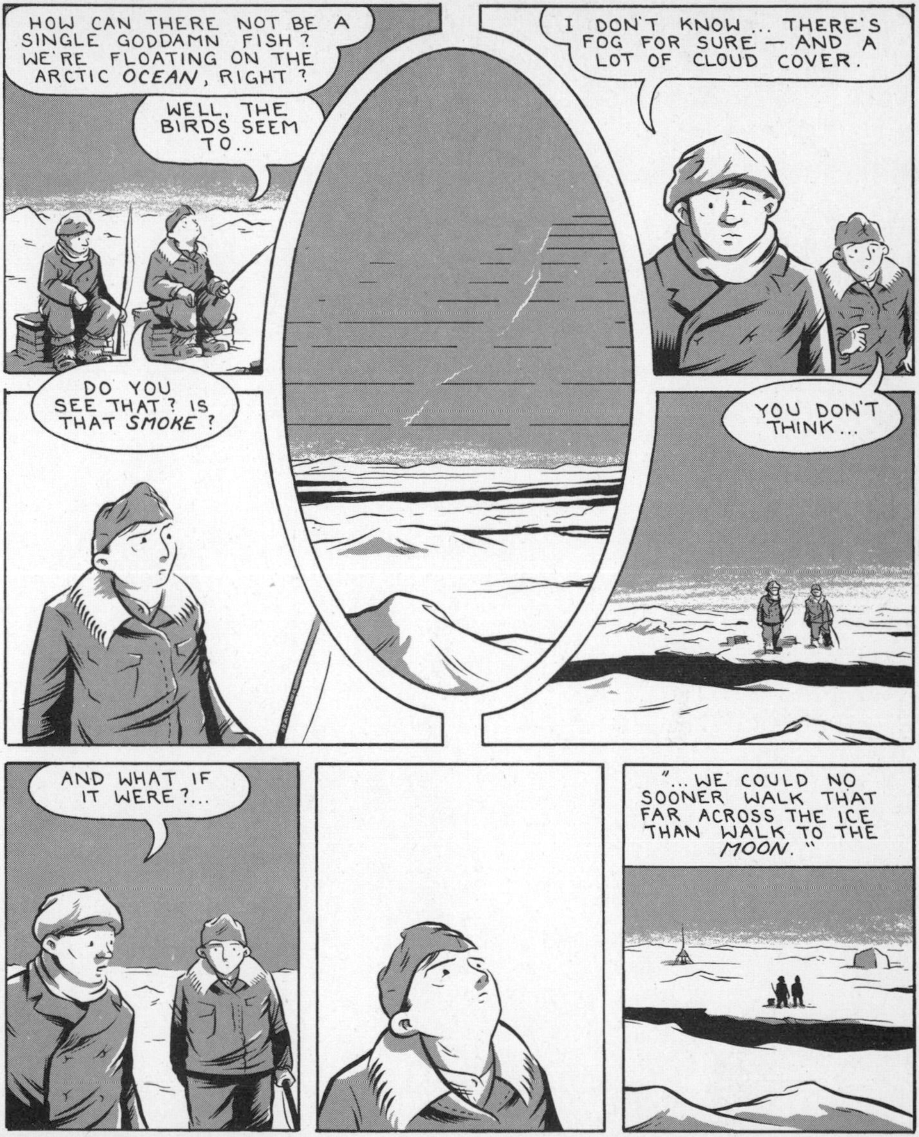
HOW CAN THERE NOT BE A SINGLE GODDAMN FISH? WE'RE FLOATING ON THE ARCTIC *OCEAN*, RIGHT?
WELL, THE BIRDS SEEM TO...
I DON'T KNOW... THERE'S FOG FOR SURE — AND A LOT OF CLOUD COVER.
DO YOU SEE THAT? IS THAT *SMOKE*?
YOU DON'T THINK...
AND WHAT IF IT WERE?...
"...WE COULD NO SOONER WALK THAT FAR ACROSS THE ICE THAN WALK TO THE *MOON*."

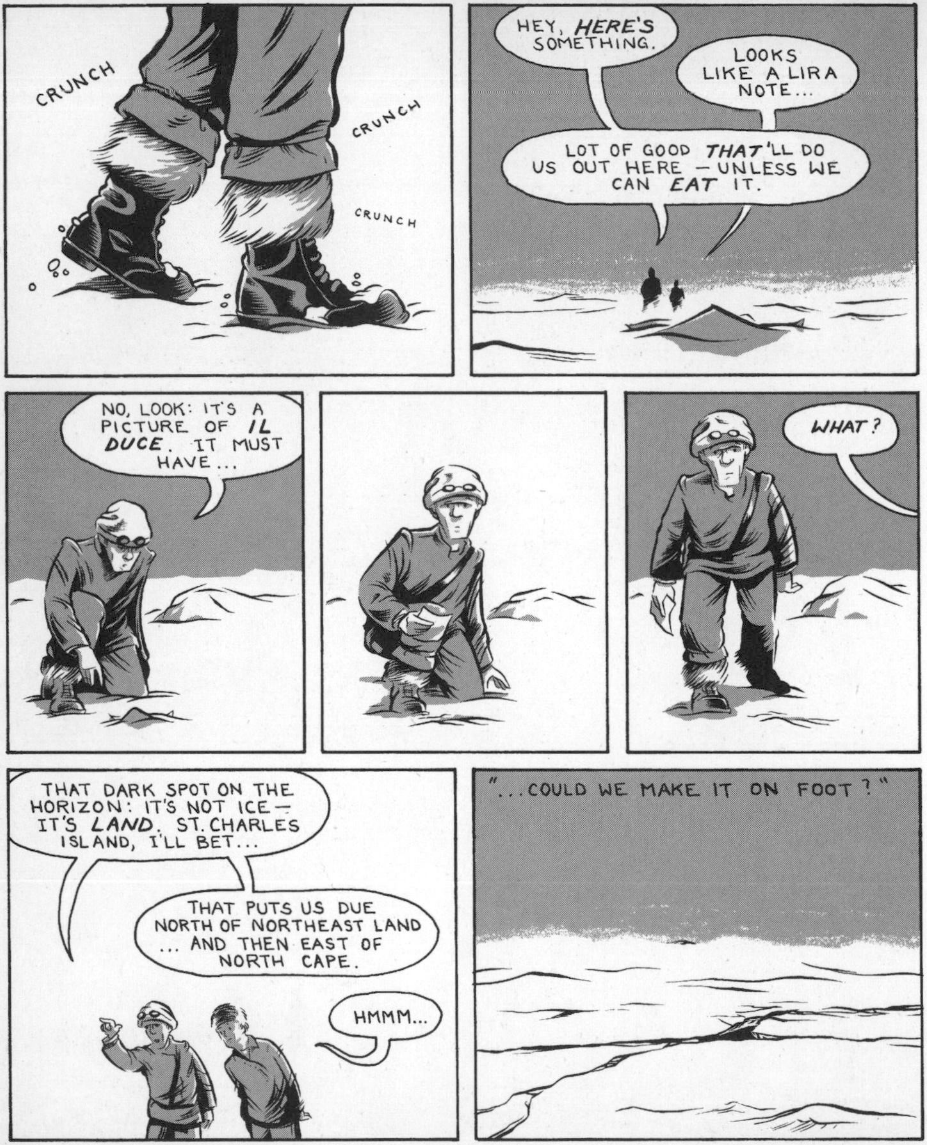
CRUNCH
CRUNCH
CRUNCH
HEY, HERE'S SOMETHING.
LOOKS LIKE A LIRA NOTE...
LOT OF GOOD THAT'LL DO US OUT HERE — UNLESS WE CAN EAT IT.
NO, LOOK: IT'S A PICTURE OF IL DUCE. IT MUST HAVE...
WHAT?
THAT DARK SPOT ON THE HORIZON: IT'S NOT ICE— IT'S LAND. ST. CHARLES ISLAND, I'LL BET...
THAT PUTS US DUE NORTH OF NORTHEAST LAND ... AND THEN EAST OF NORTH CAPE.
HMMM...
"...COULD WE MAKE IT ON FOOT?"

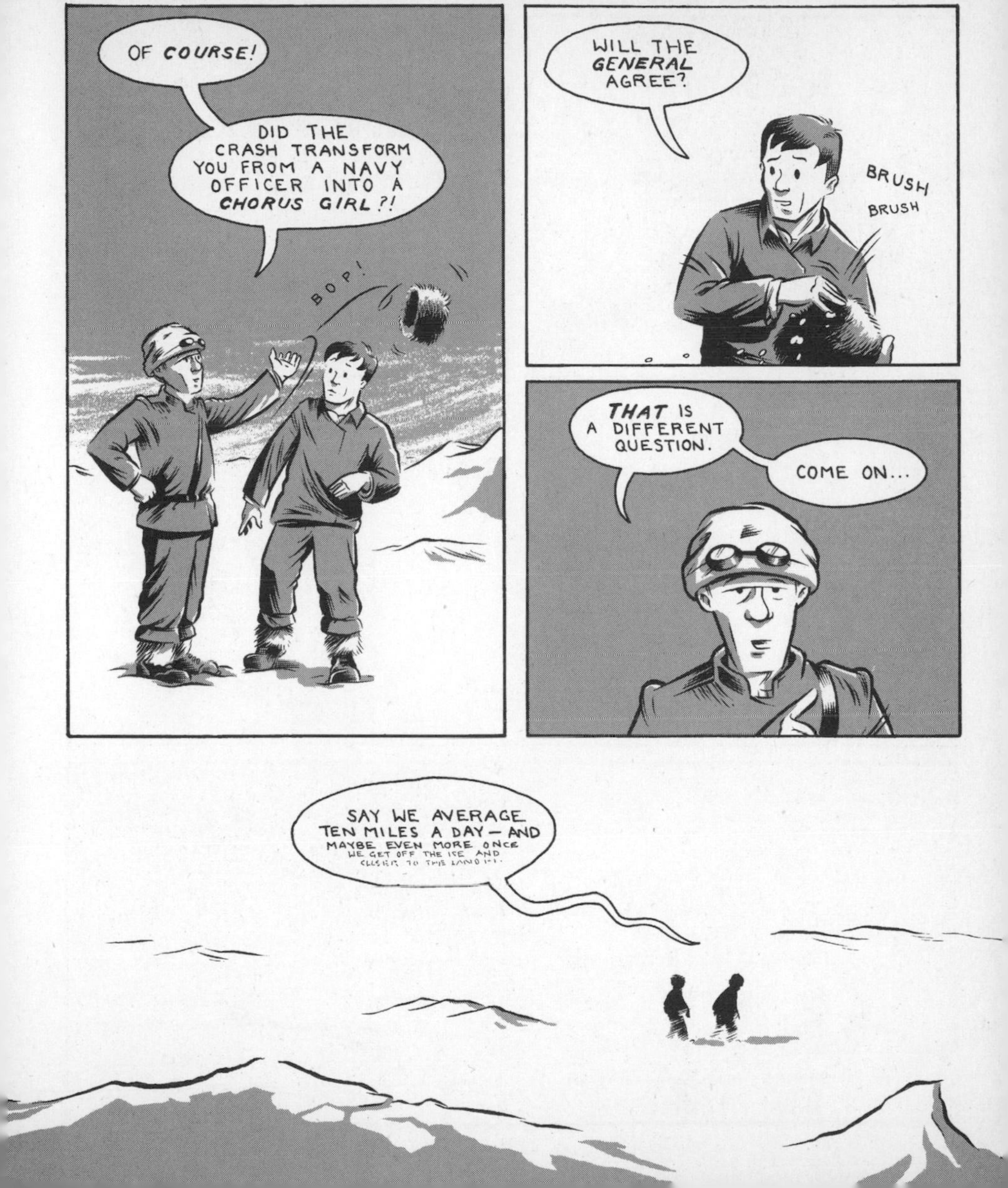
OF COURSE!
DID THE CRASH TRANSFORM YOU FROM A NAVY OFFICER INTO A CHORUS GIRL?!
BOP!
WILL THE GENERAL AGREE?
BRUSH
BRUSH
THAT IS A DIFFERENT QUESTION.
COME ON...
SAY WE AVERAGE TEN MILES A DAY — AND MAYBE EVEN MORE ONCE WE GET OFF THE ICE AND CLOSER TO THE LAND...

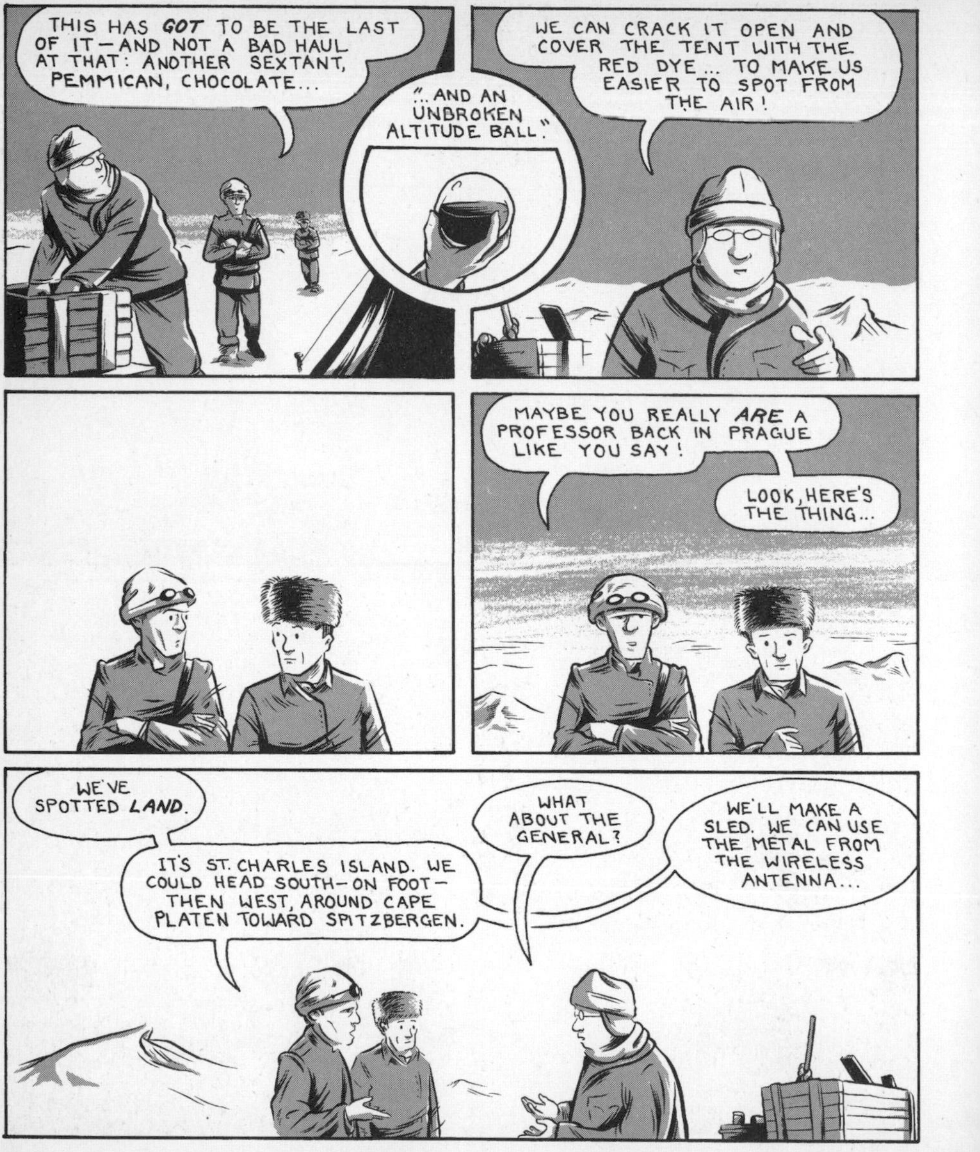
THIS HAS GOT TO BE THE LAST OF IT—AND NOT A BAD HAUL AT THAT: ANOTHER SEXTANT, PEMMICAN, CHOCOLATE...
"...AND AN UNBROKEN ALTITUDE BALL."
WE CAN CRACK IT OPEN AND COVER THE TENT WITH THE RED DYE... TO MAKE US EASIER TO SPOT FROM THE AIR!
MAYBE YOU REALLY ARE A PROFESSOR BACK IN PRAGUE LIKE YOU SAY!
LOOK, HERE'S THE THING...
WE'VE SPOTTED LAND.
IT'S ST. CHARLES ISLAND. WE COULD HEAD SOUTH—ON FOOT—THEN WEST, AROUND CAPE PLATEN TOWARD SPITZBERGEN.
WHAT ABOUT THE GENERAL?
WE'LL MAKE A SLED. WE CAN USE THE METAL FROM THE WIRELESS ANTENNA...

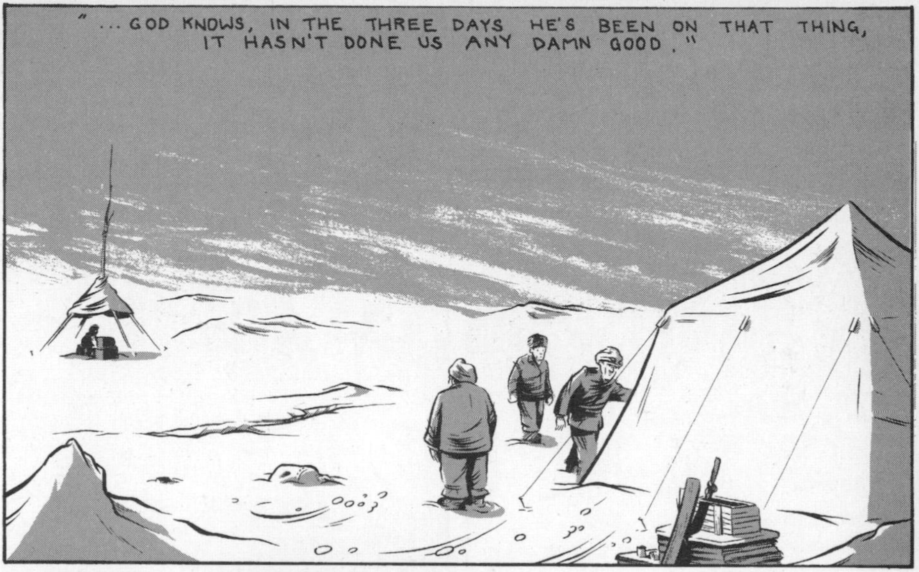
"...GOD KNOWS, IN THE THREE DAYS HE'S BEEN ON THAT THING, IT HASN'T DONE US ANY DAMN GOOD."

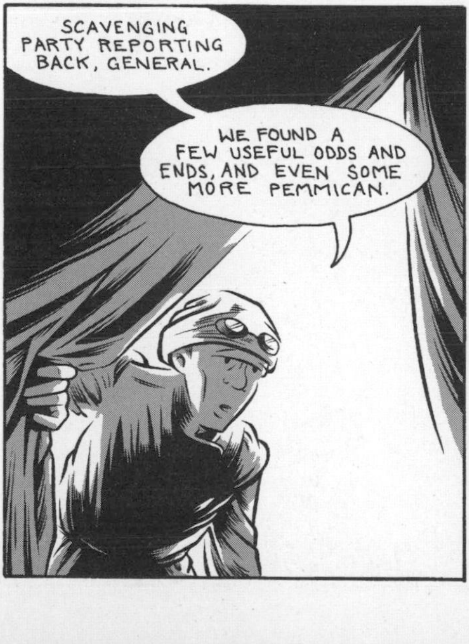
SCAVENGING PARTY REPORTING BACK, GENERAL.
WE FOUND A FEW USEFUL ODDS AND ENDS, AND EVEN SOME MORE PEMMICAN.

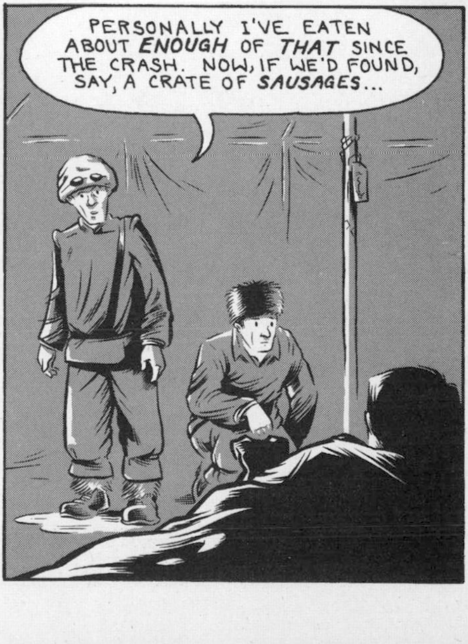
PERSONALLY I'VE EATEN ABOUT ENOUGH OF THAT SINCE THE CRASH. NOW, IF WE'D FOUND, SAY, A CRATE OF SAUSAGES...

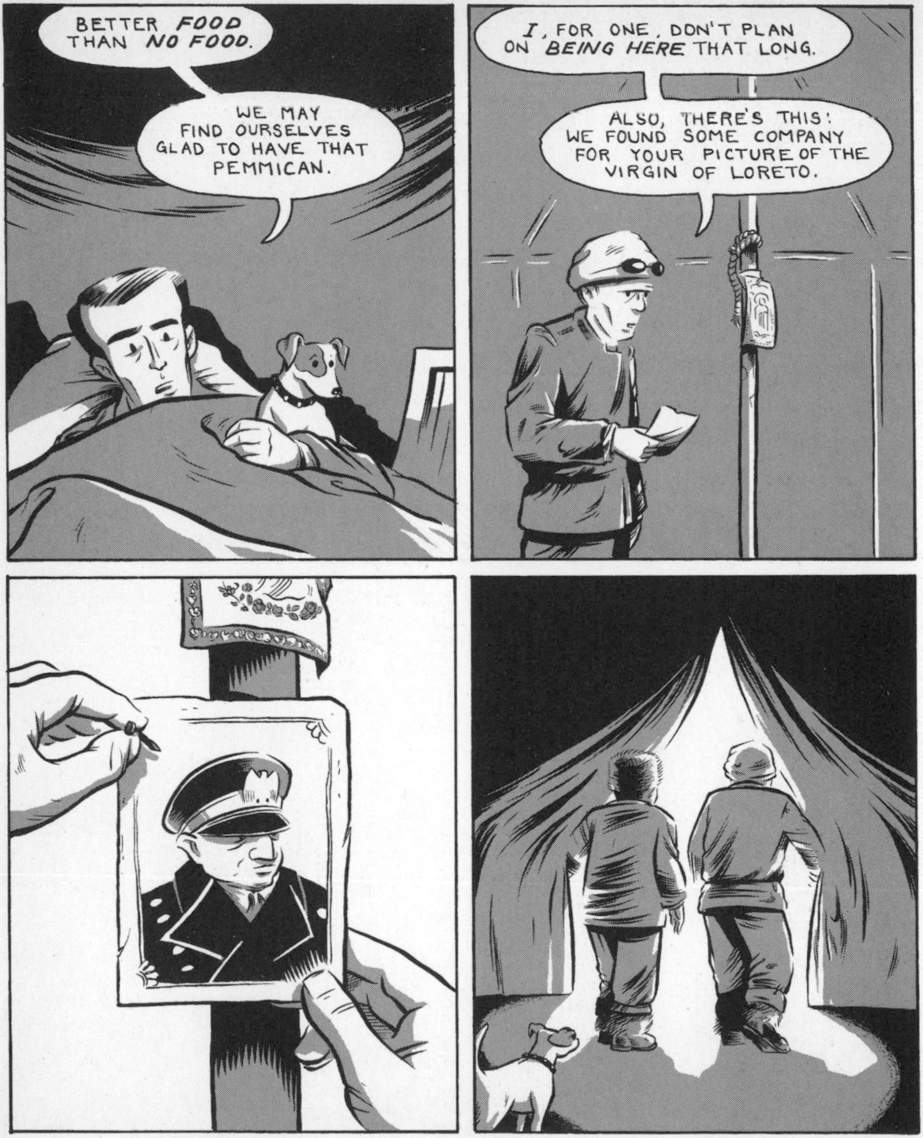
BETTER FOOD THAN NO FOOD.
WE MAY FIND OURSELVES GLAD TO HAVE THAT PEMMICAN.
I, FOR ONE, DON'T PLAN ON BEING HERE THAT LONG.
ALSO, THERE'S THIS: WE FOUND SOME COMPANY FOR YOUR PICTURE OF THE VIRGIN OF LORETO.

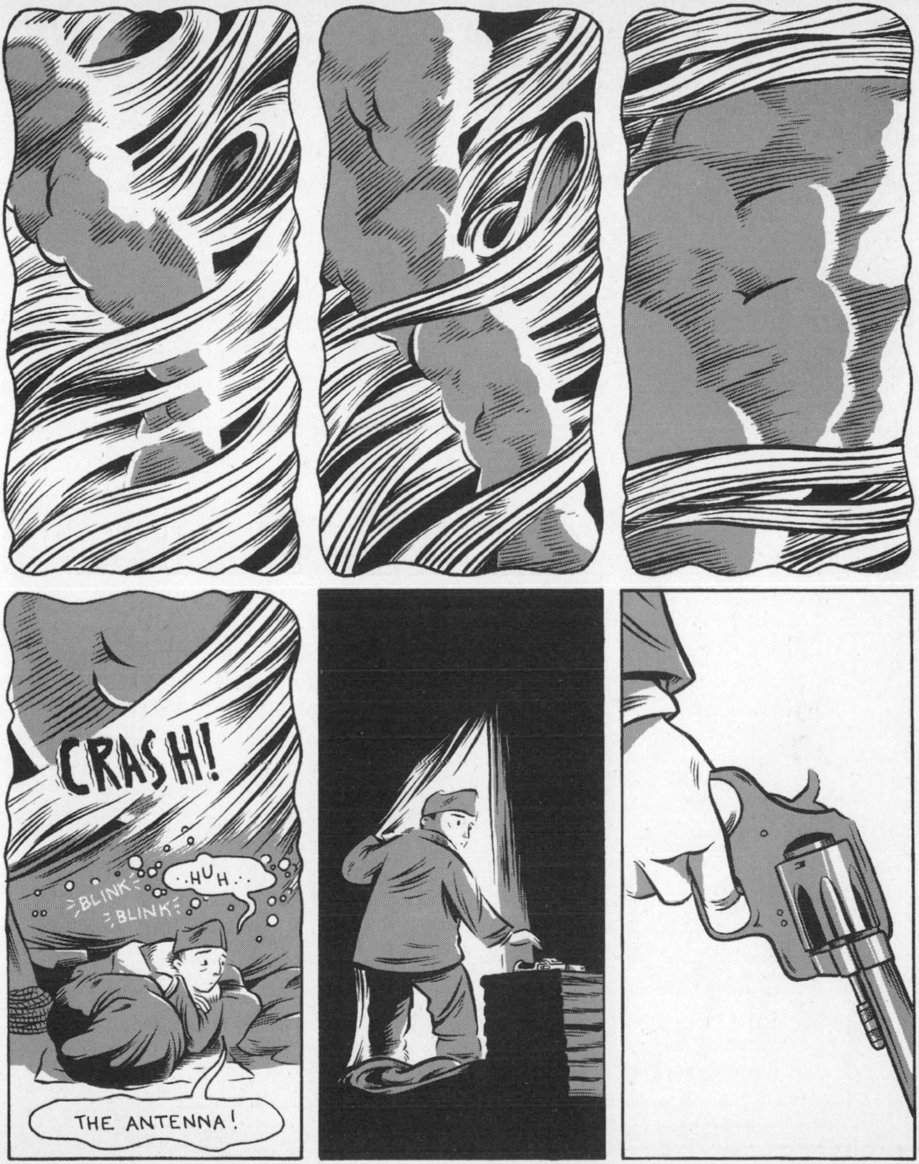
CRASH!
BLINK BLINK
..HUH...
THE ANTENNA!

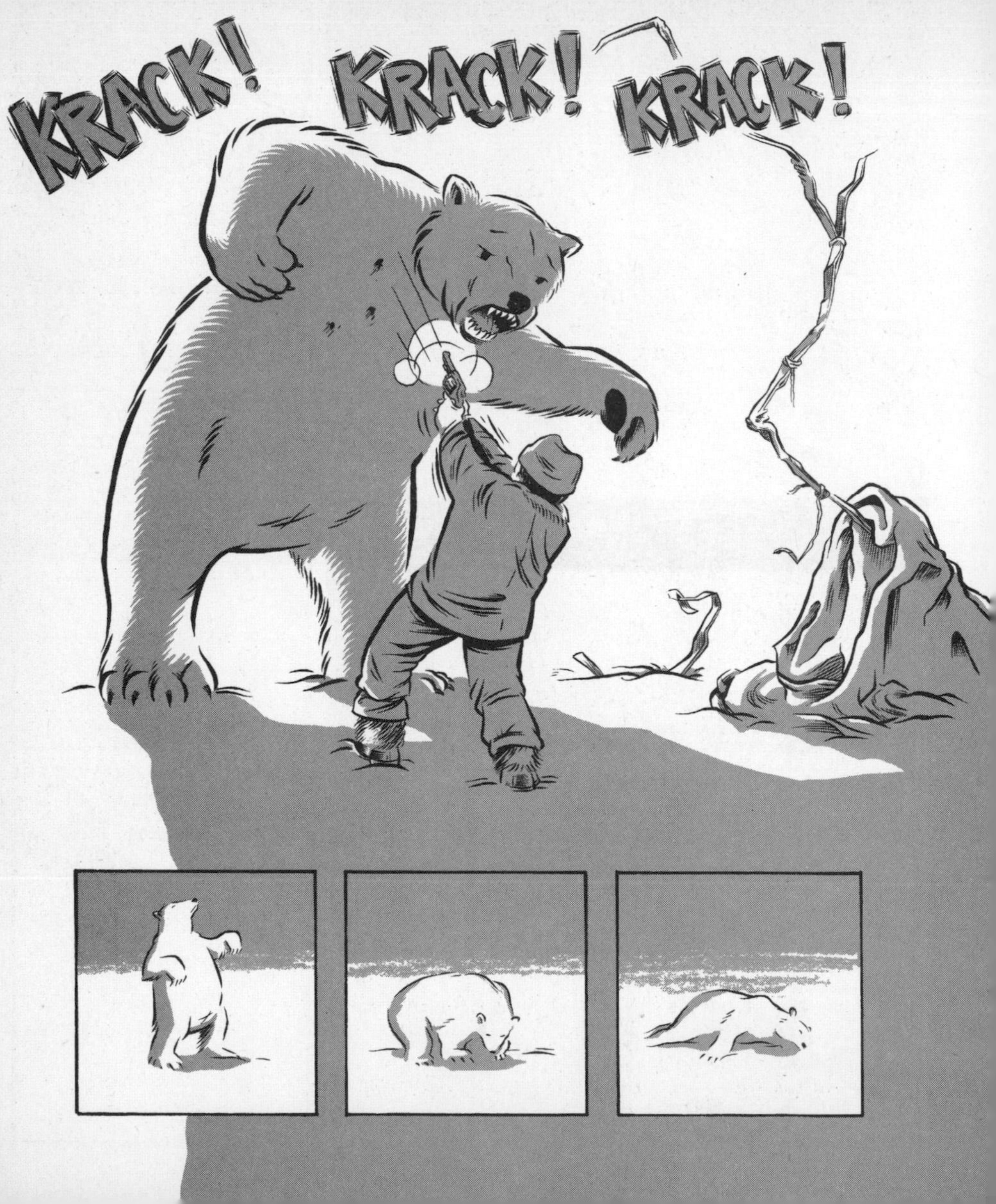
KRACK!
KRACK!
KRACK!

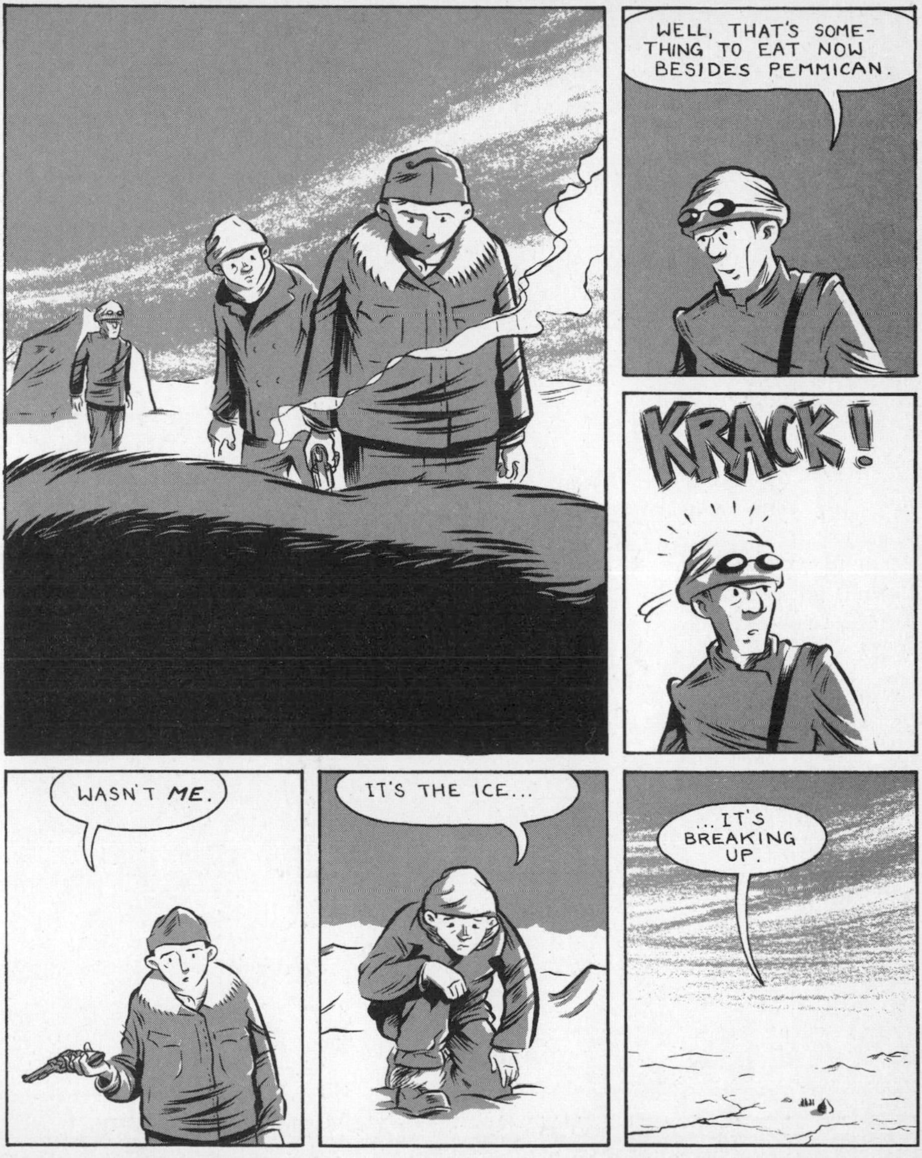
WELL, THAT'S SOME-THING TO EAT NOW BESIDES PEMMICAN.
KRACK!
WASN'T *ME*.
IT'S THE ICE...
...IT'S BREAKING UP.

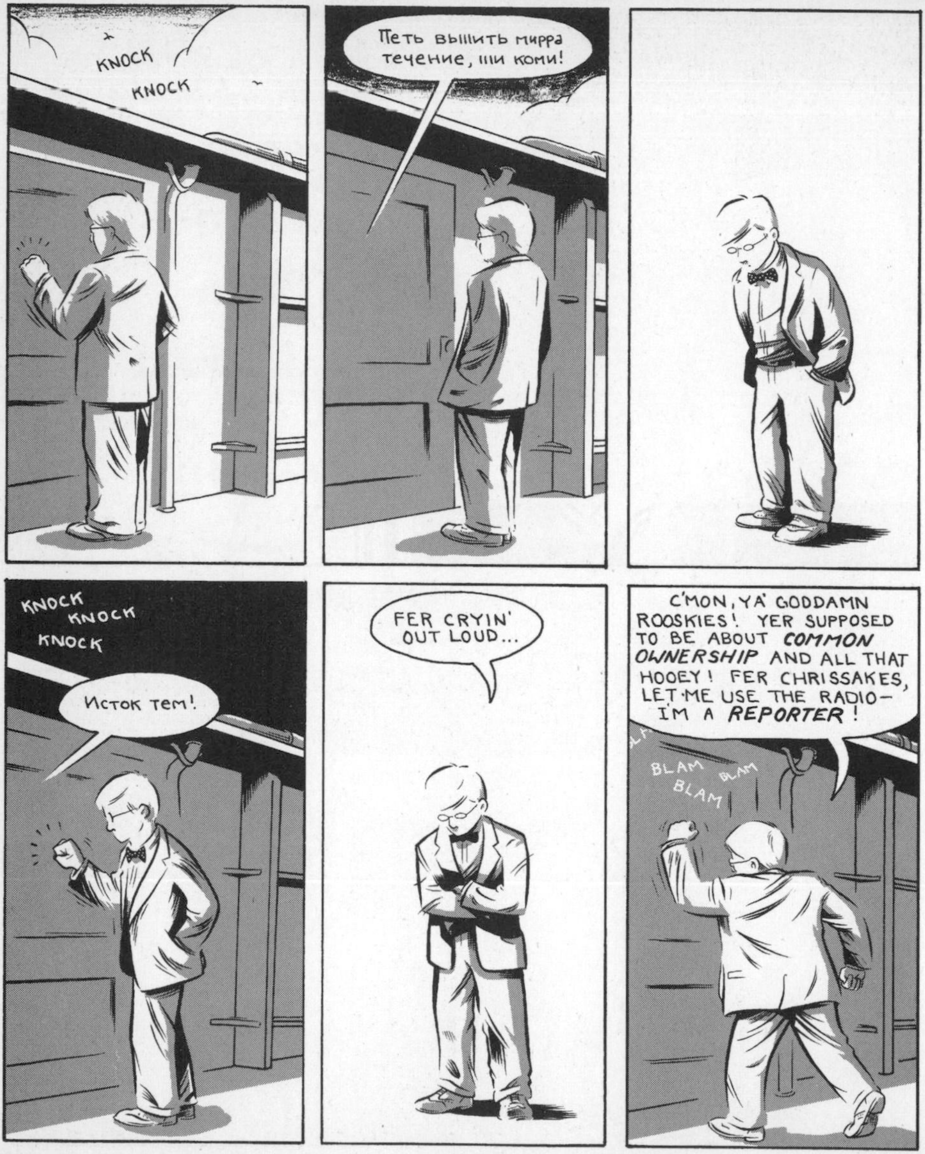
KNOCK
KNOCK
Петь вышить мирра течение, ши коми!
KNOCK
KNOCK
KNOCK
Исток тем!
FER CRYIN' OUT LOUD...
C'MON, YA' GODDAMN ROOSKIES! YER SUPPOSED TO BE ABOUT COMMON OWNERSHIP AND ALL THAT HOOEY! FER CHRISSAKES, LET ME USE THE RADIO— I'M A REPORTER!
BLAM
BLAM
BLAM

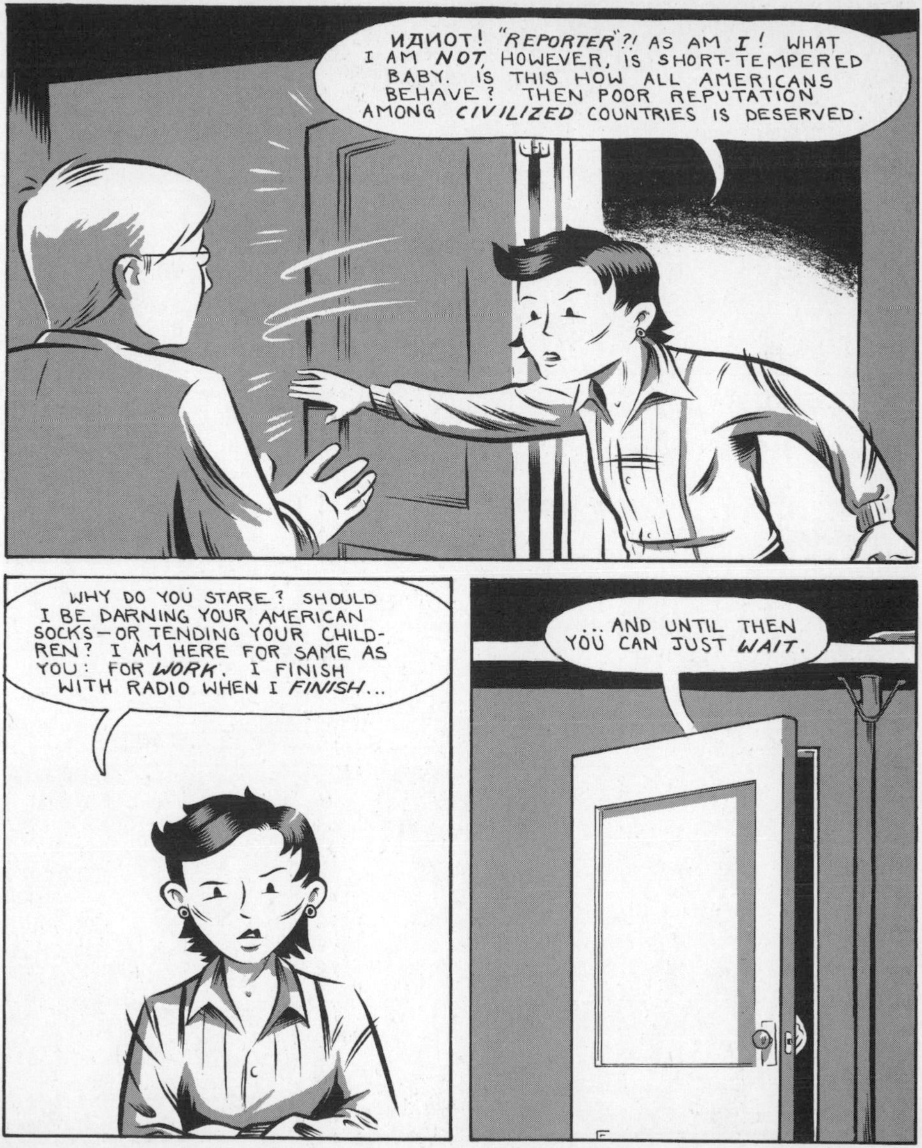
ИДИОТ! "REPORTER"?! AS AM I! WHAT I AM NOT, HOWEVER, IS SHORT-TEMPERED BABY. IS THIS HOW ALL AMERICANS BEHAVE? THEN POOR REPUTATION AMONG CIVILIZED COUNTRIES IS DESERVED.
WHY DO YOU STARE? SHOULD I BE DARNING YOUR AMERICAN SOCKS—OR TENDING YOUR CHILDREN? I AM HERE FOR SAME AS YOU: FOR WORK. I FINISH WITH RADIO WHEN I FINISH...
...AND UNTIL THEN YOU CAN JUST WAIT.

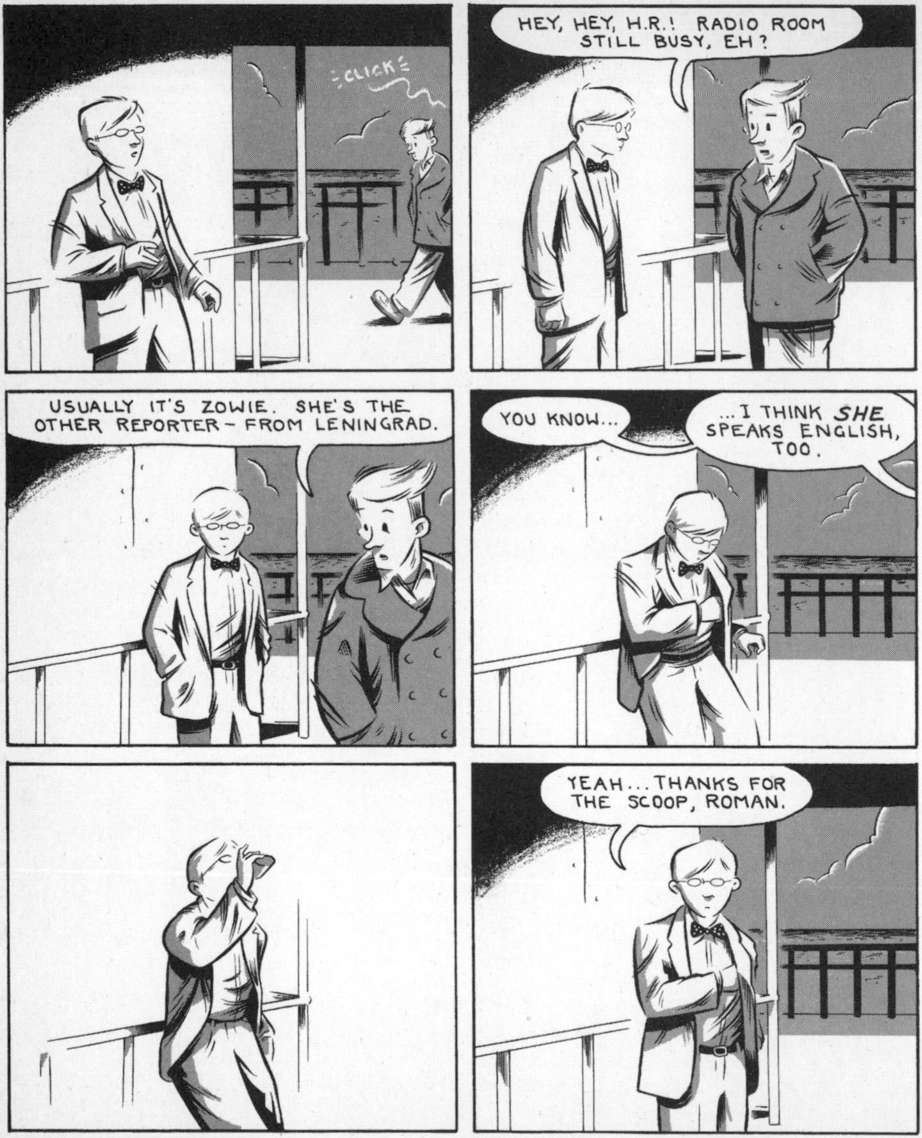
CLICK
HEY, HEY, H.R.! RADIO ROOM STILL BUSY, EH?
USUALLY IT'S ZOWIE. SHE'S THE OTHER REPORTER – FROM LENINGRAD.
YOU KNOW...
...I THINK SHE SPEAKS ENGLISH, TOO.
YEAH... THANKS FOR THE SCOOP, ROMAN.

III

Contact

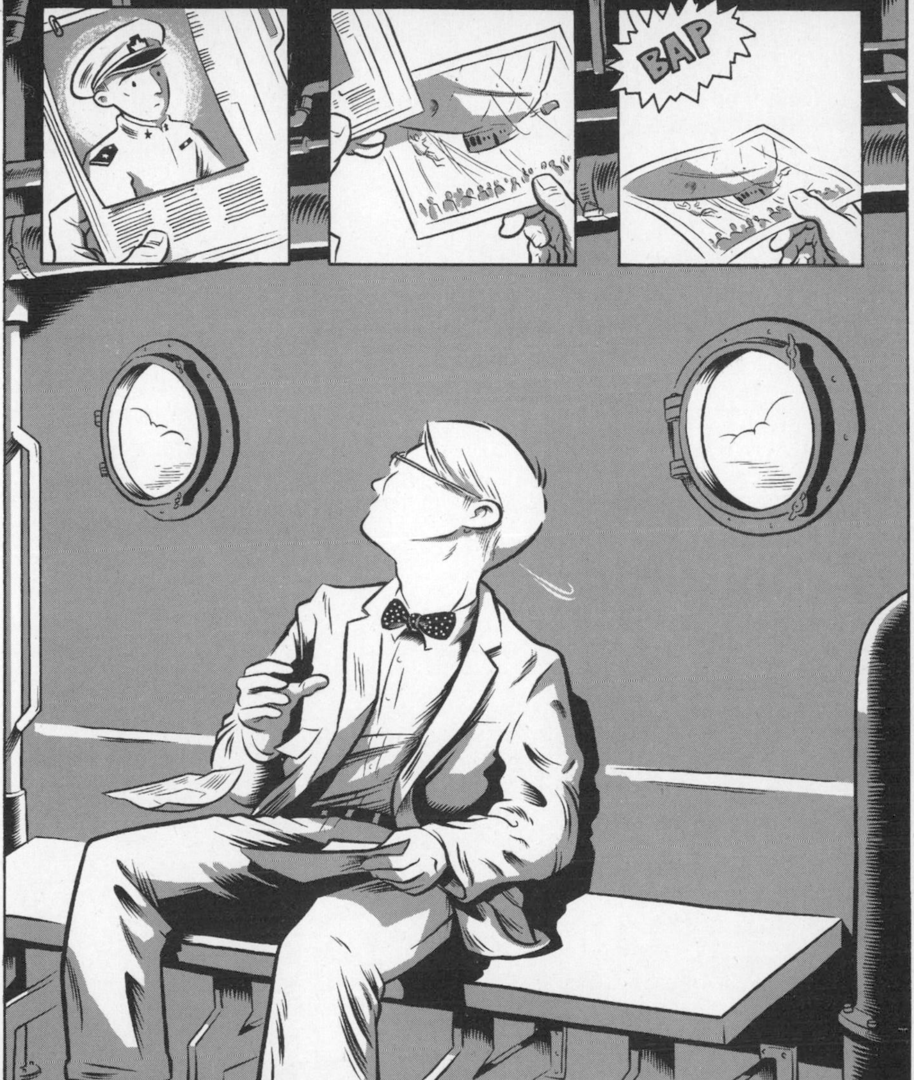
BAP

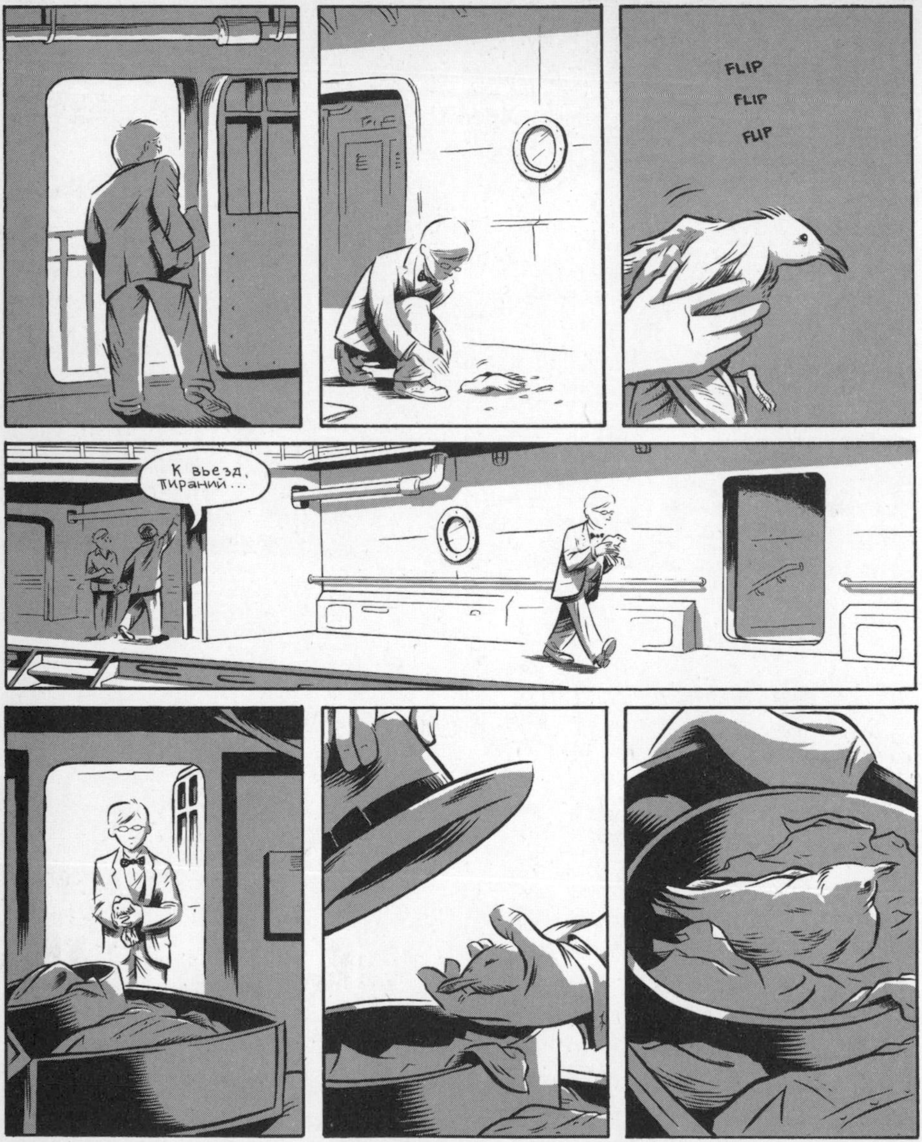
FLIP
FLIP
FLIP
К въезд, Пираний...

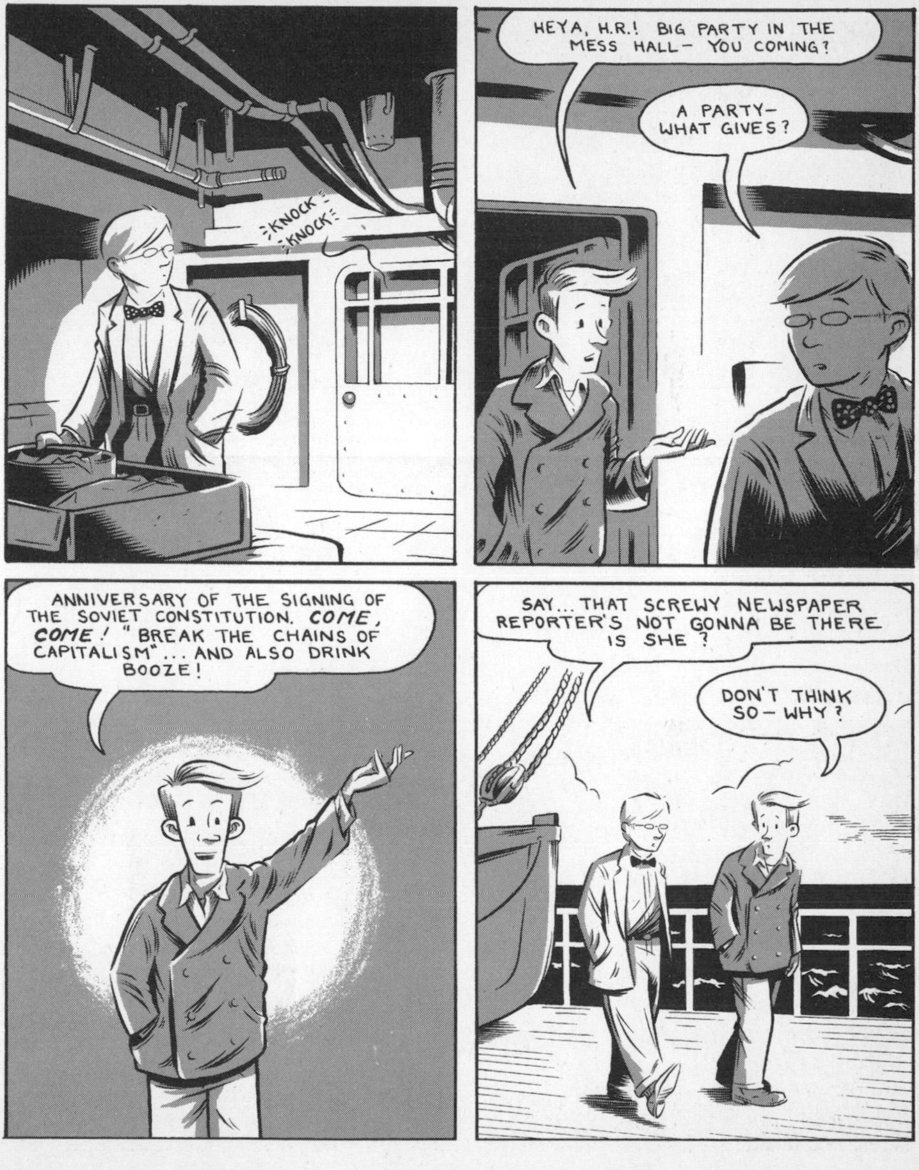
KNOCK KNOCK
HEYA, H.R.! BIG PARTY IN THE MESS HALL– YOU COMING?
A PARTY– WHAT GIVES?
ANNIVERSARY OF THE SIGNING OF THE SOVIET CONSTITUTION. COME, COME! "BREAK THE CHAINS OF CAPITALISM"... AND ALSO DRINK BOOZE!
SAY... THAT SCREWY NEWSPAPER REPORTER'S NOT GONNA BE THERE IS SHE?
DON'T THINK SO– WHY?

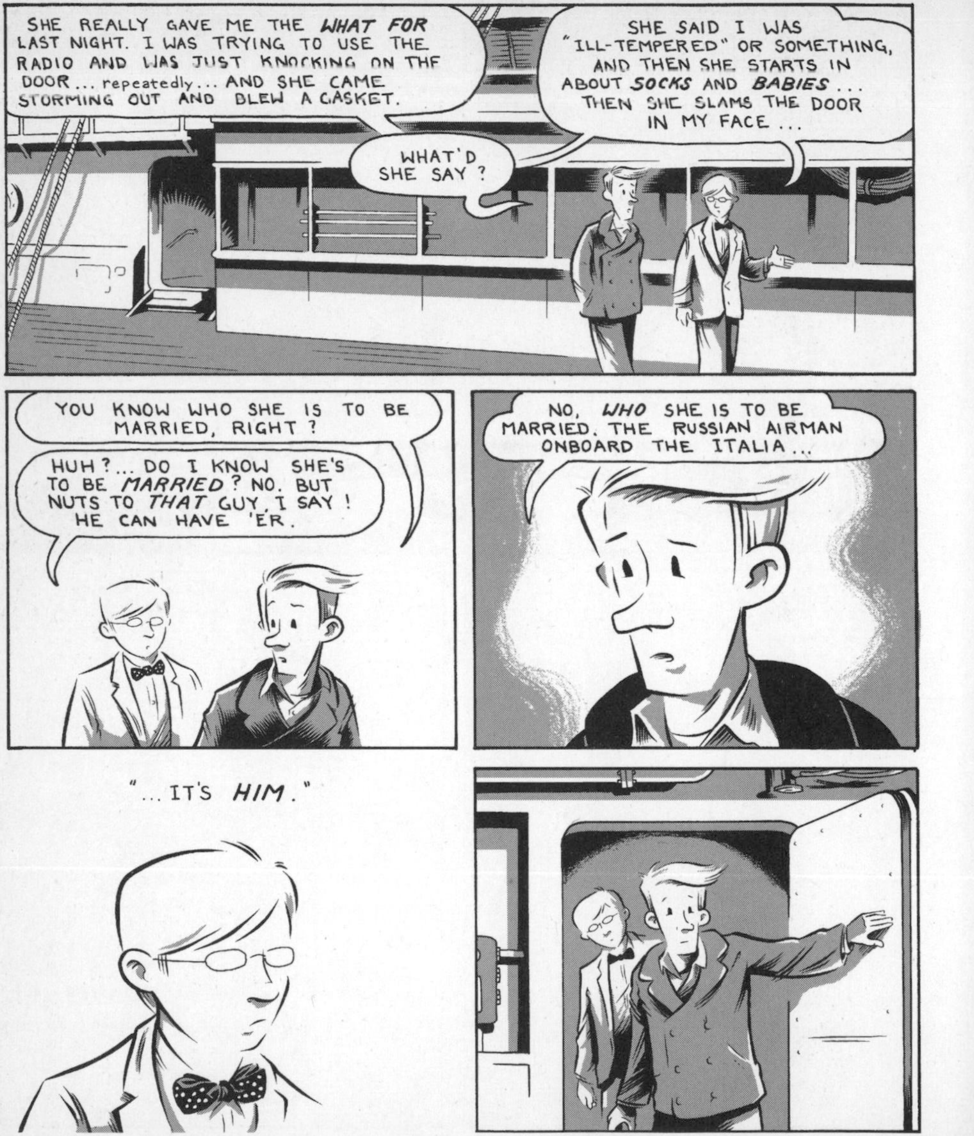
SHE REALLY GAVE ME THE WHAT FOR LAST NIGHT. I WAS TRYING TO USE THE RADIO AND WAS JUST KNOCKING ON THE DOOR... repeatedly... AND SHE CAME STORMING OUT AND BLEW A GASKET.
WHAT'D SHE SAY?
SHE SAID I WAS "ILL-TEMPERED" OR SOMETHING, AND THEN SHE STARTS IN ABOUT SOCKS AND BABIES... THEN SHE SLAMS THE DOOR IN MY FACE...
YOU KNOW WHO SHE IS TO BE MARRIED, RIGHT?
HUH?... DO I KNOW SHE'S TO BE MARRIED? NO. BUT NUTS TO THAT GUY, I SAY! HE CAN HAVE 'ER.
NO, WHO SHE IS TO BE MARRIED. THE RUSSIAN AIRMAN ONBOARD THE ITALIA...
"...IT'S HIM."

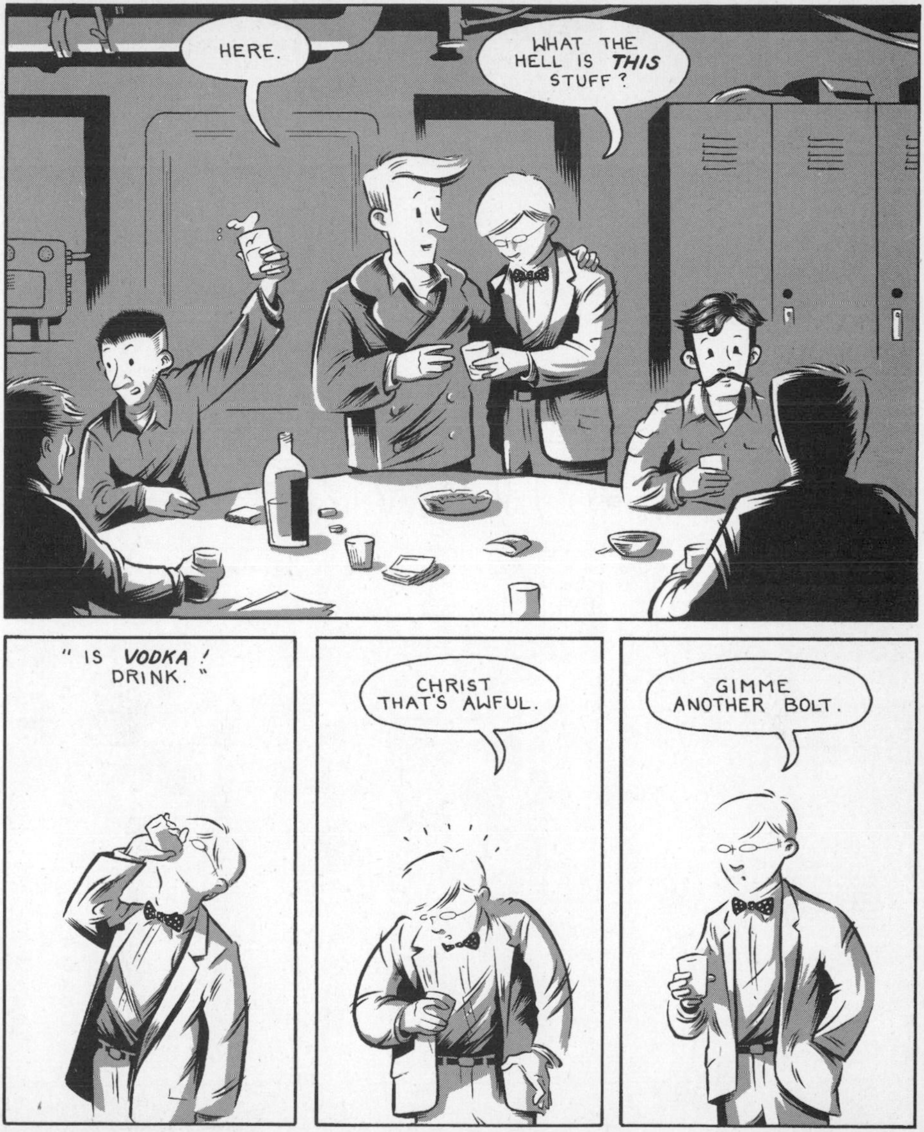
HERE.
WHAT THE HELL IS THIS STUFF?
" IS VODKA! DRINK. "
CHRIST THAT'S AWFUL.
GIMME ANOTHER BOLT.

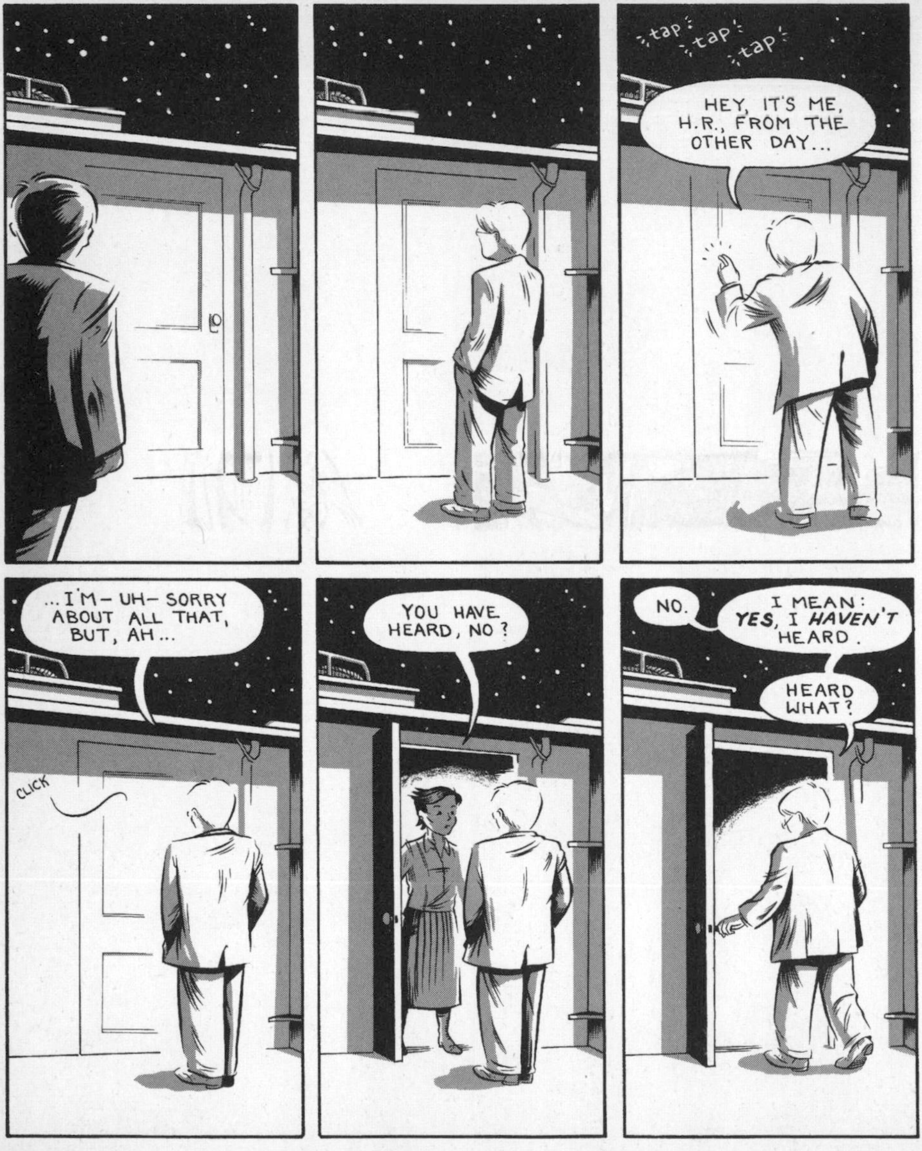
tap
tap
tap
HEY, IT'S ME, H.R., FROM THE OTHER DAY...
... I'M– UH– SORRY ABOUT ALL THAT, BUT, AH...
CLICK
YOU HAVE HEARD, NO?
NO.
I MEAN: YES, I HAVEN'T HEARD.
HEARD WHAT?

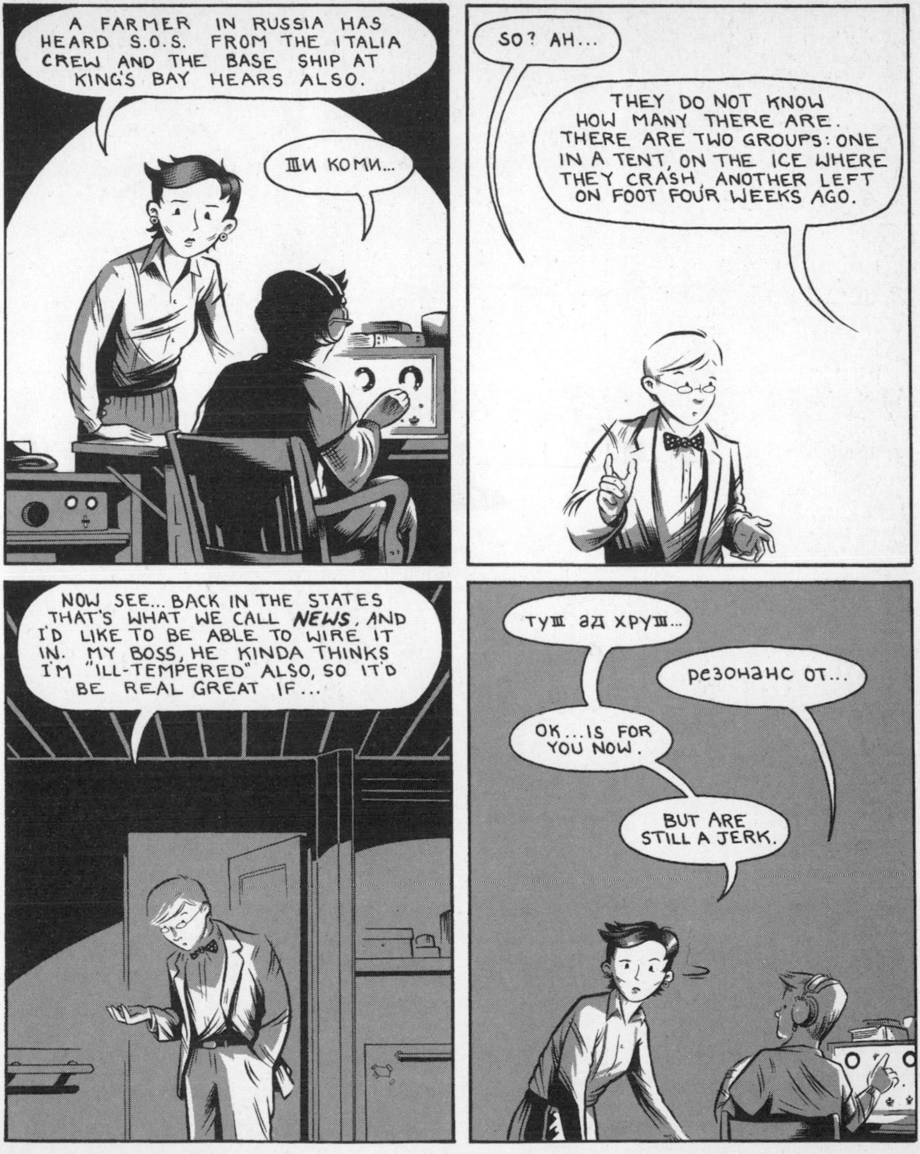
A FARMER IN RUSSIA HAS HEARD S.O.S. FROM THE ITALIA CREW AND THE BASE SHIP AT KING'S BAY HEARS ALSO.
ШИ КОМИ...
SO? AH...
THEY DO NOT KNOW HOW MANY THERE ARE. THERE ARE TWO GROUPS: ONE IN A TENT, ON THE ICE WHERE THEY CRASH, ANOTHER LEFT ON FOOT FOUR WEEKS AGO.
NOW SEE... BACK IN THE STATES THAT'S WHAT WE CALL ***NEWS***, AND I'D LIKE TO BE ABLE TO WIRE IT IN. MY BOSS, HE KINDA THINKS I'M "ILL-TEMPERED" ALSO, SO IT'D BE REAL GREAT IF...
ТУШ ад ХРУШ...
резонанс от...
OK... IS FOR YOU NOW.
BUT ARE STILL A JERK.

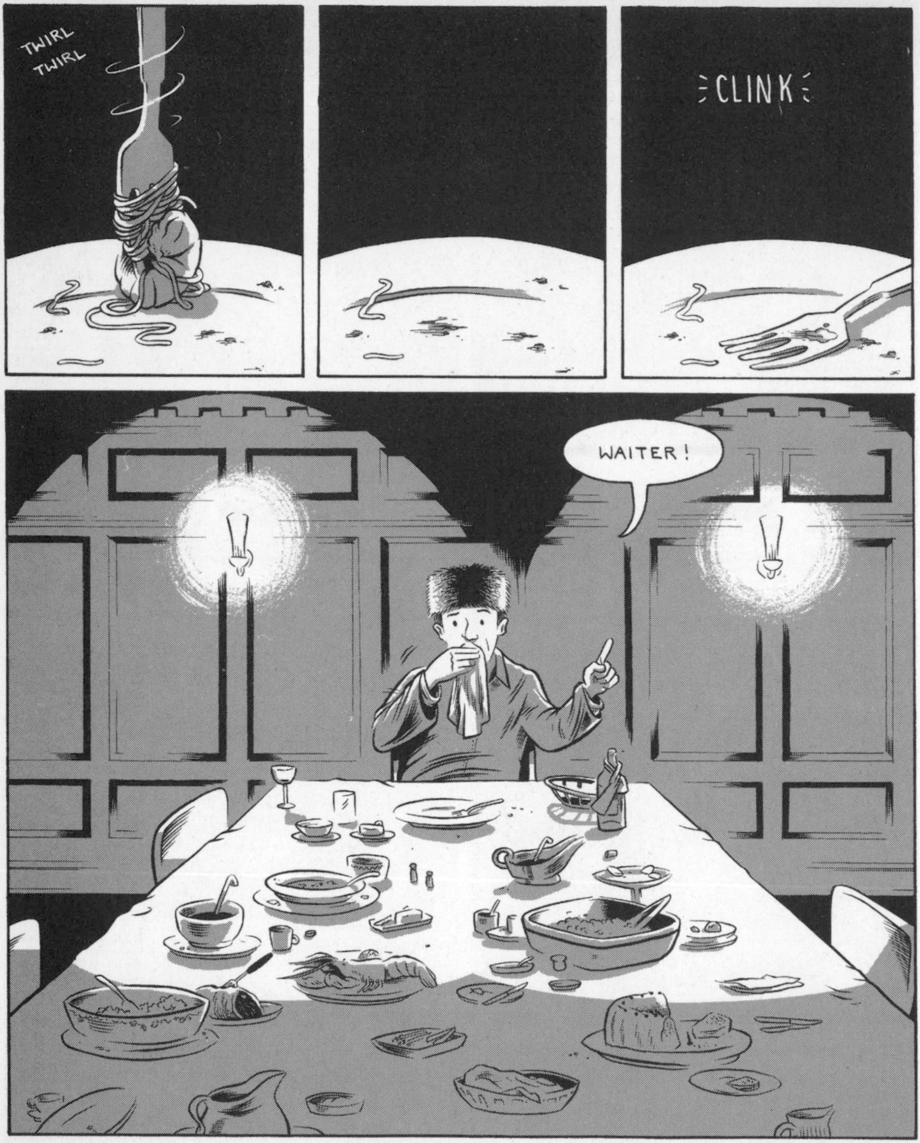
TWIRL
TWIRL
CLINK
WAITER!

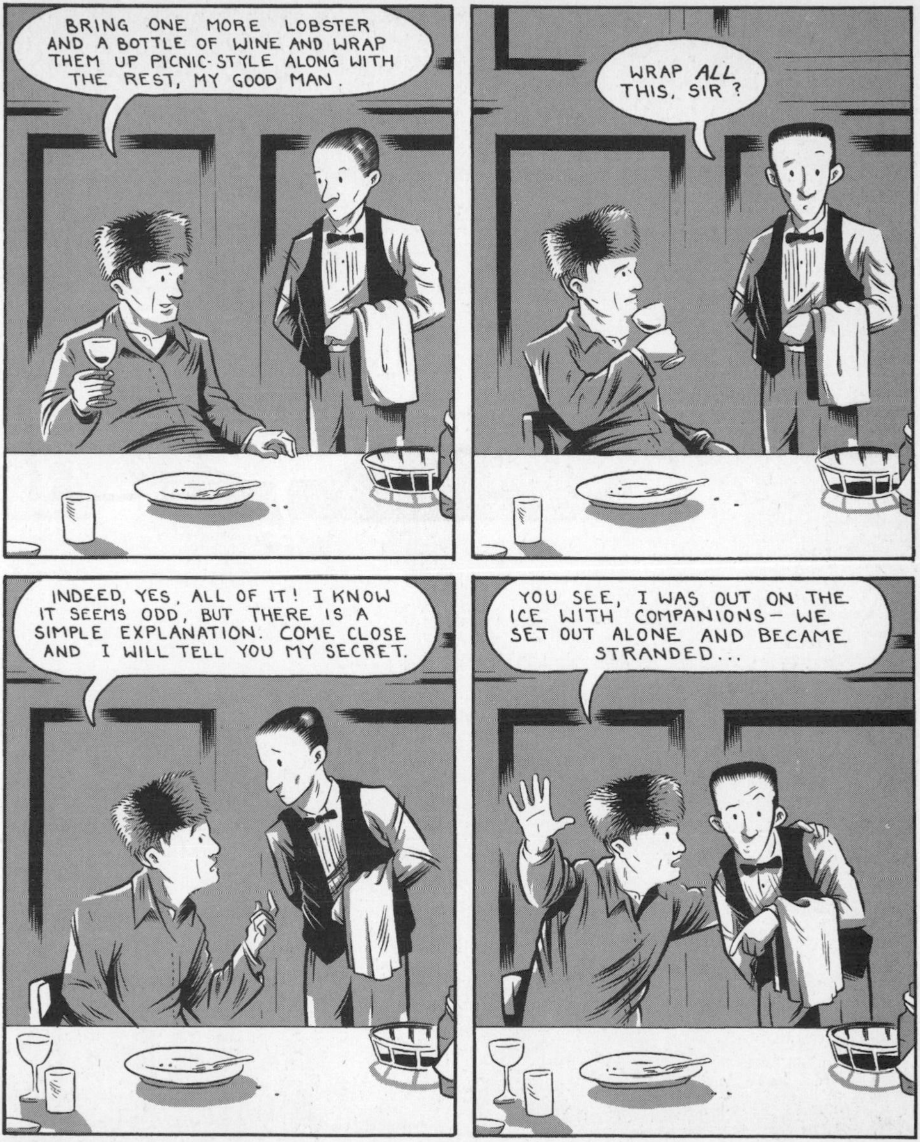
BRING ONE MORE LOBSTER AND A BOTTLE OF WINE AND WRAP THEM UP PICNIC-STYLE ALONG WITH THE REST, MY GOOD MAN.
WRAP ALL THIS, SIR?
INDEED, YES, ALL OF IT! I KNOW IT SEEMS ODD, BUT THERE IS A SIMPLE EXPLANATION. COME CLOSE AND I WILL TELL YOU MY SECRET.
YOU SEE, I WAS OUT ON THE ICE WITH COMPANIONS– WE SET OUT ALONE AND BECAME STRANDED...

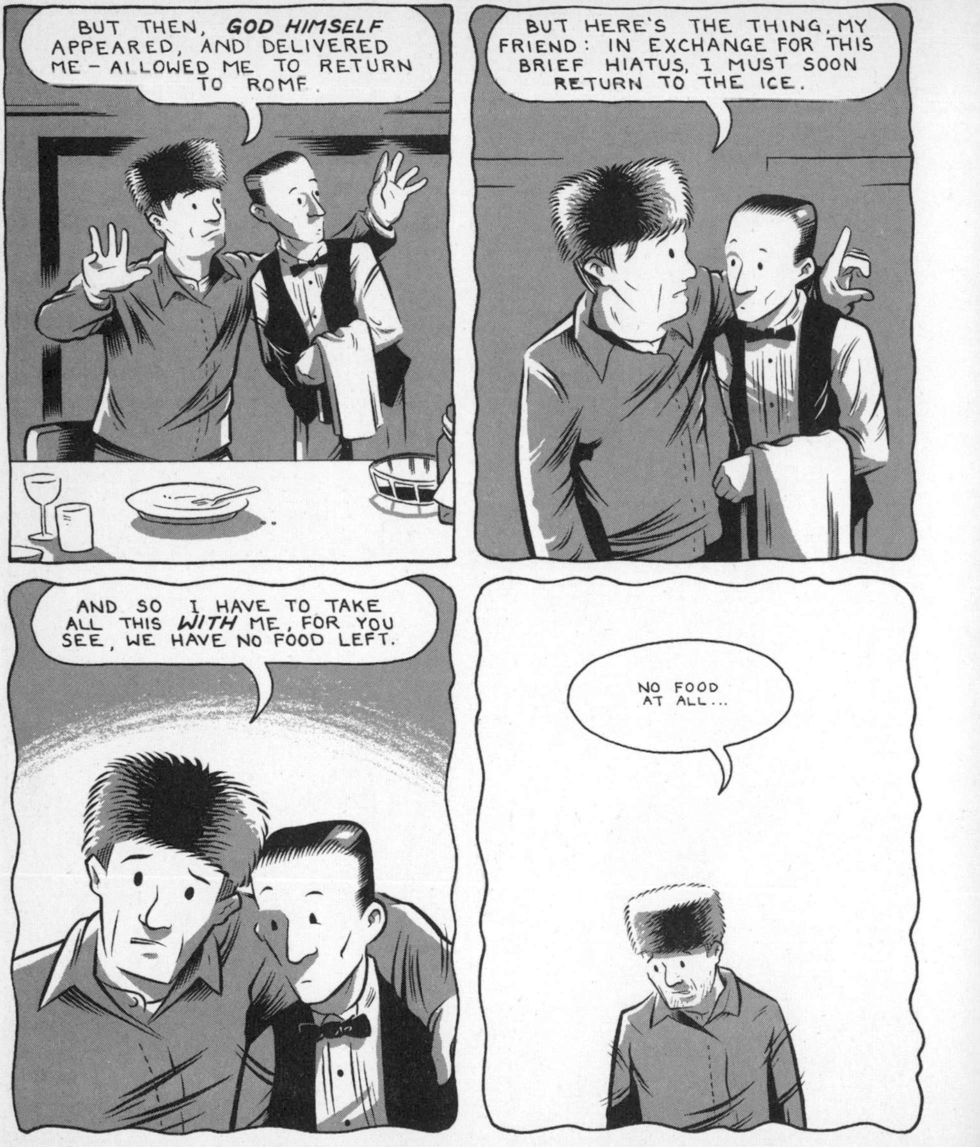
BUT THEN, GOD HIMSELF APPEARED, AND DELIVERED ME - ALLOWED ME TO RETURN TO ROMF.
BUT HERE'S THE THING, MY FRIEND: IN EXCHANGE FOR THIS BRIEF HIATUS, I MUST SOON RETURN TO THE ICE.
AND SO I HAVE TO TAKE ALL THIS WITH ME, FOR YOU SEE, WE HAVE NO FOOD LEFT.
NO FOOD AT ALL...

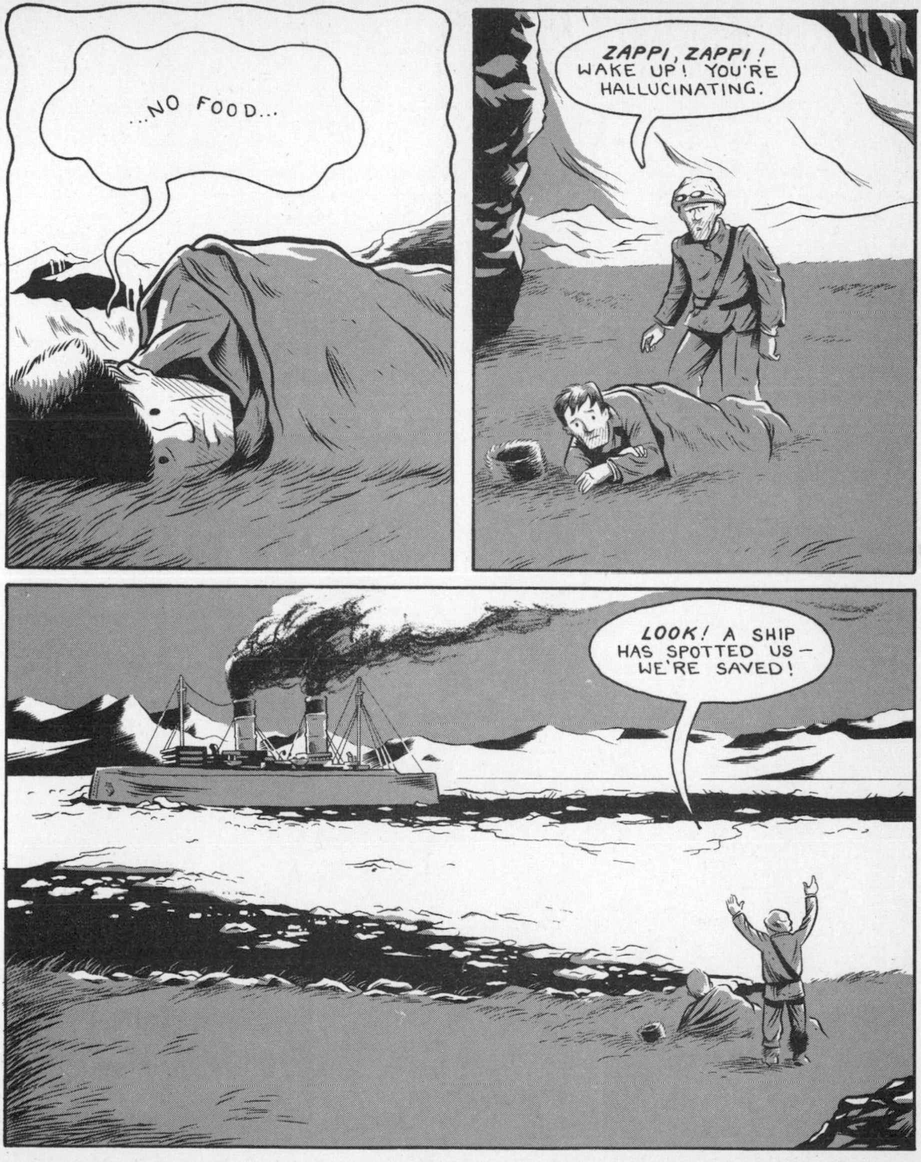
...NO FOOD...
ZAPPI, ZAPPI! WAKE UP! YOU'RE HALLUCINATING.
LOOK! A SHIP HAS SPOTTED US— WE'RE SAVED!

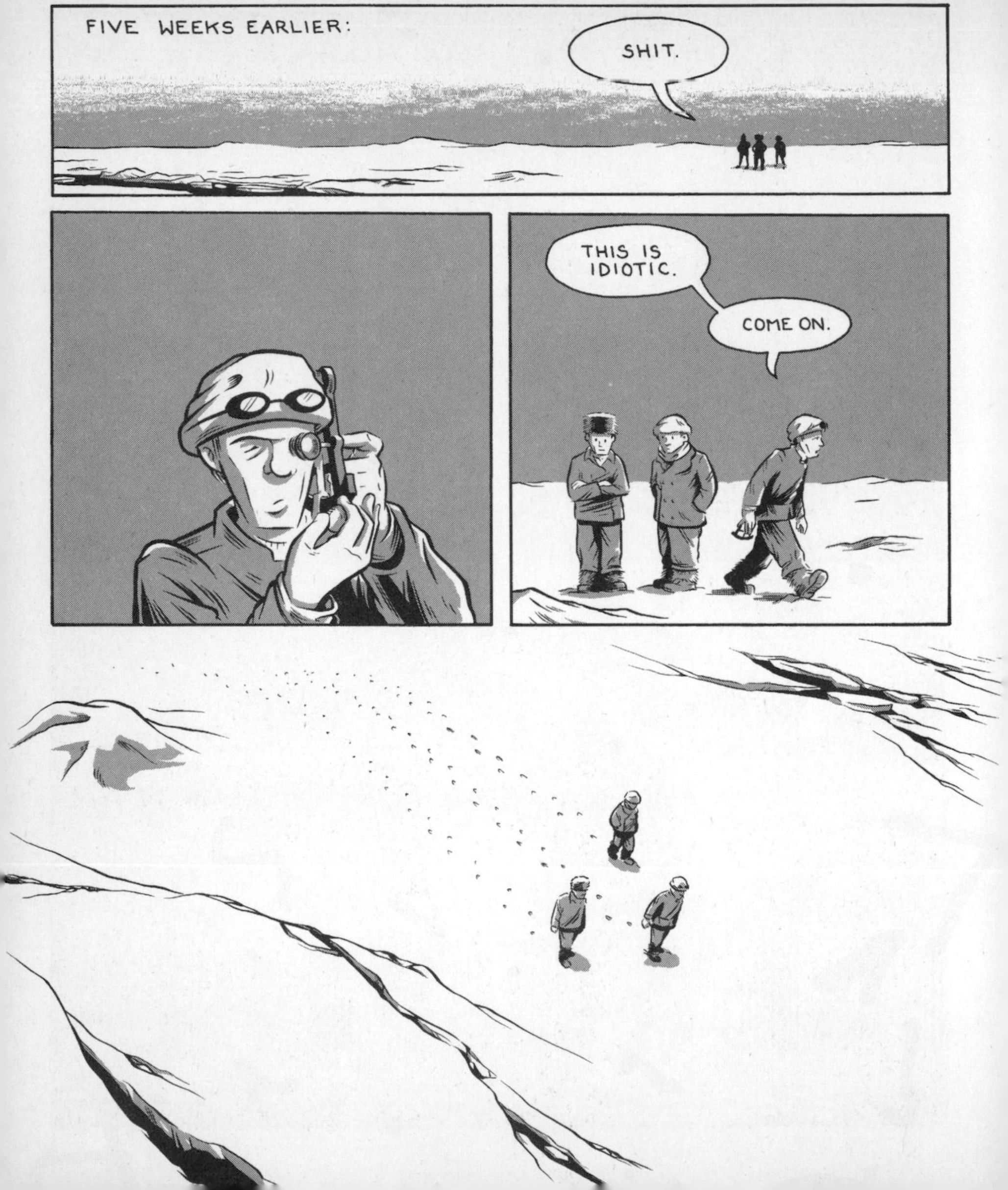
FIVE WEEKS EARLIER:
SHIT.
THIS IS IDIOTIC.
COME ON.

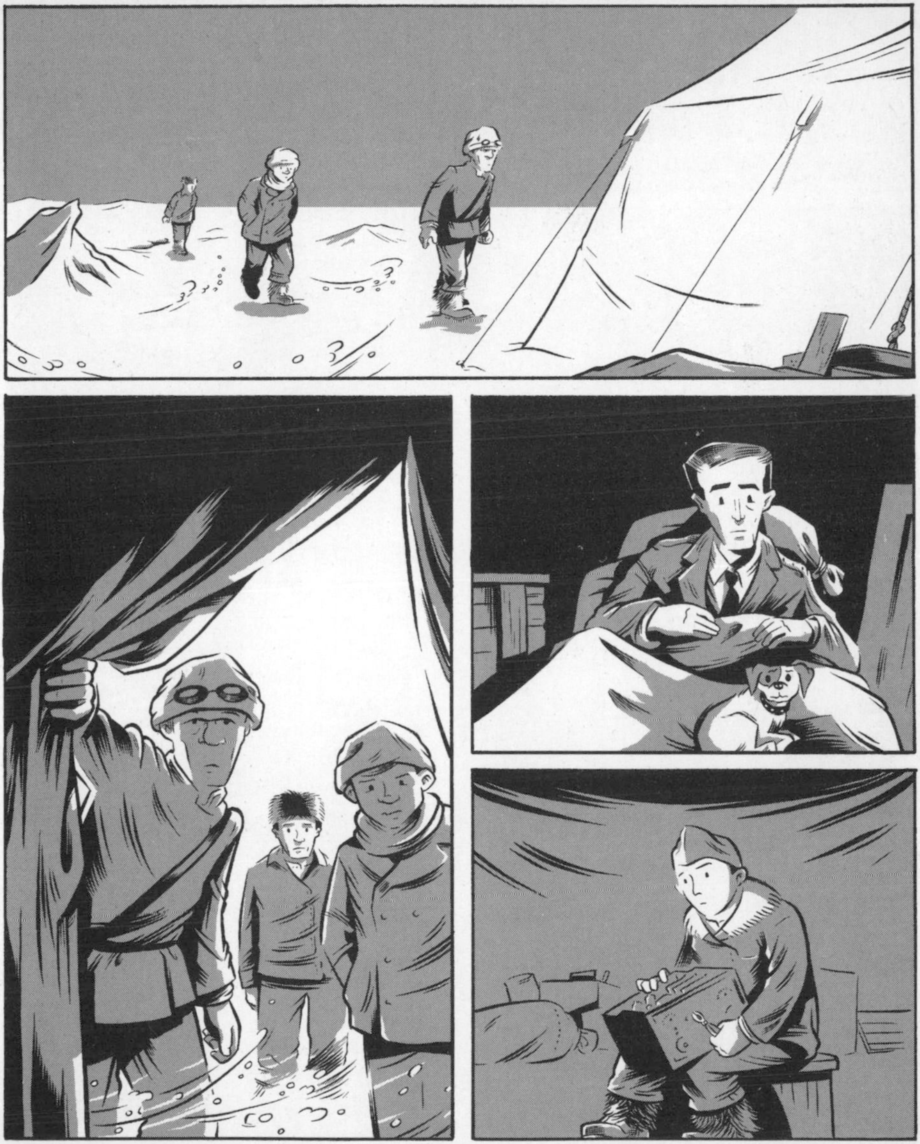

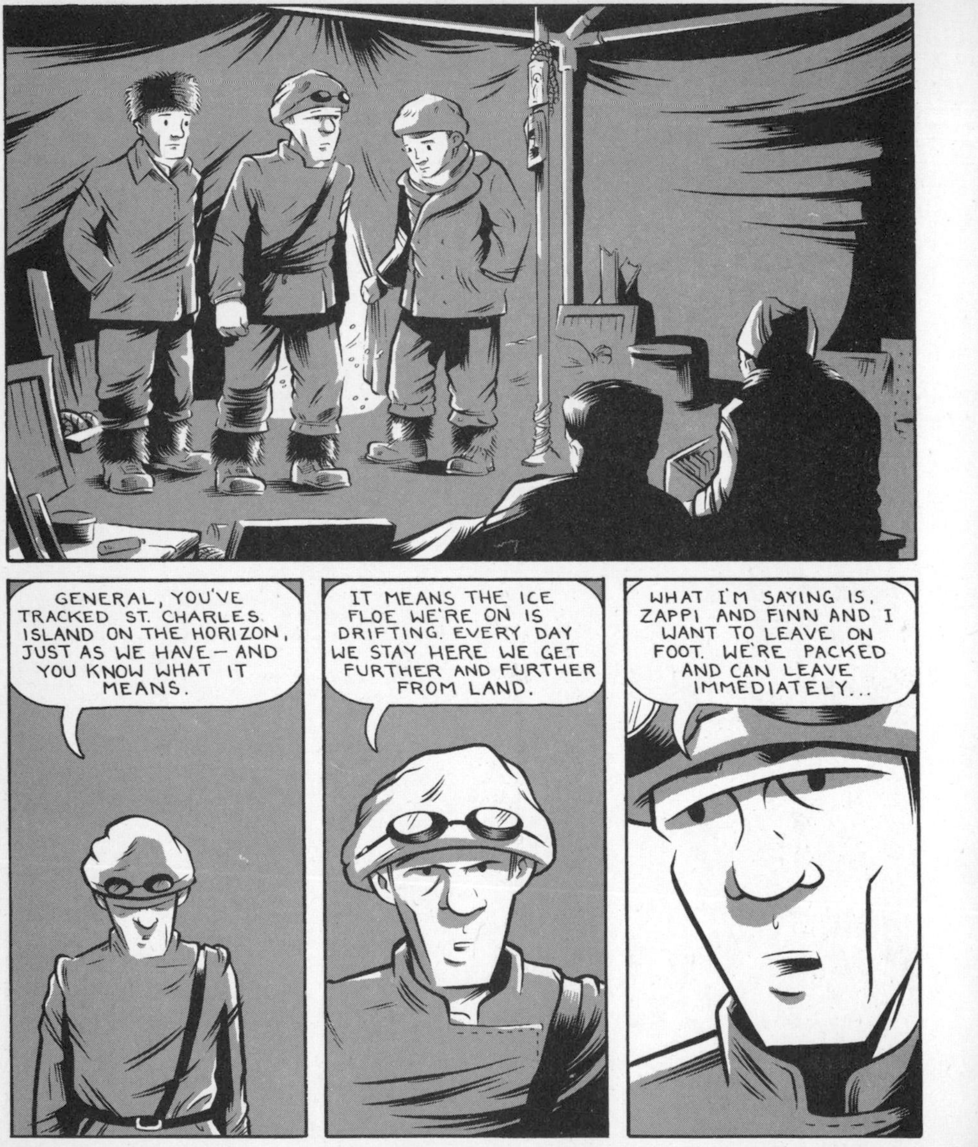
GENERAL, YOU'VE TRACKED ST. CHARLES ISLAND ON THE HORIZON, JUST AS WE HAVE— AND YOU KNOW WHAT IT MEANS.
IT MEANS THE ICE FLOE WE'RE ON IS DRIFTING. EVERY DAY WE STAY HERE WE GET FURTHER AND FURTHER FROM LAND.
WHAT I'M SAYING IS, ZAPPI AND FINN AND I WANT TO LEAVE ON FOOT. WE'RE PACKED AND CAN LEAVE IMMEDIATELY...

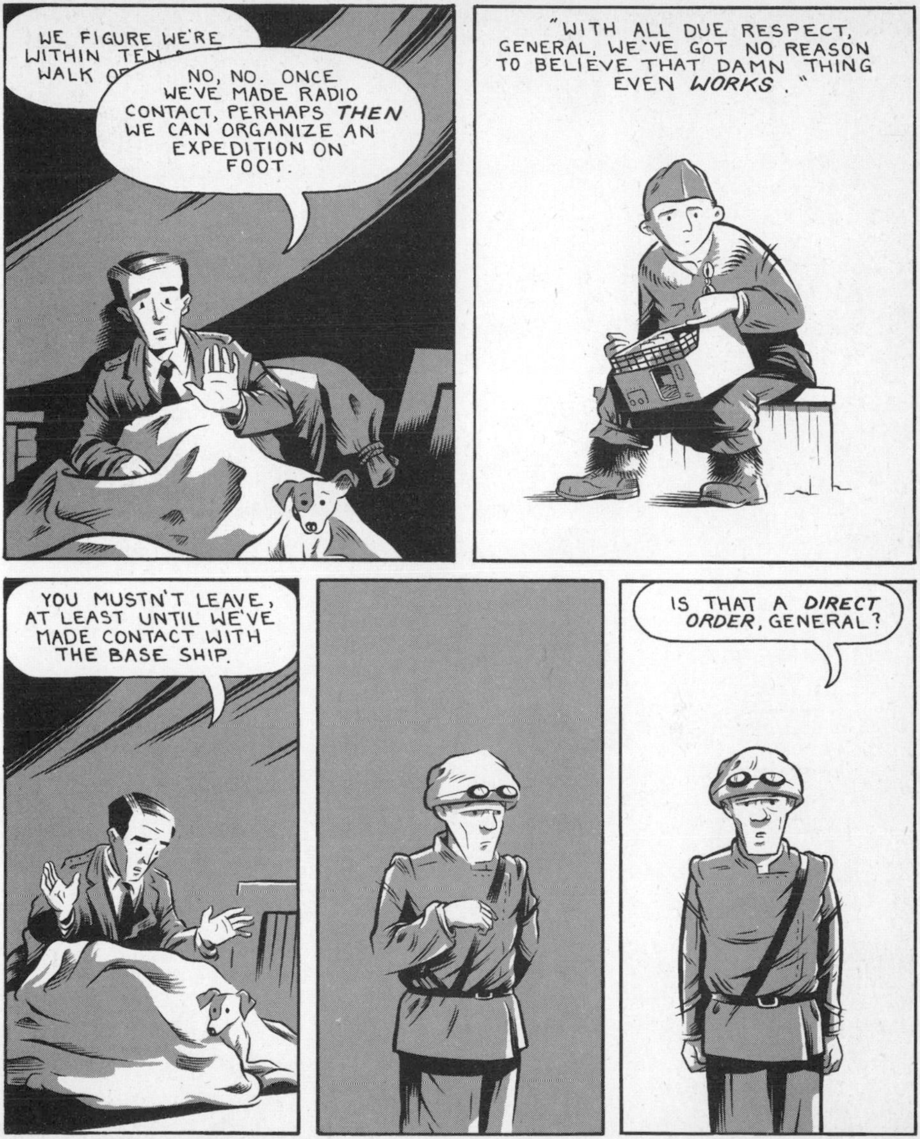
WE FIGURE WE'RE WITHIN TEN
WALK
NO, NO. ONCE WE'VE MADE RADIO CONTACT, PERHAPS *THEN* WE CAN ORGANIZE AN EXPEDITION ON FOOT.
"WITH ALL DUE RESPECT, GENERAL, WE'VE GOT NO REASON TO BELIEVE THAT DAMN THING EVEN *WORKS*."
YOU MUSTN'T LEAVE, AT LEAST UNTIL WE'VE MADE CONTACT WITH THE BASE SHIP.
IS THAT A *DIRECT ORDER*, GENERAL?

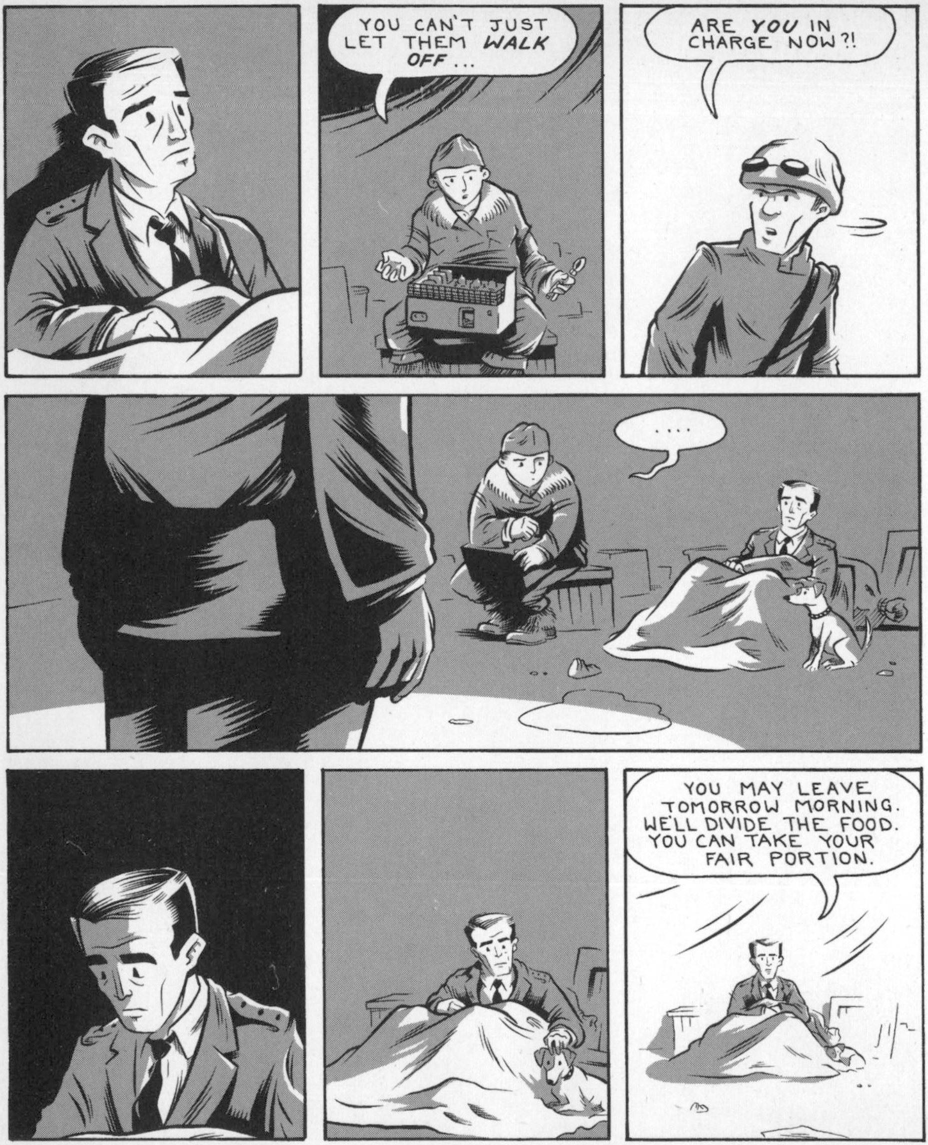
YOU CAN'T JUST LET THEM WALK OFF ...
ARE YOU IN CHARGE NOW?!
....
YOU MAY LEAVE TOMORROW MORNING. WE'LL DIVIDE THE FOOD. YOU CAN TAKE YOUR FAIR PORTION.

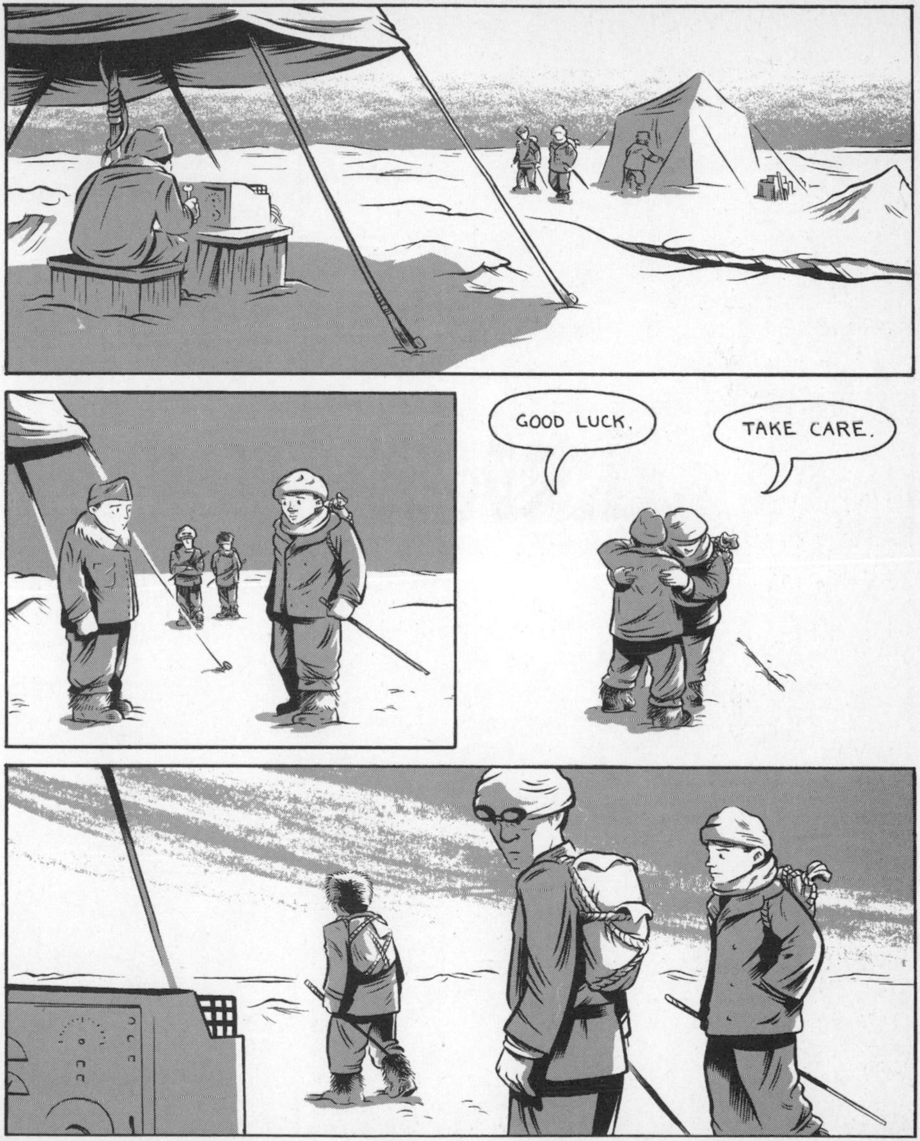
GOOD LUCK.
TAKE CARE.

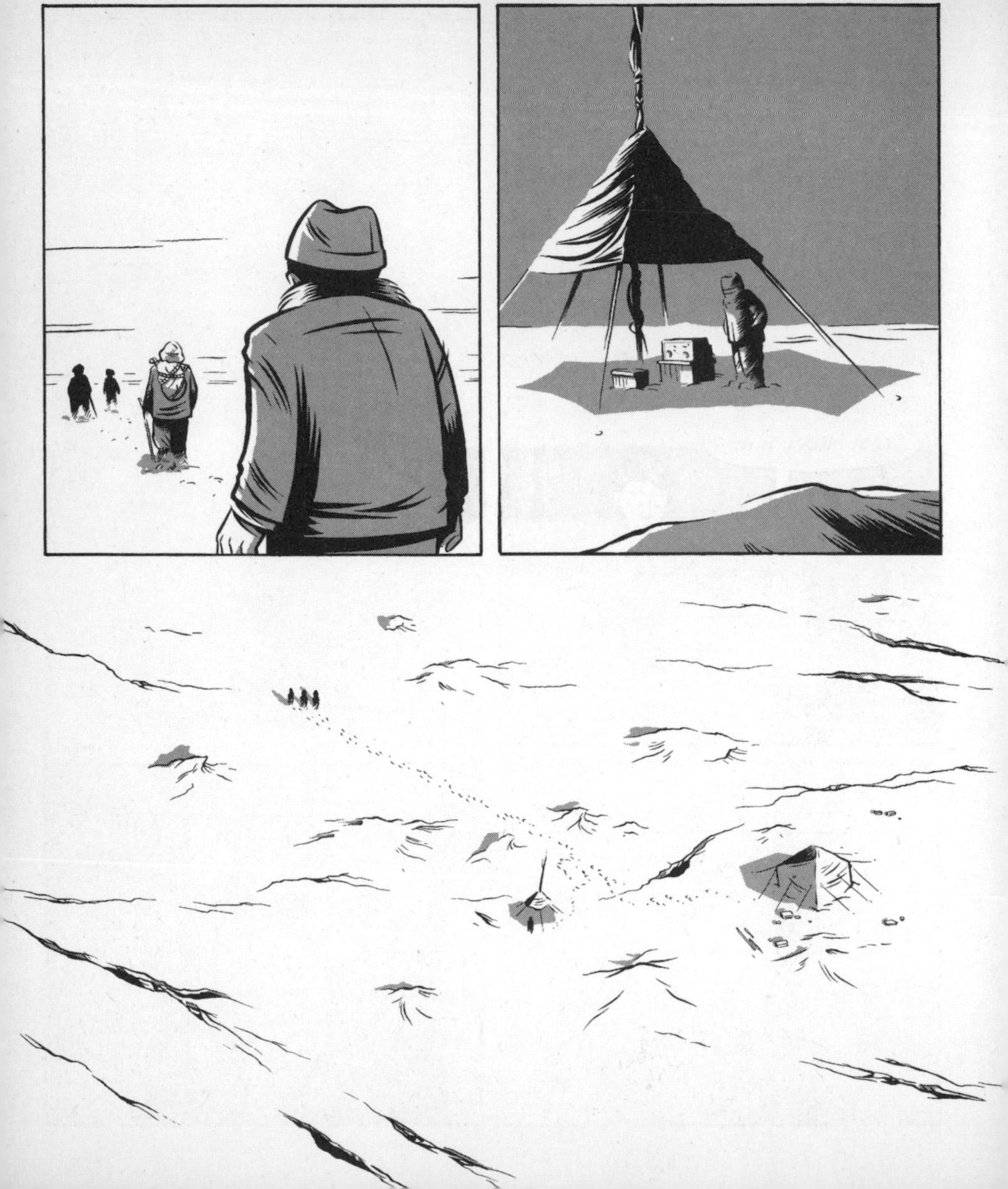

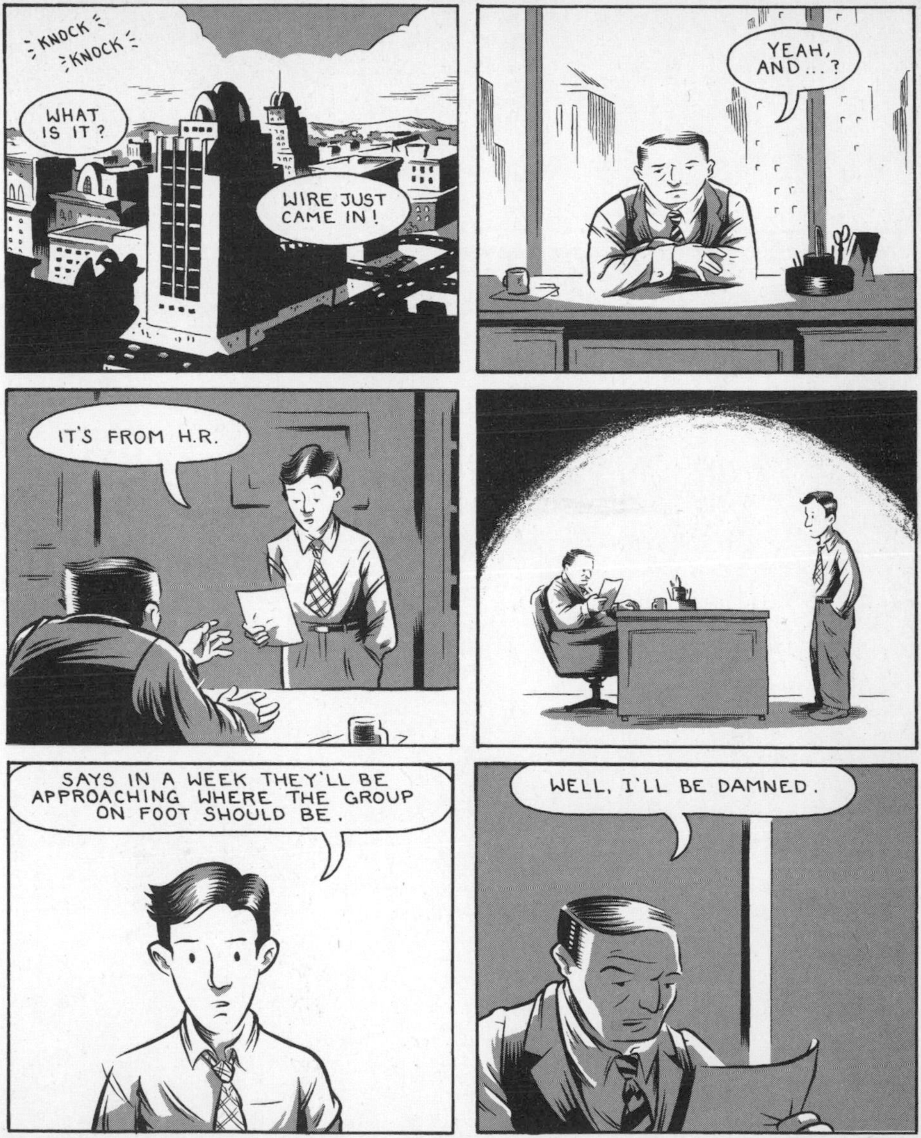
KNOCK KNOCK
WHAT IS IT?
WIRE JUST CAME IN!
YEAH, AND...?
IT'S FROM H.R.
SAYS IN A WEEK THEY'LL BE APPROACHING WHERE THE GROUP ON FOOT SHOULD BE.
WELL, I'LL BE DAMNED.

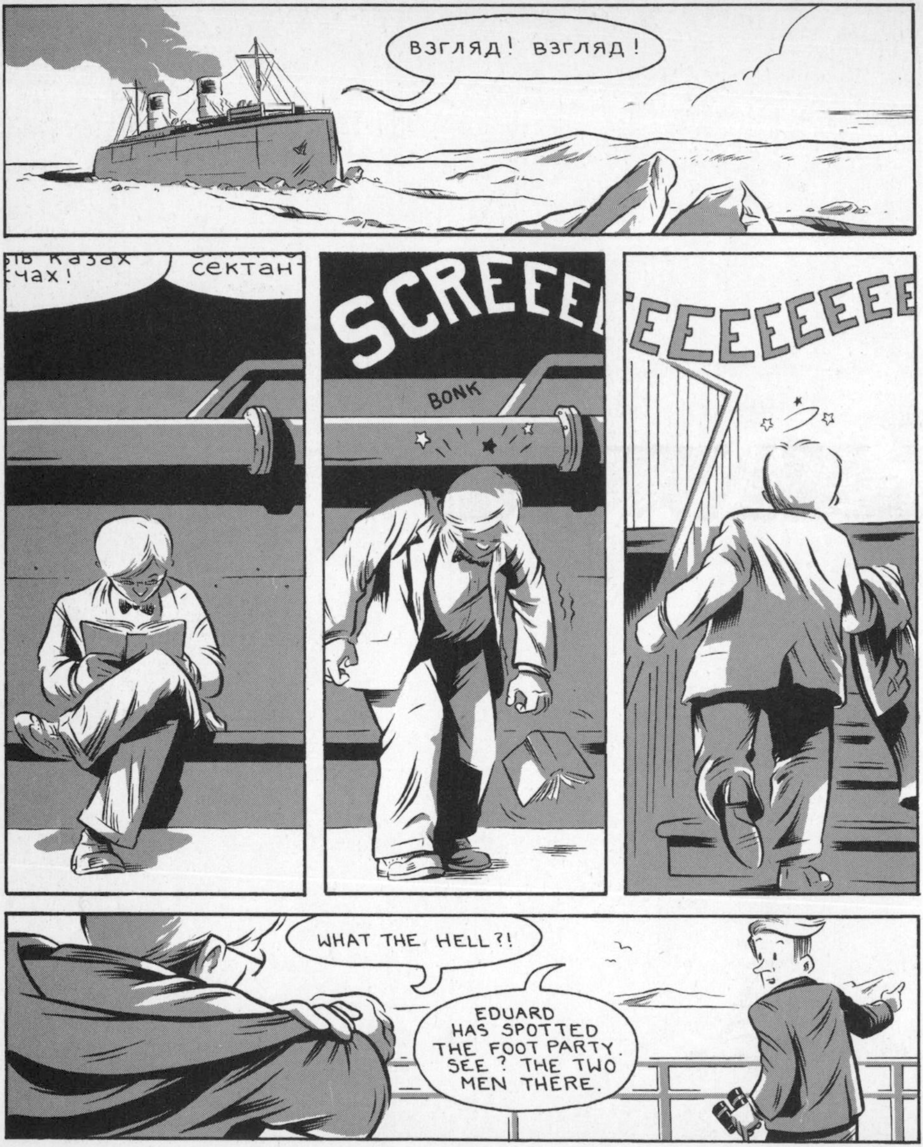

ВЗГЛЯД! ВЗГЛЯД!
SCREEEEEEEEEEEEEE
BONK
WHAT THE HELL?!
EDUARD HAS SPOTTED THE FOOT PARTY. SEE? THE TWO MEN THERE.

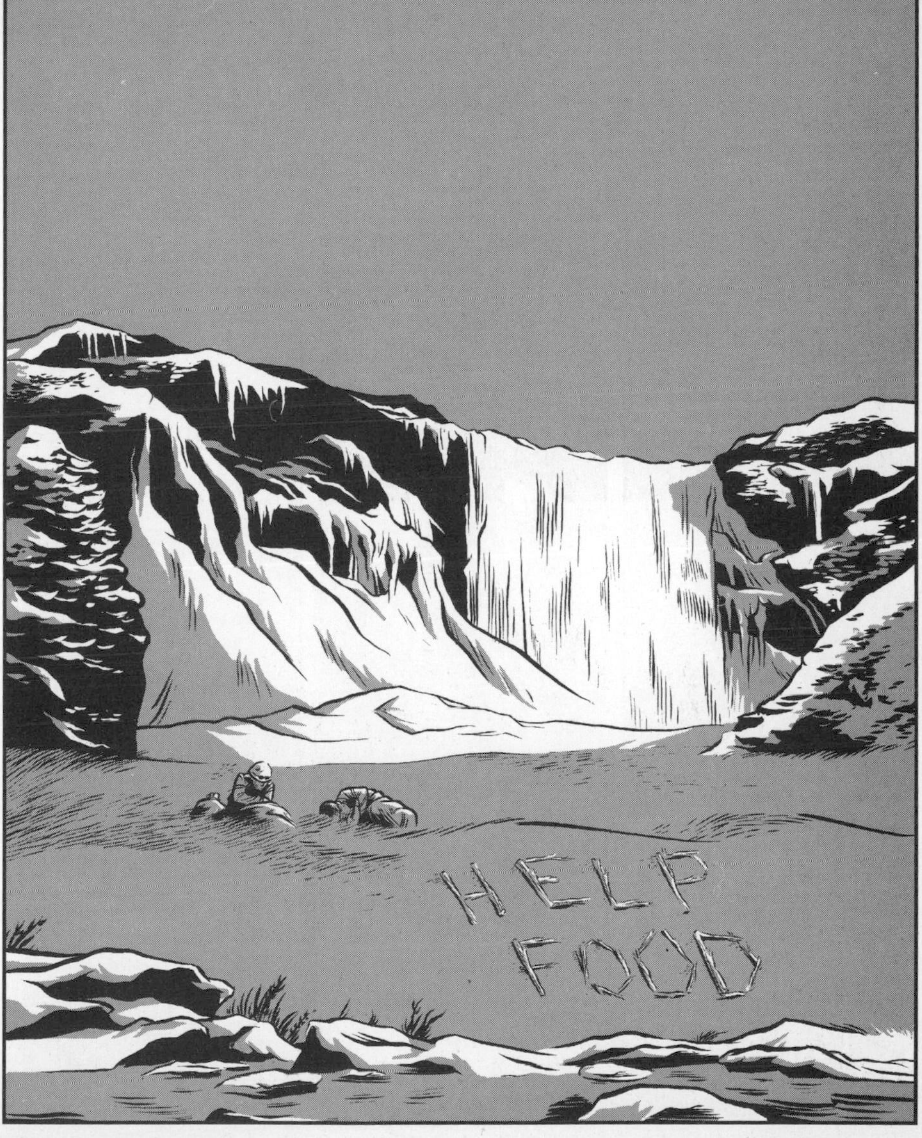
HELP
FOOD

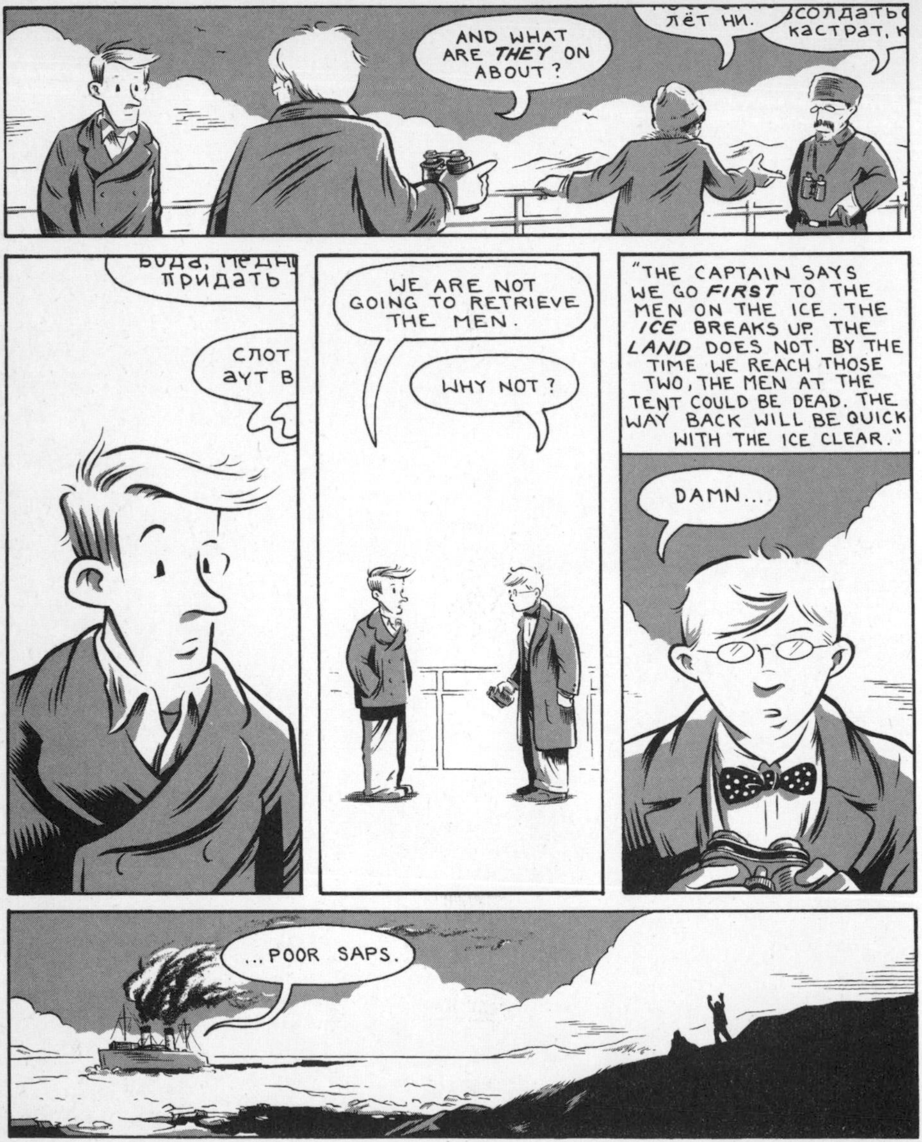
AND WHAT ARE *THEY* ON ABOUT?
лёт ни.
кастрат,
придать
WE ARE NOT GOING TO RETRIEVE THE MEN.
WHY NOT?
"THE CAPTAIN SAYS WE GO *FIRST* TO THE MEN ON THE ICE. THE *ICE* BREAKS UP. THE *LAND* DOES NOT. BY THE TIME WE REACH THOSE TWO, THE MEN AT THE TENT COULD BE DEAD. THE WAY BACK WILL BE QUICK WITH THE ICE CLEAR."
DAMN...
...POOR SAPS.

IV

Grounded

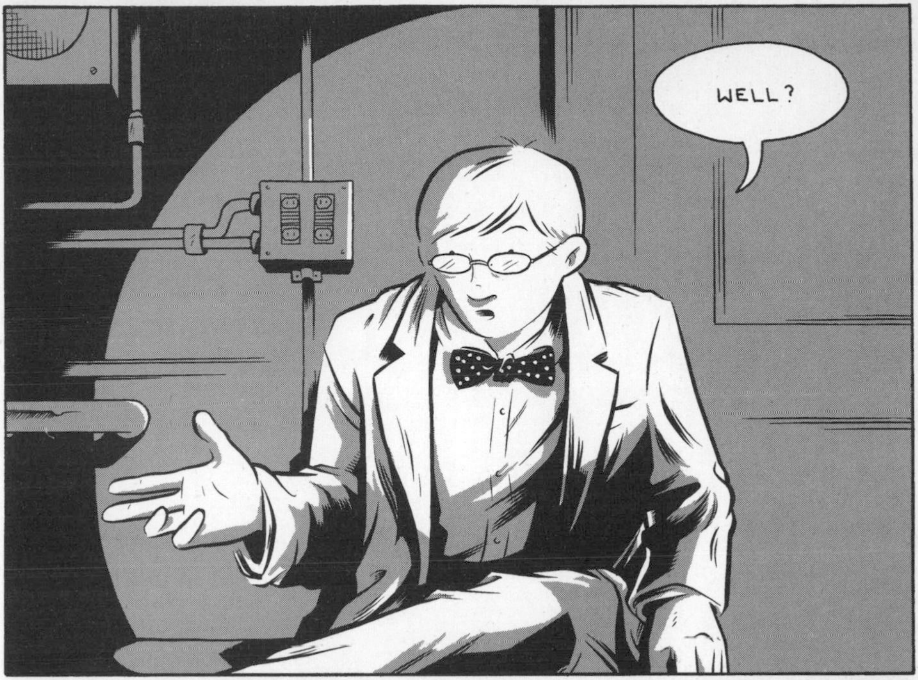
WELL?

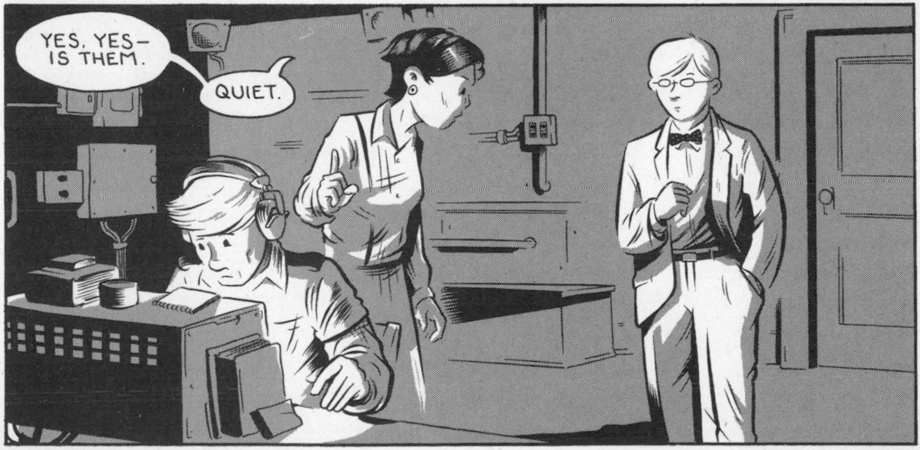
YES. YES—
IS THEM.
QUIET.

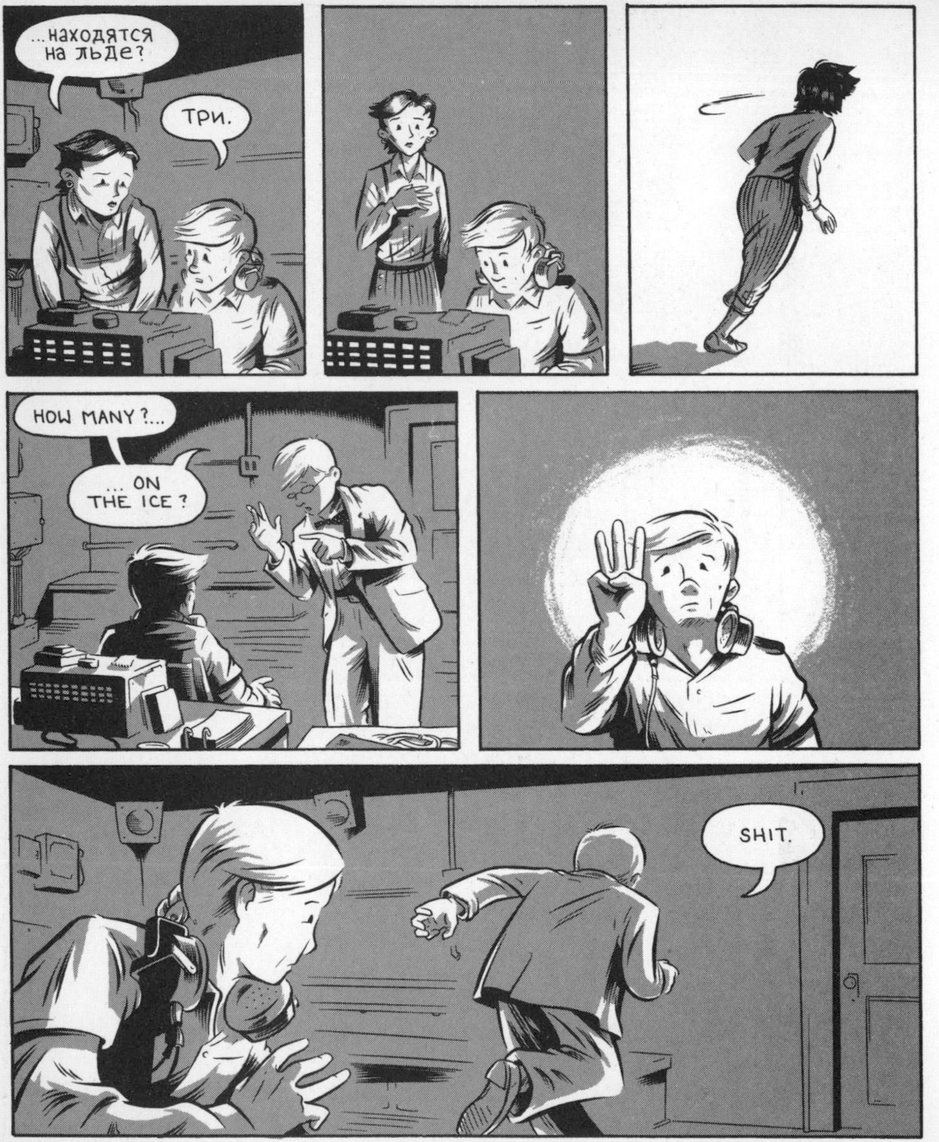
...находятся
на льде?
Три.
HOW MANY ?...
... ON
THE ICE ?
SHIT.

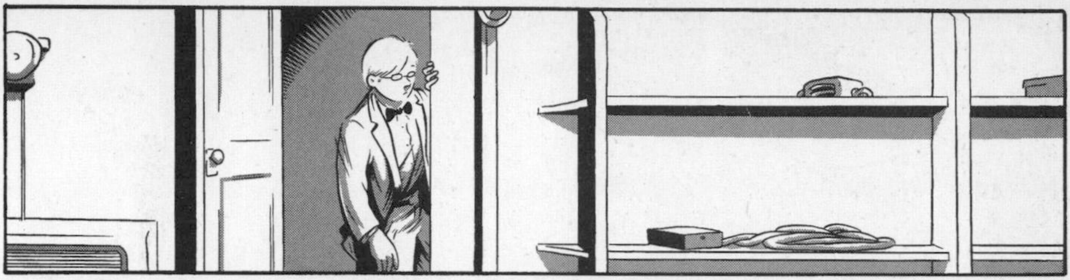

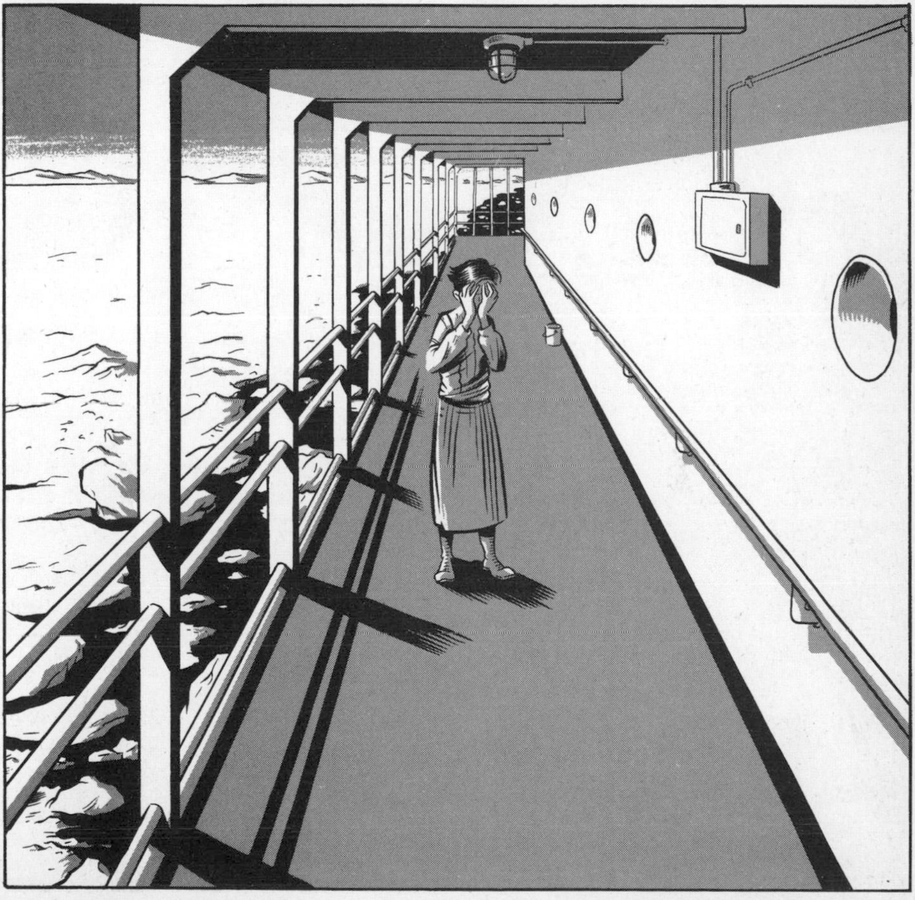

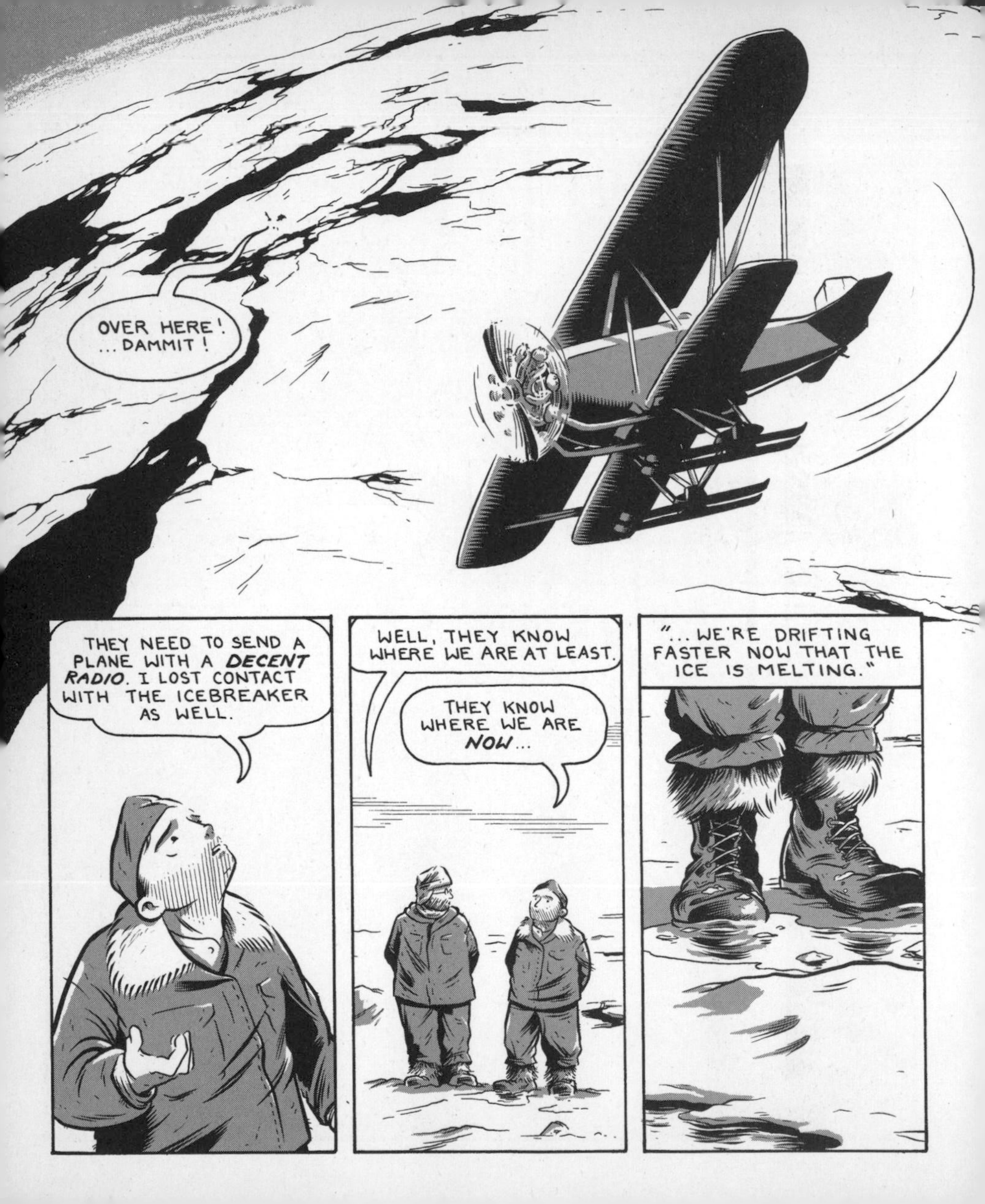
OVER HERE! ...DAMMIT!
THEY NEED TO SEND A PLANE WITH A DECENT RADIO. I LOST CONTACT WITH THE ICEBREAKER AS WELL.
WELL, THEY KNOW WHERE WE ARE AT LEAST.
THEY KNOW WHERE WE ARE NOW...
"...WE'RE DRIFTING FASTER NOW THAT THE ICE IS MELTING."

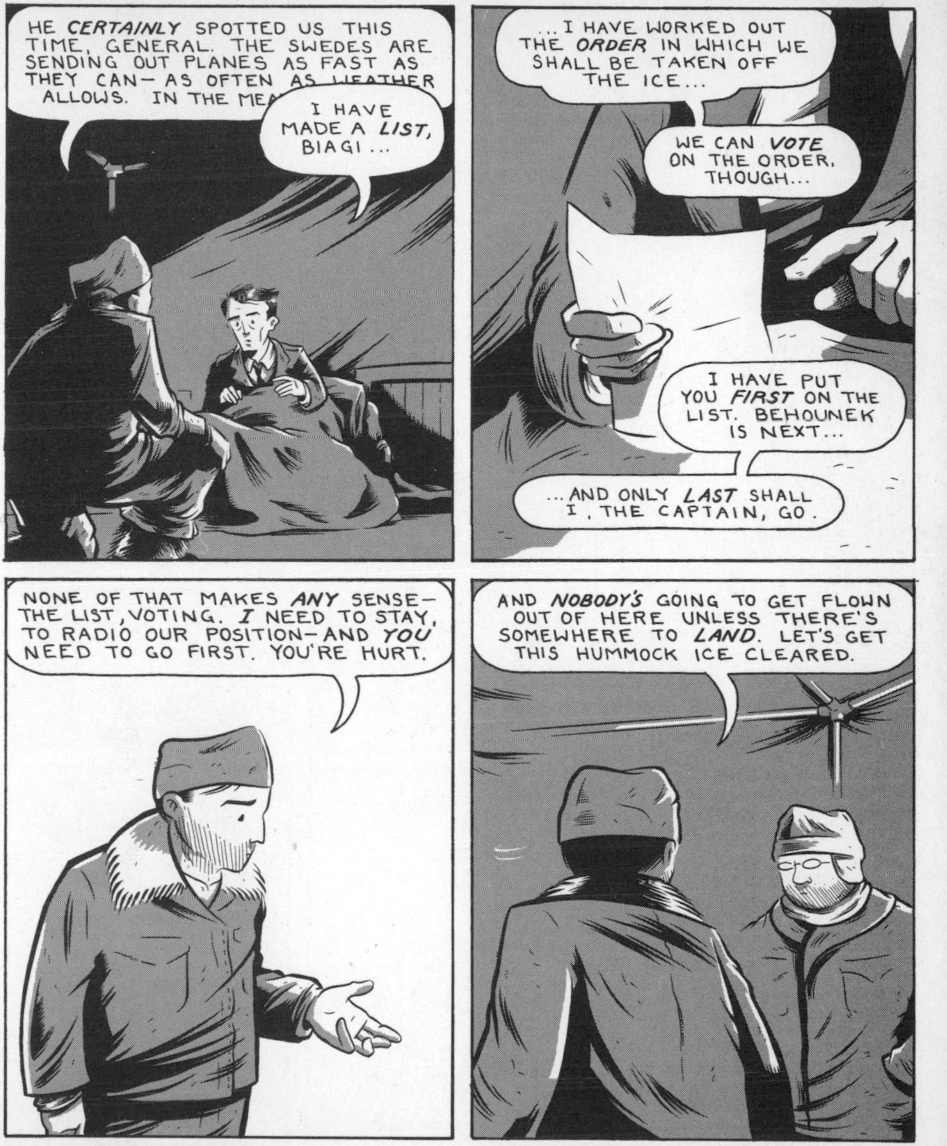
HE CERTAINLY SPOTTED US THIS TIME, GENERAL. THE SWEDES ARE SENDING OUT PLANES AS FAST AS THEY CAN— AS OFTEN AS WEATHER ALLOWS. IN THE MEA
I HAVE MADE A LIST, BIAGI...
...I HAVE WORKED OUT THE ORDER IN WHICH WE SHALL BE TAKEN OFF THE ICE...
WE CAN VOTE ON THE ORDER, THOUGH...
I HAVE PUT YOU FIRST ON THE LIST. BEHOUNEK IS NEXT...
...AND ONLY LAST SHALL I, THE CAPTAIN, GO.
NONE OF THAT MAKES ANY SENSE— THE LIST, VOTING. I NEED TO STAY, TO RADIO OUR POSITION— AND YOU NEED TO GO FIRST. YOU'RE HURT.
AND NOBODY'S GOING TO GET FLOWN OUT OF HERE UNLESS THERE'S SOMEWHERE TO LAND. LET'S GET THIS HUMMOCK ICE CLEARED.

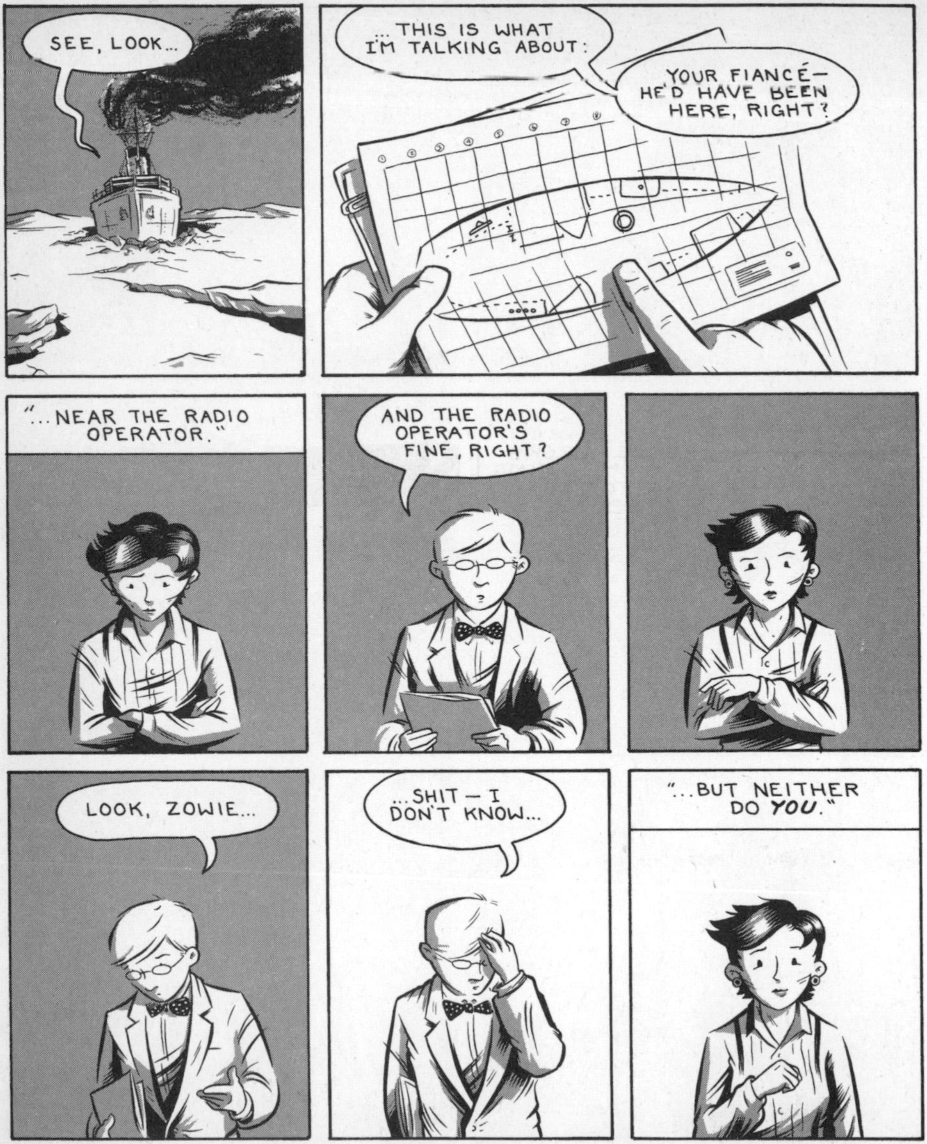
SEE, LOOK...
... THIS IS WHAT I'M TALKING ABOUT:
YOUR FIANCÉ— HE'D HAVE BEEN HERE, RIGHT?
"... NEAR THE RADIO OPERATOR."
AND THE RADIO OPERATOR'S FINE, RIGHT?
LOOK, ZOWIE...
... SHIT — I DON'T KNOW...
"... BUT NEITHER DO *YOU*."

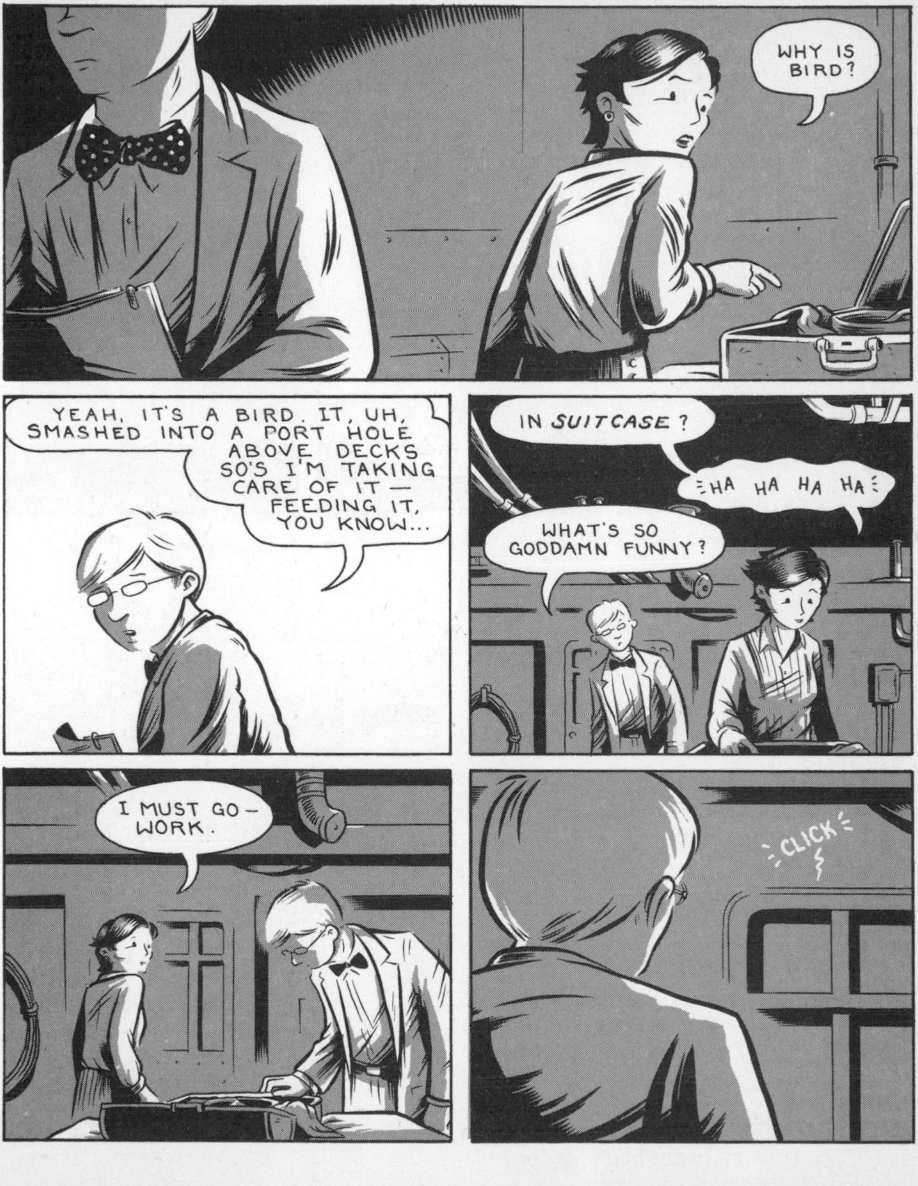
WHY IS BIRD?
YEAH, IT'S A BIRD. IT, UH, SMASHED INTO A PORT HOLE ABOVE DECKS SO'S I'M TAKING CARE OF IT — FEEDING IT, YOU KNOW...
IN SUITCASE?
HA HA HA HA
WHAT'S SO GODDAMN FUNNY?
I MUST GO — WORK.
CLICK

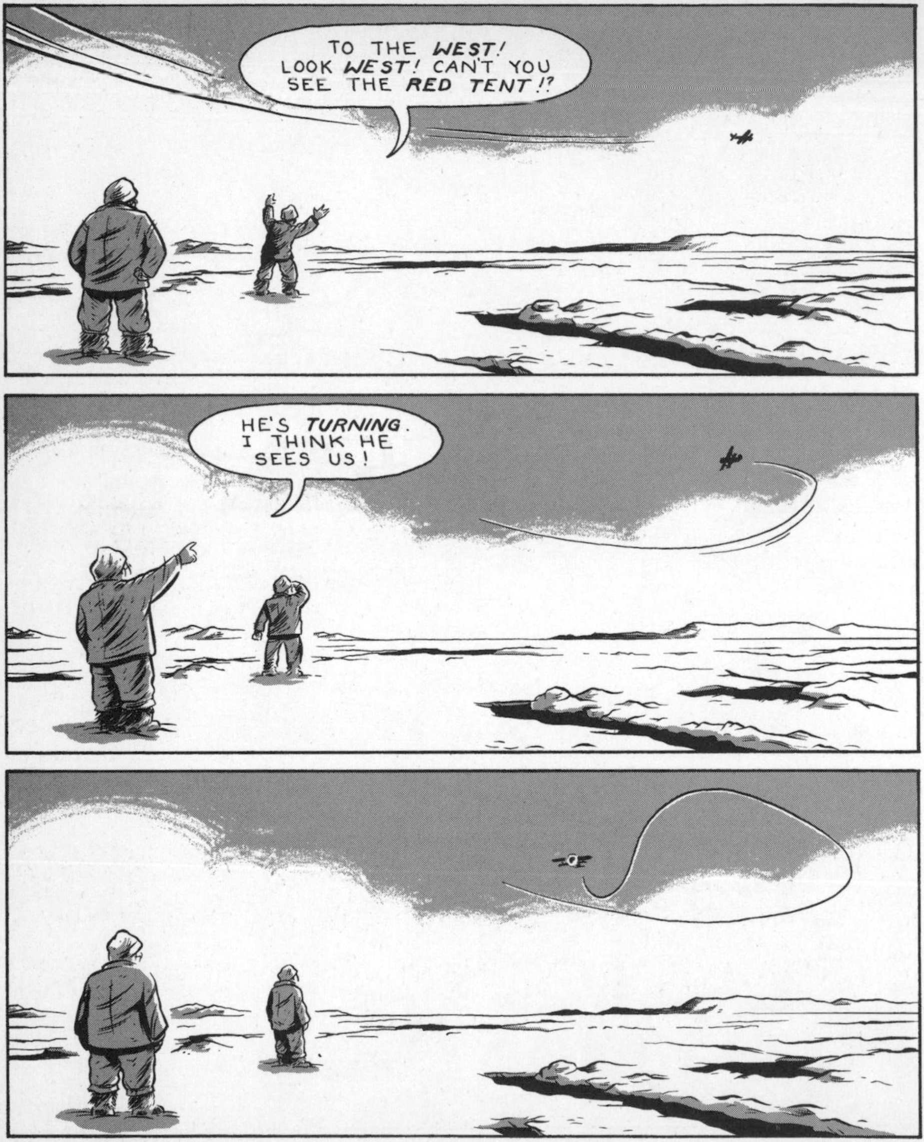
TO THE WEST! LOOK WEST! CAN'T YOU SEE THE RED TENT!?
HE'S TURNING. I THINK HE SEES US!

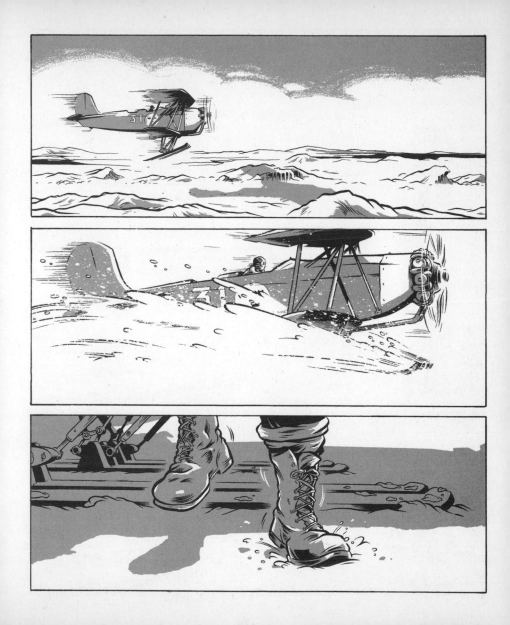

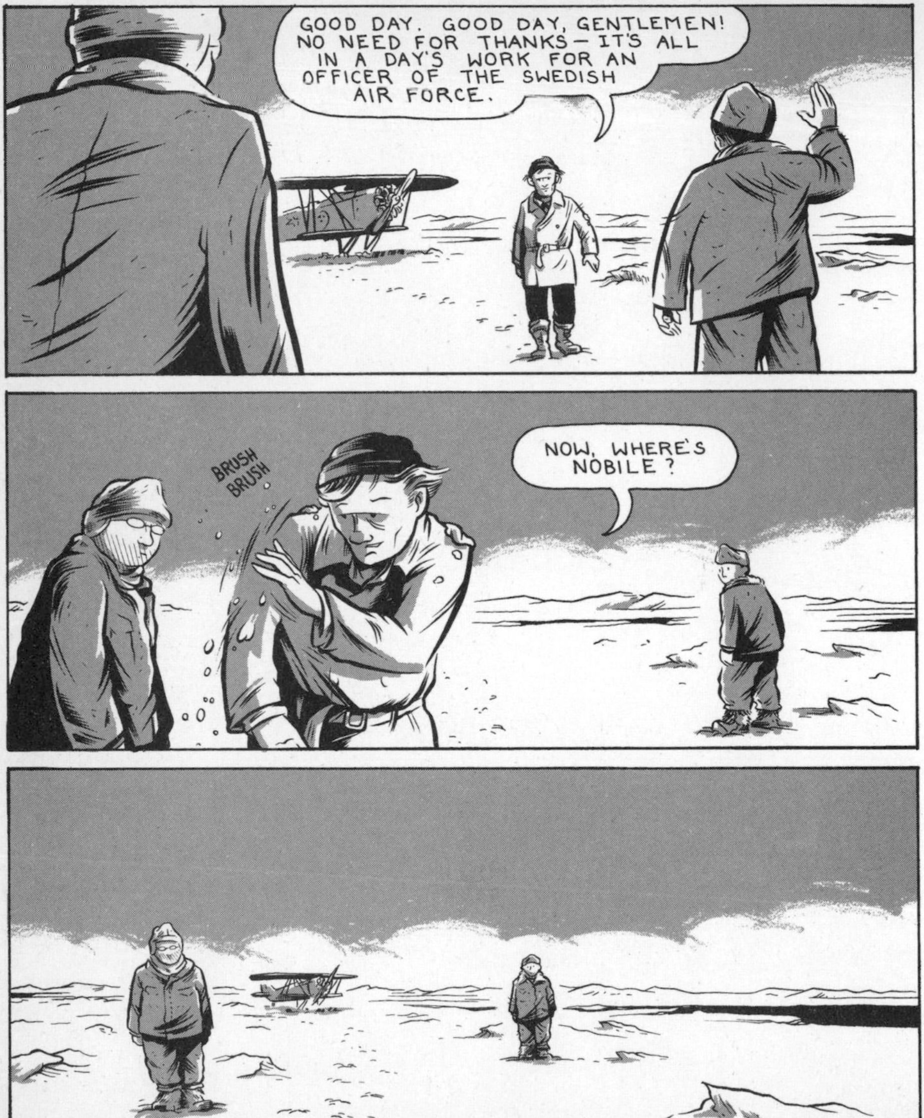
GOOD DAY. GOOD DAY, GENTLEMEN! NO NEED FOR THANKS — IT'S ALL IN A DAY'S WORK FOR AN OFFICER OF THE SWEDISH AIR FORCE.
BRUSH BRUSH
NOW, WHERE'S NOBILE?

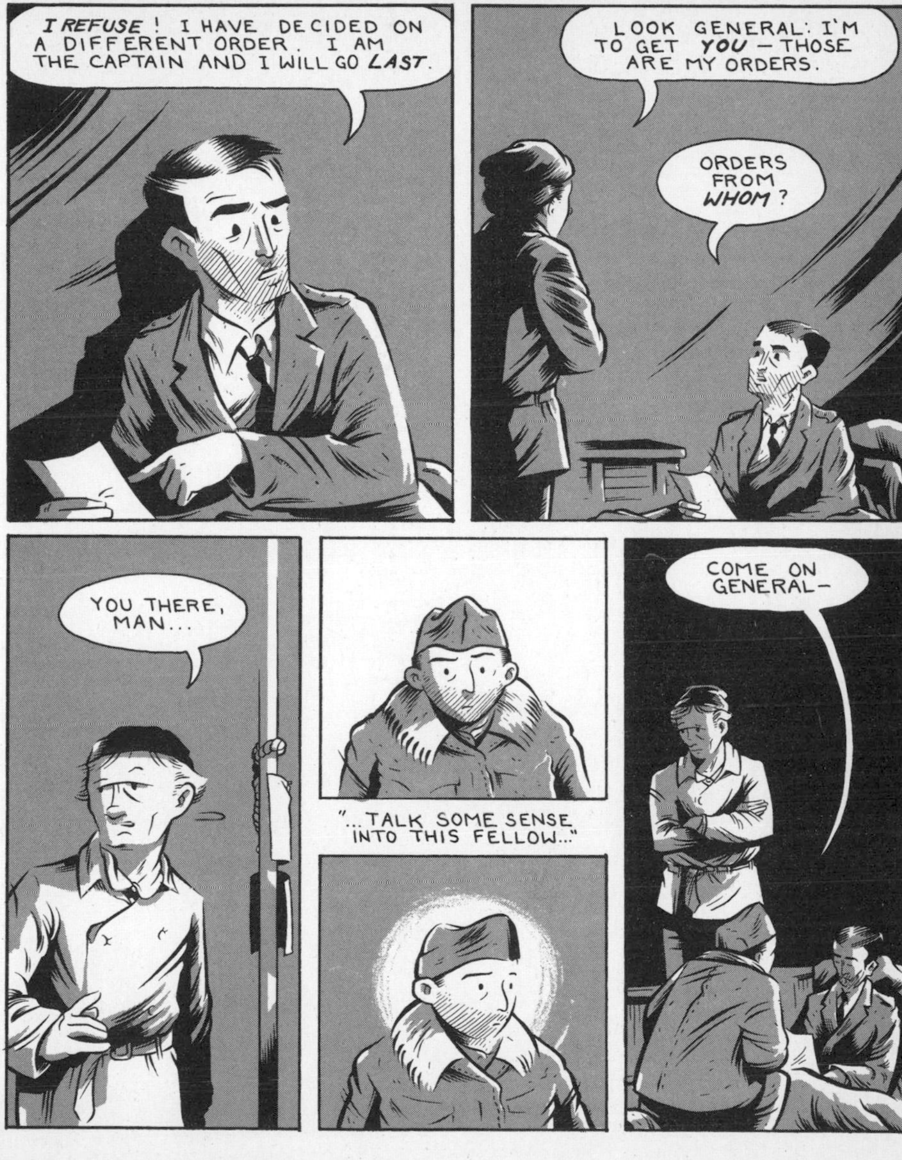
I REFUSE! I HAVE DECIDED ON A DIFFERENT ORDER. I AM THE CAPTAIN AND I WILL GO LAST.
LOOK GENERAL: I'M TO GET YOU — THOSE ARE MY ORDERS.
ORDERS FROM WHOM?
YOU THERE, MAN...
"...TALK SOME SENSE INTO THIS FELLOW..."
COME ON GENERAL—

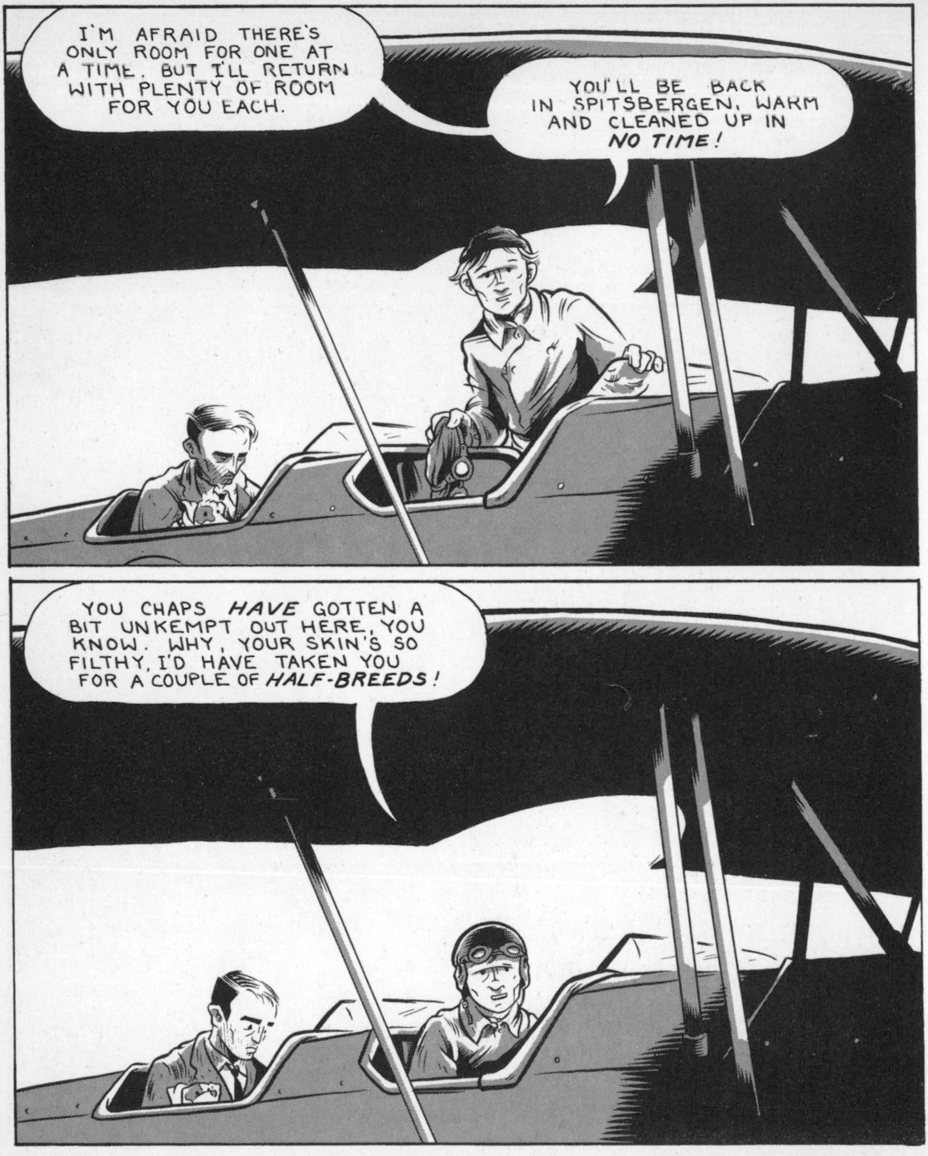
I'M AFRAID THERE'S ONLY ROOM FOR ONE AT A TIME. BUT I'LL RETURN WITH PLENTY OF ROOM FOR YOU EACH.
YOU'LL BE BACK IN SPITSBERGEN, WARM AND CLEANED UP IN NO TIME!
YOU CHAPS HAVE GOTTEN A BIT UNKEMPT OUT HERE, YOU KNOW. WHY, YOUR SKIN'S SO FILTHY, I'D HAVE TAKEN YOU FOR A COUPLE OF HALF-BREEDS!

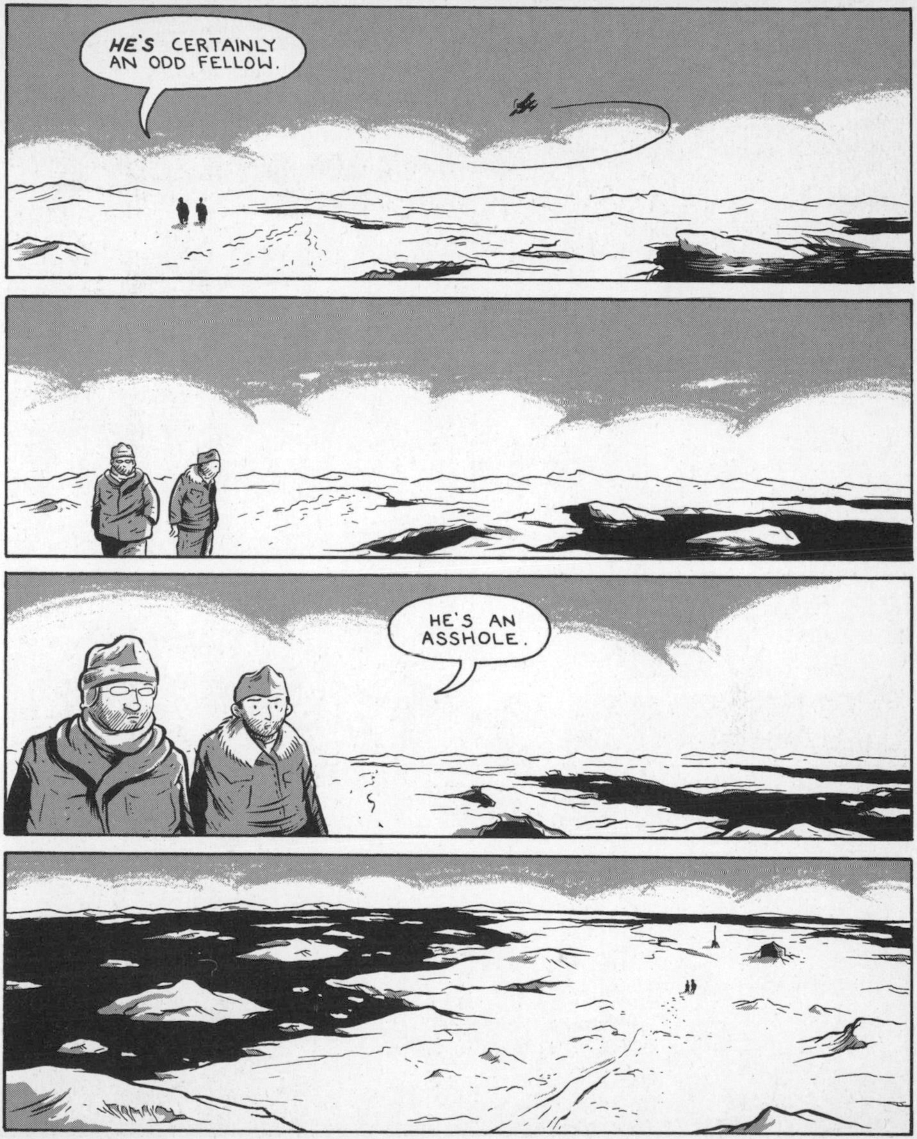
HE'S CERTAINLY AN ODD FELLOW.
HE'S AN ASSHOLE.

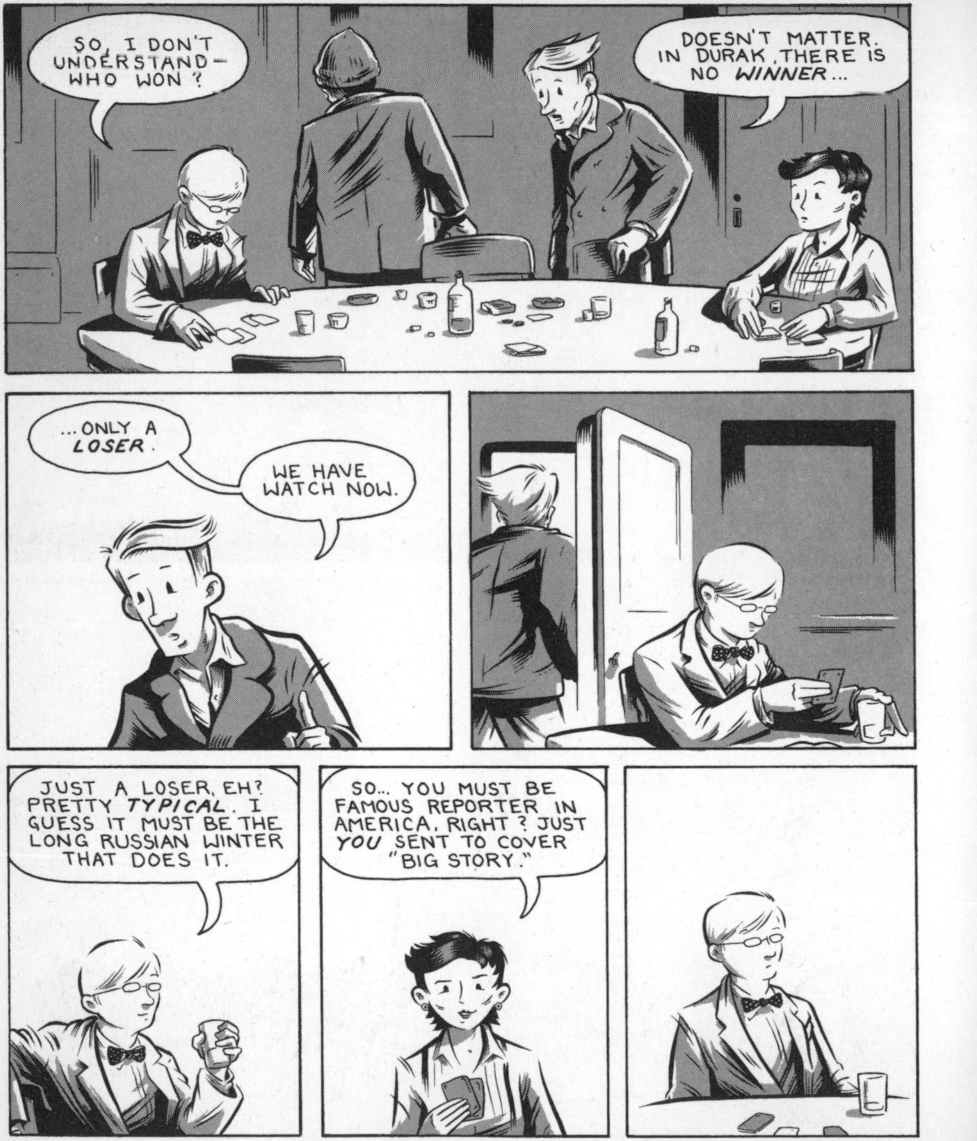
SO, I DON'T UNDERSTAND— WHO WON ?
DOESN'T MATTER. IN DURAK, THERE IS NO WINNER...
...ONLY A LOSER.
WE HAVE WATCH NOW.
JUST A LOSER, EH? PRETTY TYPICAL. I GUESS IT MUST BE THE LONG RUSSIAN WINTER THAT DOES IT.
SO... YOU MUST BE FAMOUS REPORTER IN AMERICA, RIGHT ? JUST YOU SENT TO COVER "BIG STORY."

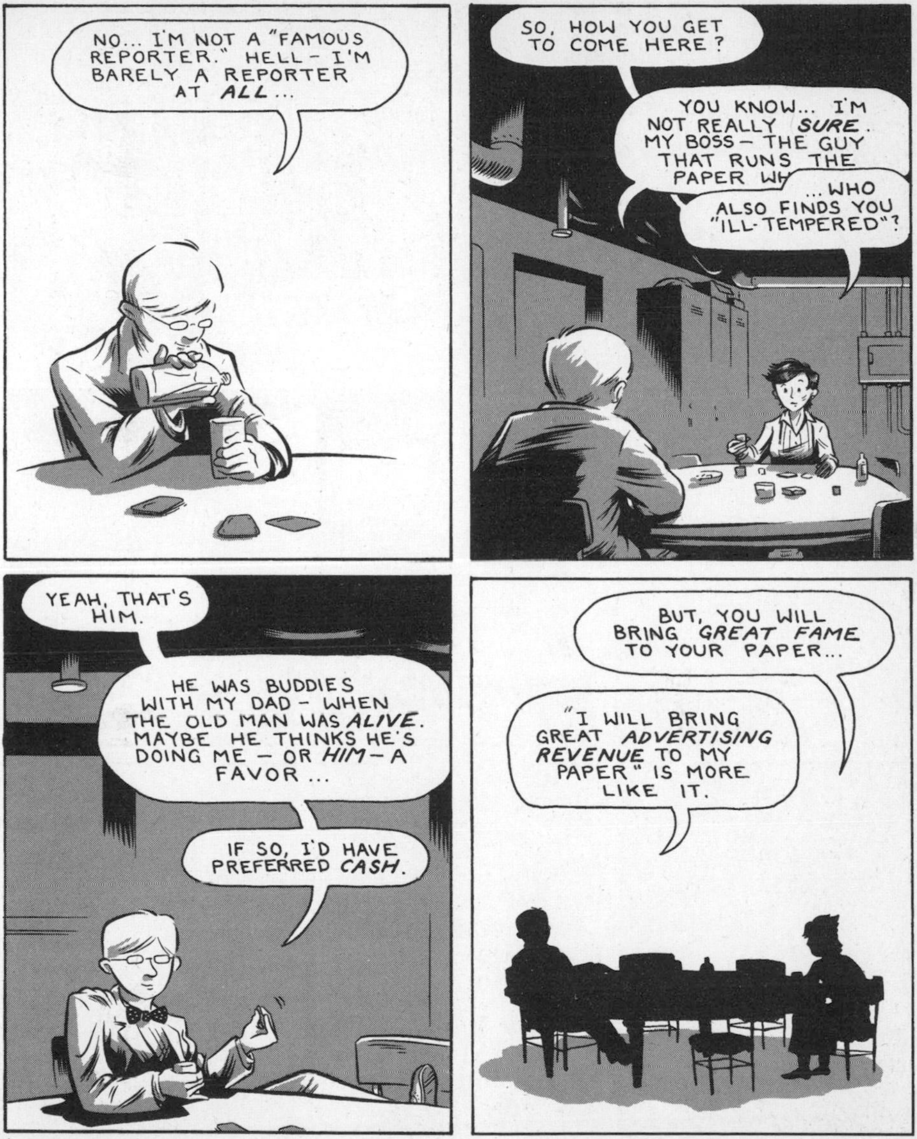
NO... I'M NOT A "FAMOUS REPORTER." HELL - I'M BARELY A REPORTER AT ALL...
SO, HOW YOU GET TO COME HERE?
YOU KNOW... I'M NOT REALLY SURE. MY BOSS - THE GUY THAT RUNS THE PAPER WH
...WHO ALSO FINDS YOU "ILL-TEMPERED"?
YEAH, THAT'S HIM.
HE WAS BUDDIES WITH MY DAD - WHEN THE OLD MAN WAS ALIVE. MAYBE HE THINKS HE'S DOING ME - OR HIM - A FAVOR...
IF SO, I'D HAVE PREFERRED CASH.
BUT, YOU WILL BRING GREAT FAME TO YOUR PAPER...
"I WILL BRING GREAT ADVERTISING REVENUE TO MY PAPER" IS MORE LIKE IT.

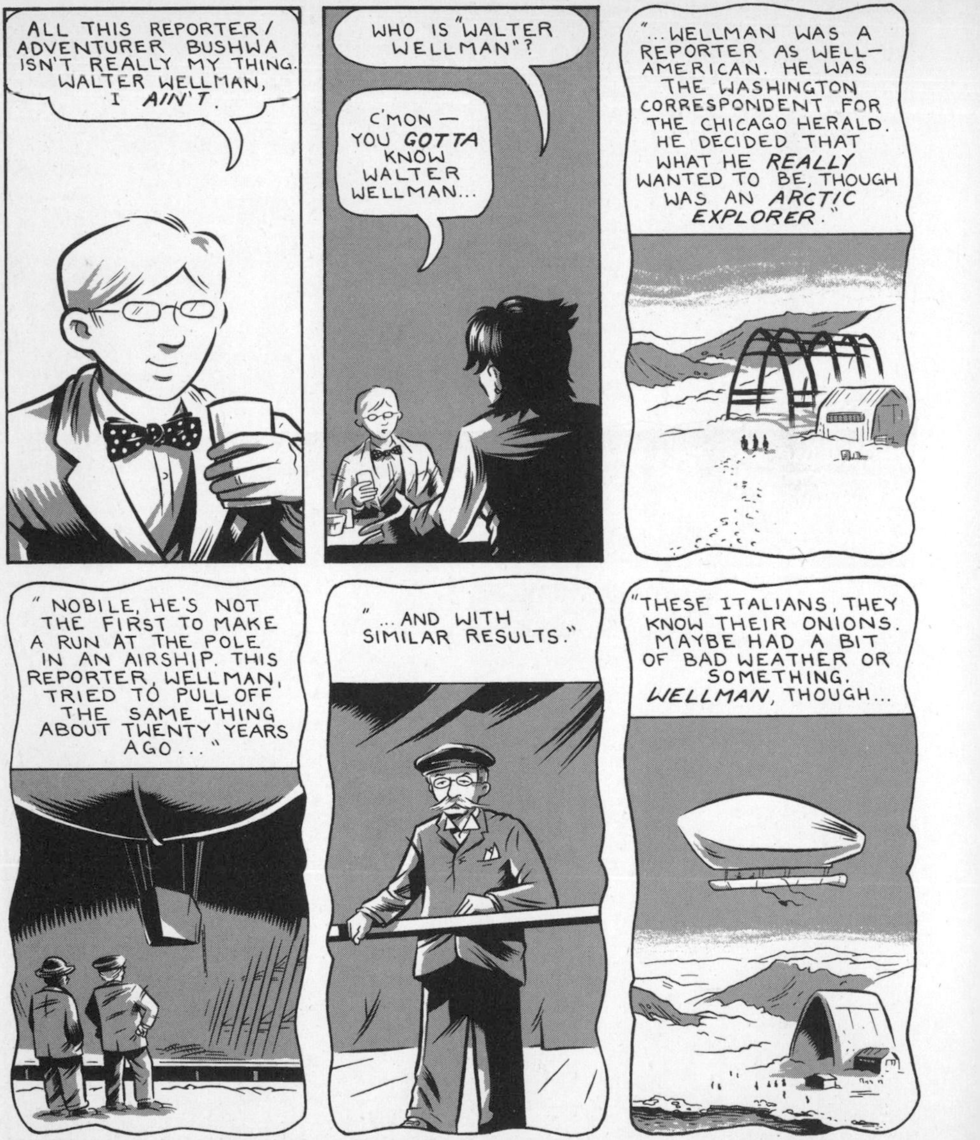
ALL THIS REPORTER/ ADVENTURER BUSHWA ISN'T REALLY MY THING. WALTER WELLMAN, I AIN'T.
WHO IS "WALTER WELLMAN"?
C'MON — YOU GOTTA KNOW WALTER WELLMAN...
"...WELLMAN WAS A REPORTER AS WELL— AMERICAN. HE WAS THE WASHINGTON CORRESPONDENT FOR THE CHICAGO HERALD. HE DECIDED THAT WHAT HE REALLY WANTED TO BE, THOUGH WAS AN ARCTIC EXPLORER."
"NOBILE, HE'S NOT THE FIRST TO MAKE A RUN AT THE POLE IN AN AIRSHIP. THIS REPORTER, WELLMAN, TRIED TO PULL OFF THE SAME THING ABOUT TWENTY YEARS AGO..."
"...AND WITH SIMILAR RESULTS."
"THESE ITALIANS, THEY KNOW THEIR ONIONS. MAYBE HAD A BIT OF BAD WEATHER OR SOMETHING. WELLMAN, THOUGH...

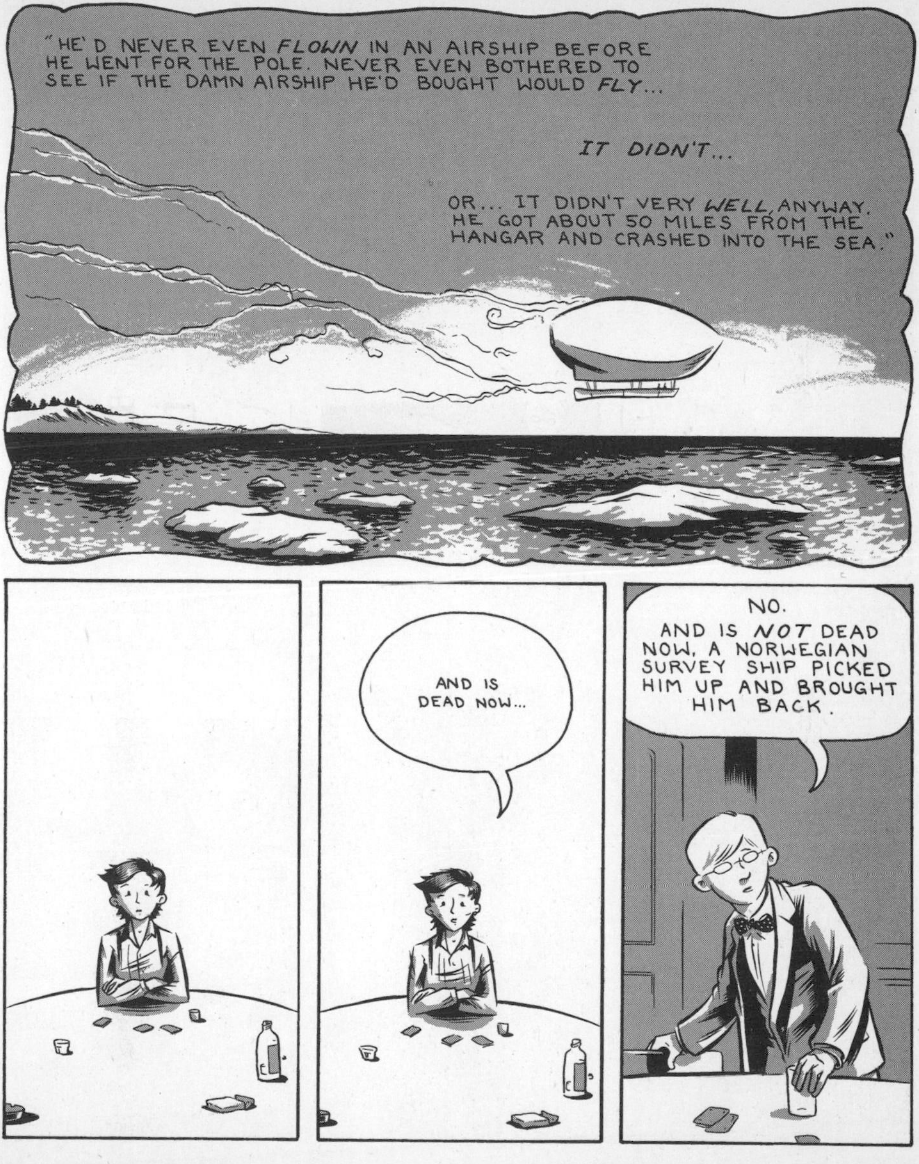
"HE'D NEVER EVEN FLOWN IN AN AIRSHIP BEFORE HE WENT FOR THE POLE. NEVER EVEN BOTHERED TO SEE IF THE DAMN AIRSHIP HE'D BOUGHT WOULD FLY...
IT DIDN'T...
OR... IT DIDN'T VERY WELL, ANYWAY. HE GOT ABOUT 50 MILES FROM THE HANGAR AND CRASHED INTO THE SEA."
AND IS DEAD NOW...
NO. AND IS NOT DEAD NOW. A NORWEGIAN SURVEY SHIP PICKED HIM UP AND BROUGHT HIM BACK.

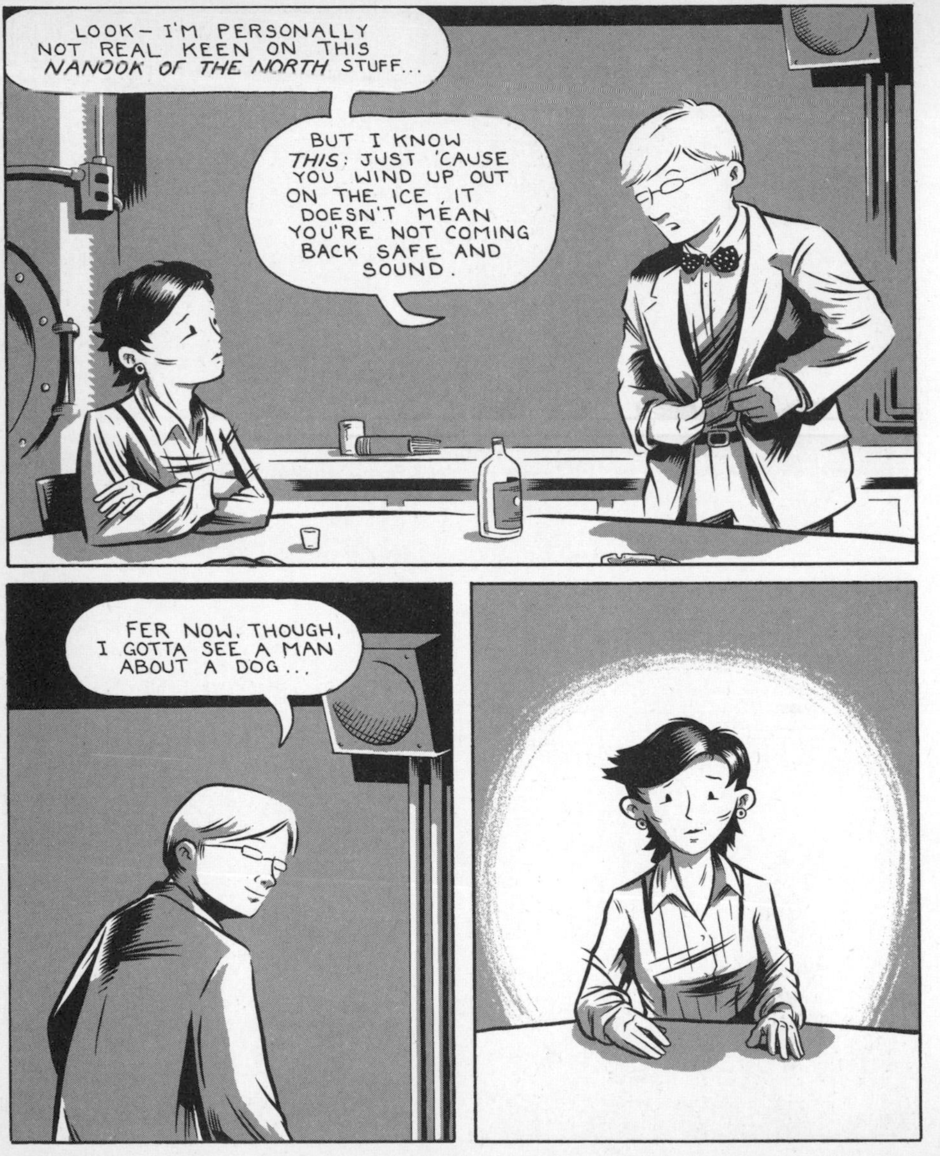
LOOK— I'M PERSONALLY NOT REAL KEEN ON THIS *NANOOK OF THE NORTH* STUFF...
BUT I KNOW *THIS*: JUST 'CAUSE YOU WIND UP OUT ON THE ICE, IT DOESN'T MEAN YOU'RE NOT COMING BACK SAFE AND SOUND.
FER NOW, THOUGH, I GOTTA SEE A MAN ABOUT A DOG...

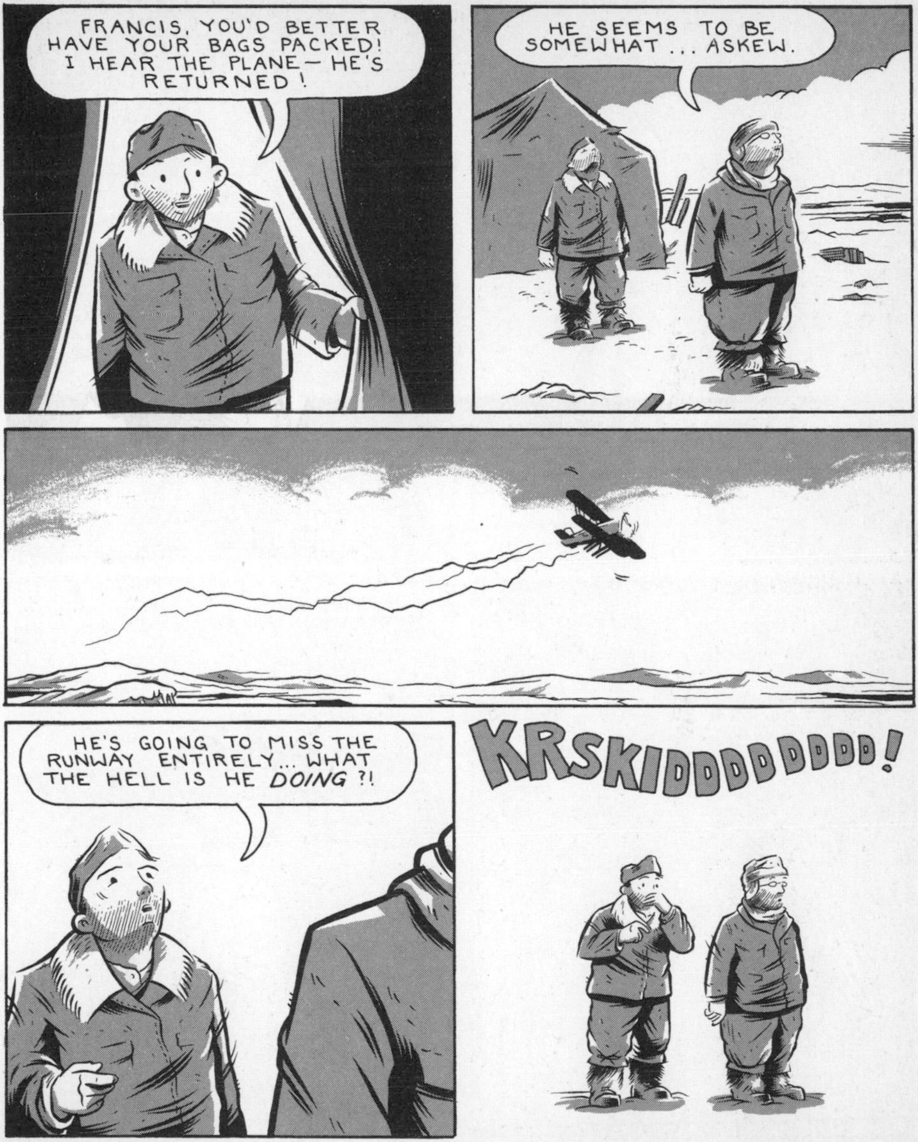
FRANCIS, YOU'D BETTER HAVE YOUR BAGS PACKED! I HEAR THE PLANE— HE'S RETURNED!
HE SEEMS TO BE SOMEWHAT ... ASKEW.
HE'S GOING TO MISS THE RUNWAY ENTIRELY... WHAT THE HELL IS HE *DOING* ?!
KRSKIDDDDDDDDD!

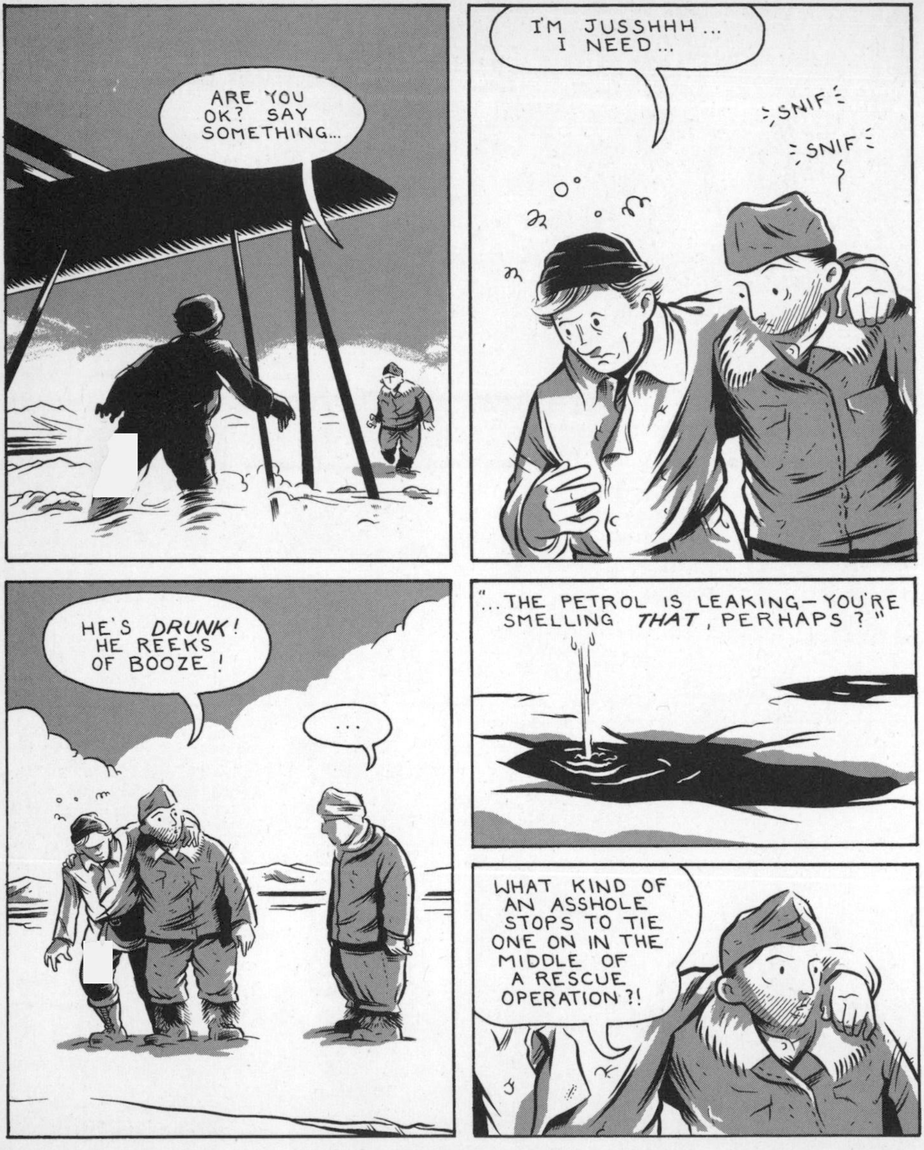
ARE YOU OK? SAY SOMETHING...
I'M JUSSHHH... I NEED...
SNIF
SNIF
HE'S *DRUNK*! HE REEKS OF BOOZE!
...
"...THE PETROL IS LEAKING—YOU'RE SMELLING *THAT*, PERHAPS?"
WHAT KIND OF AN ASSHOLE STOPS TO TIE ONE ON IN THE MIDDLE OF A RESCUE OPERATION?!

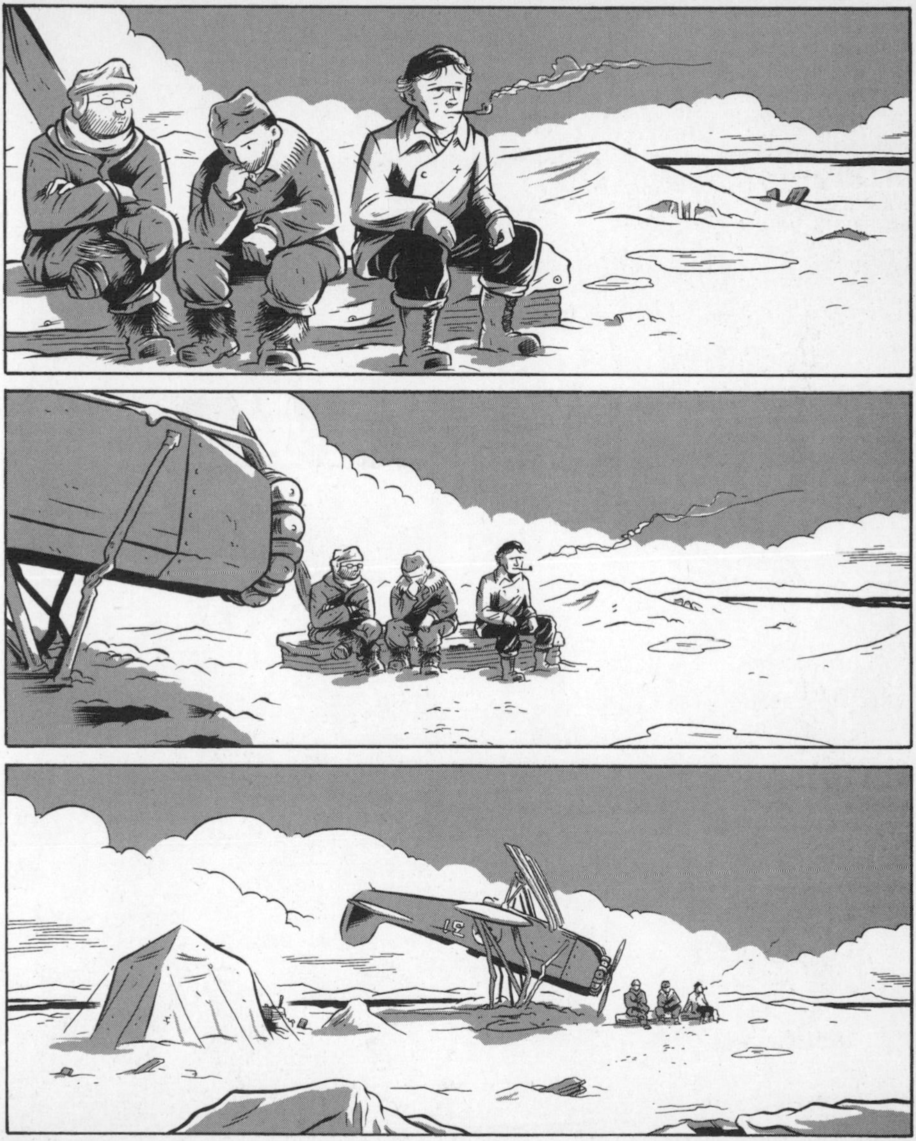

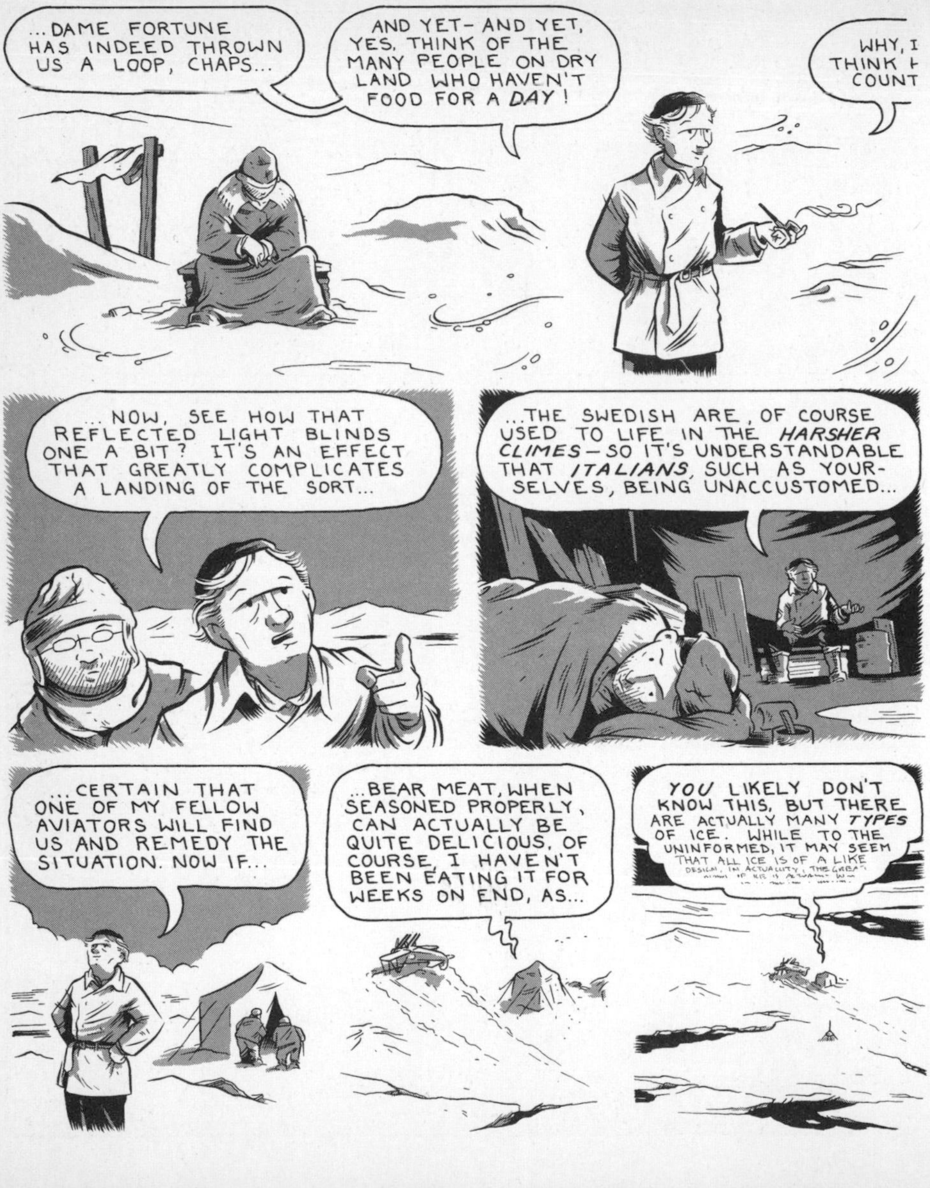
...DAME FORTUNE HAS INDEED THROWN US A LOOP, CHAPS...
AND YET- AND YET, YES, THINK OF THE MANY PEOPLE ON DRY LAND WHO HAVEN'T FOOD FOR A DAY!
WHY, I THINK
...NOW, SEE HOW THAT REFLECTED LIGHT BLINDS ONE A BIT? IT'S AN EFFECT THAT GREATLY COMPLICATES A LANDING OF THE SORT...
...THE SWEDISH ARE, OF COURSE USED TO LIFE IN THE HARSHER CLIMES—SO IT'S UNDERSTANDABLE THAT ITALIANS, SUCH AS YOURSELVES, BEING UNACCUSTOMED...
...CERTAIN THAT ONE OF MY FELLOW AVIATORS WILL FIND US AND REMEDY THE SITUATION. NOW IF...
...BEAR MEAT, WHEN SEASONED PROPERLY, CAN ACTUALLY BE QUITE DELICIOUS. OF COURSE, I HAVEN'T BEEN EATING IT FOR WEEKS ON END, AS...
YOU LIKELY DON'T KNOW THIS, BUT THERE ARE ACTUALLY MANY TYPES OF ICE. WHILE TO THE UNINFORMED, IT MAY SEEM THAT ALL ICE IS OF A LIKE

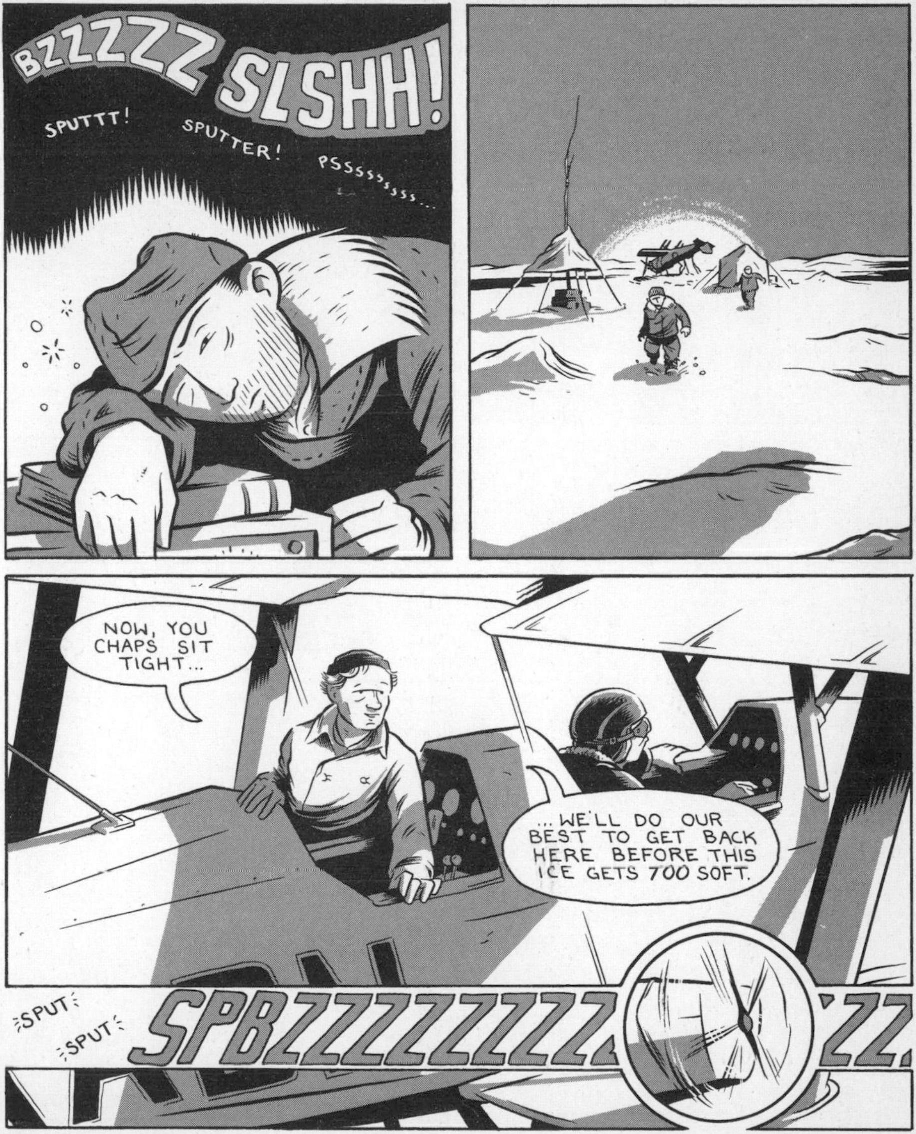
BZZZZZ SLSHH!
SPUTTT!
SPUTTER!
PSSSSSSSSS...
NOW, YOU CHAPS SIT TIGHT...
...WE'LL DO OUR BEST TO GET BACK HERE BEFORE THIS ICE GETS *TOO* SOFT.
SPUT SPUT
SPBZZZZZZZZZZ ZZ.

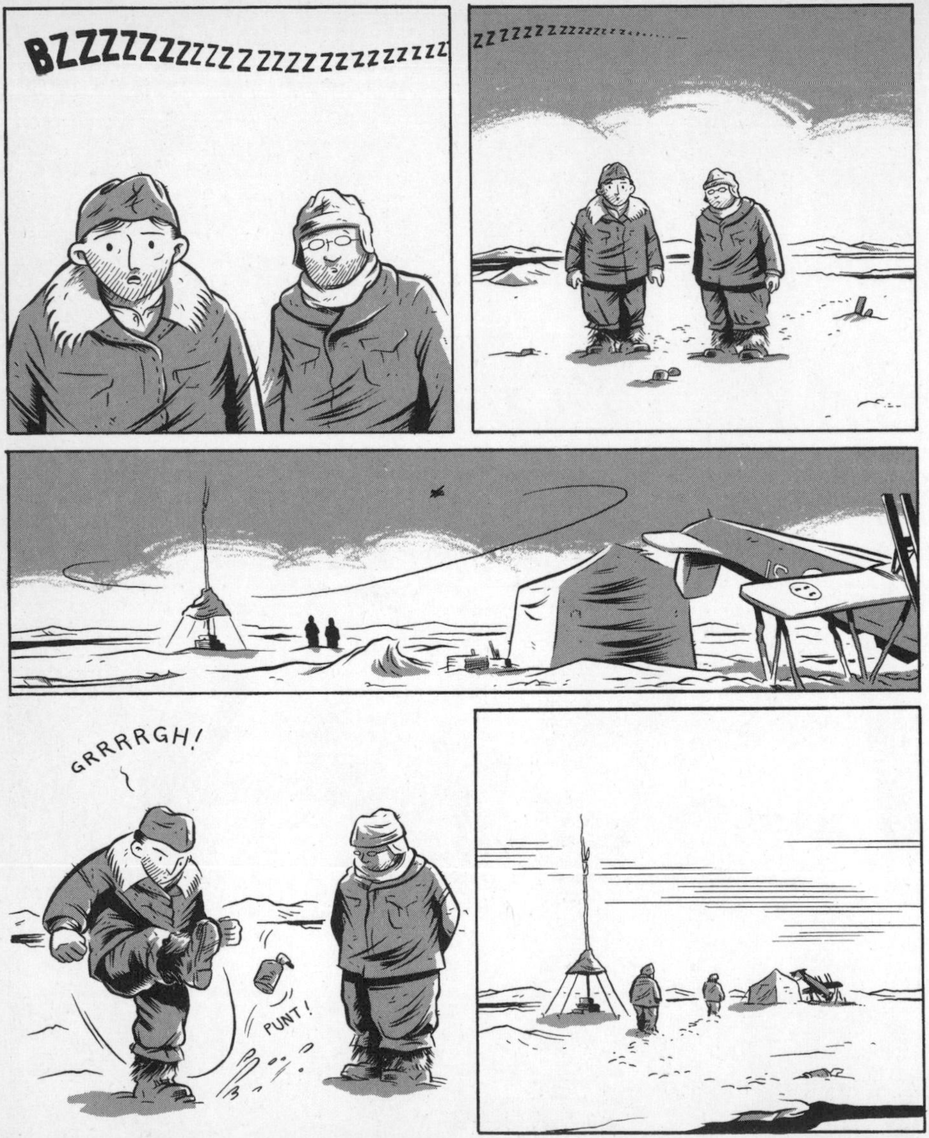
BZZZZZZZZZZZZZZZZZZZZZZZZZZ
ZZZZZZZZZZZZZZ
GRRRRGH!
PUNT!

V

Release

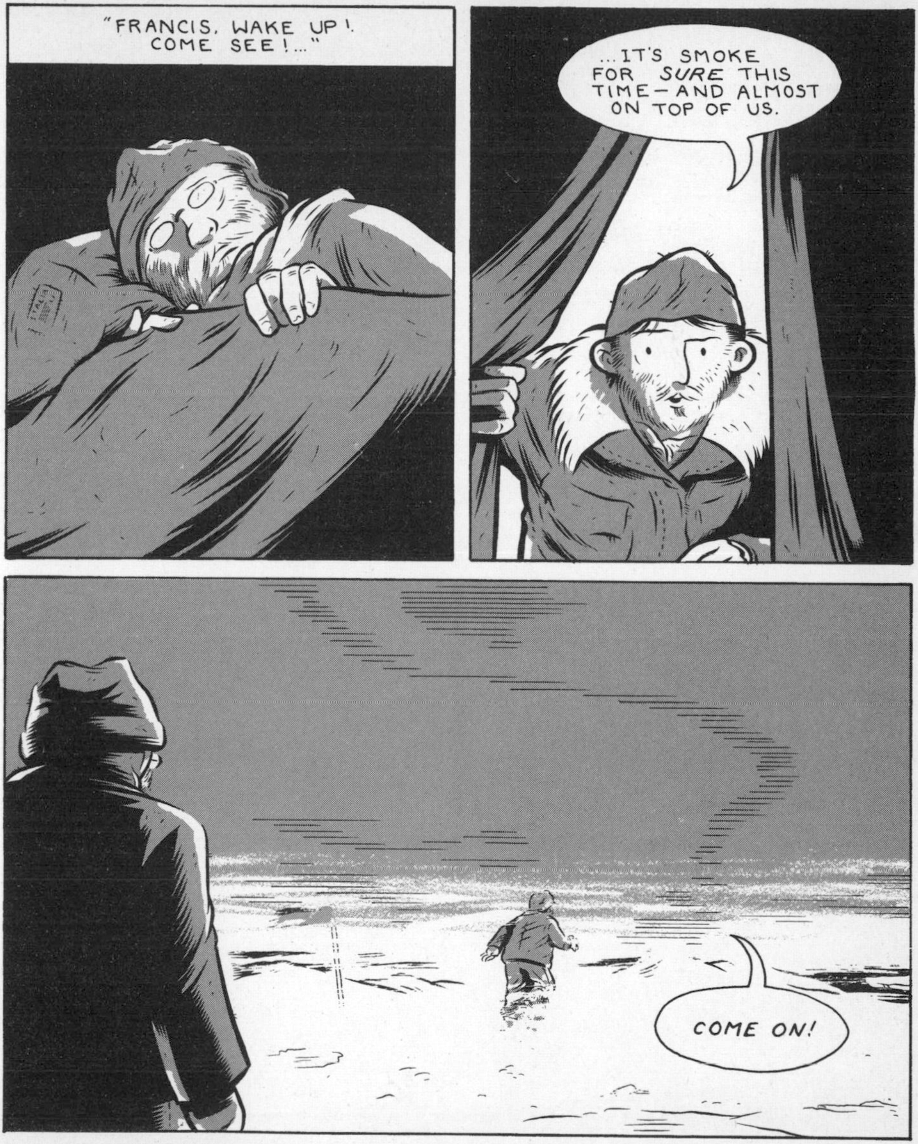
"FRANCIS. WAKE UP!
COME SEE!..."
...IT'S SMOKE FOR SURE THIS TIME—AND ALMOST ON TOP OF US.
COME ON!

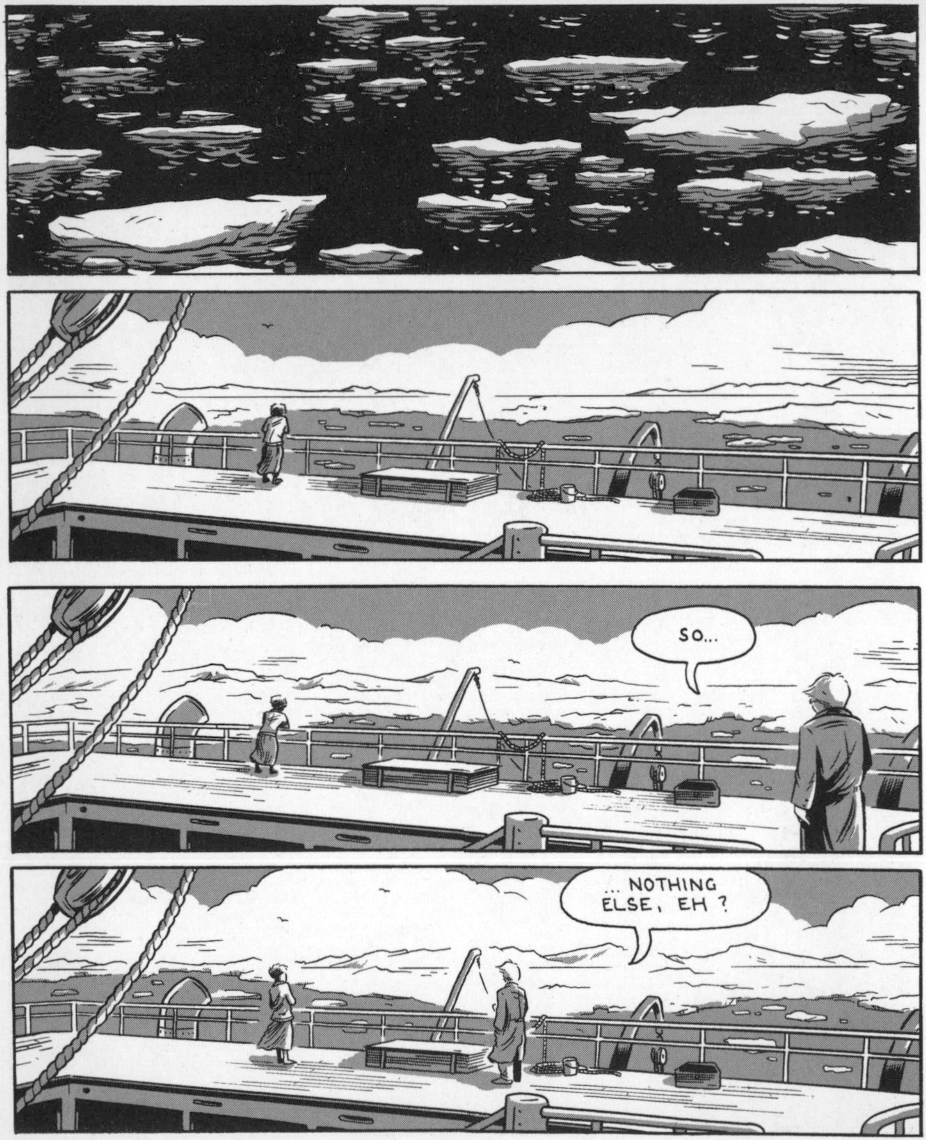
SO...
... NOTHING ELSE, EH ?

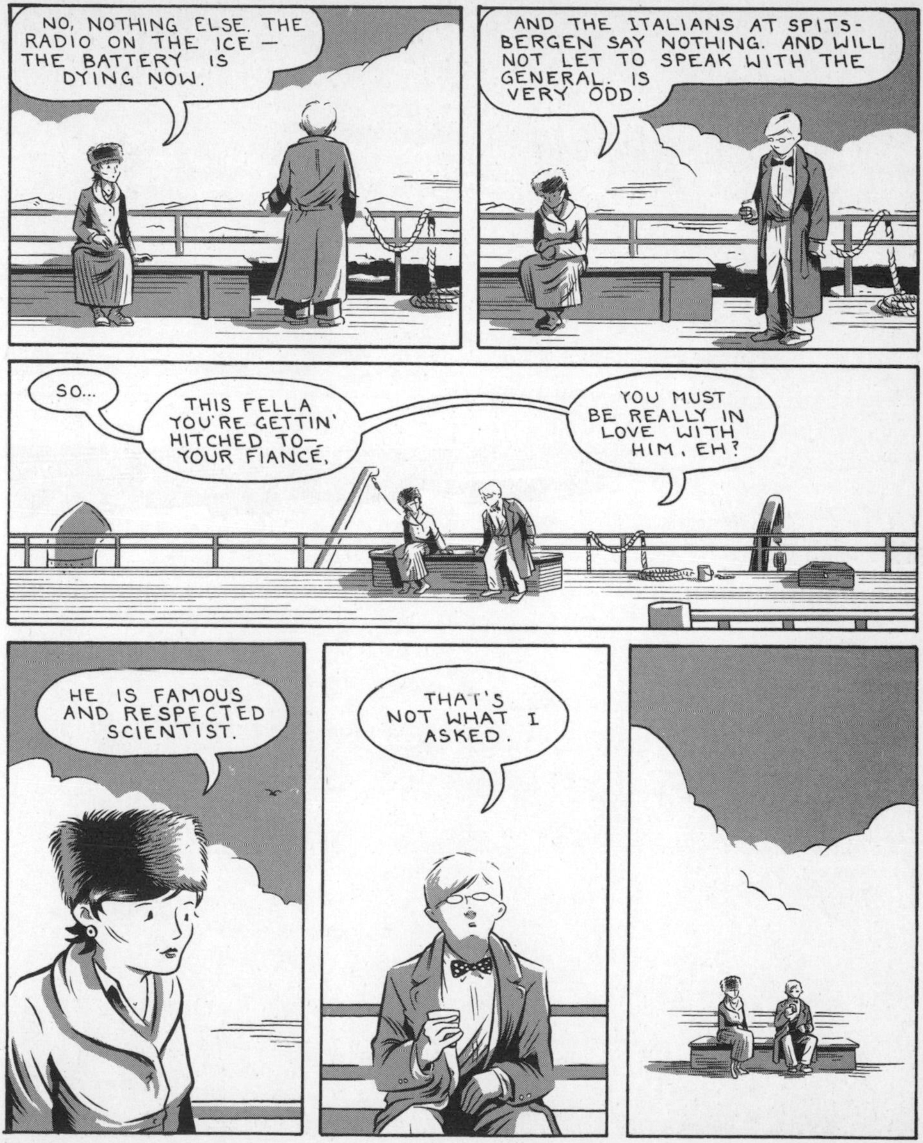
NO, NOTHING ELSE. THE RADIO ON THE ICE — THE BATTERY IS DYING NOW.
AND THE ITALIANS AT SPITS-BERGEN SAY NOTHING. AND WILL NOT LET TO SPEAK WITH THE GENERAL. IS VERY ODD.
SO...
THIS FELLA YOU'RE GETTIN' HITCHED TO— YOUR FIANCÉ,
YOU MUST BE REALLY IN LOVE WITH HIM, EH?
HE IS FAMOUS AND RESPECTED SCIENTIST.
THAT'S NOT WHAT I ASKED.

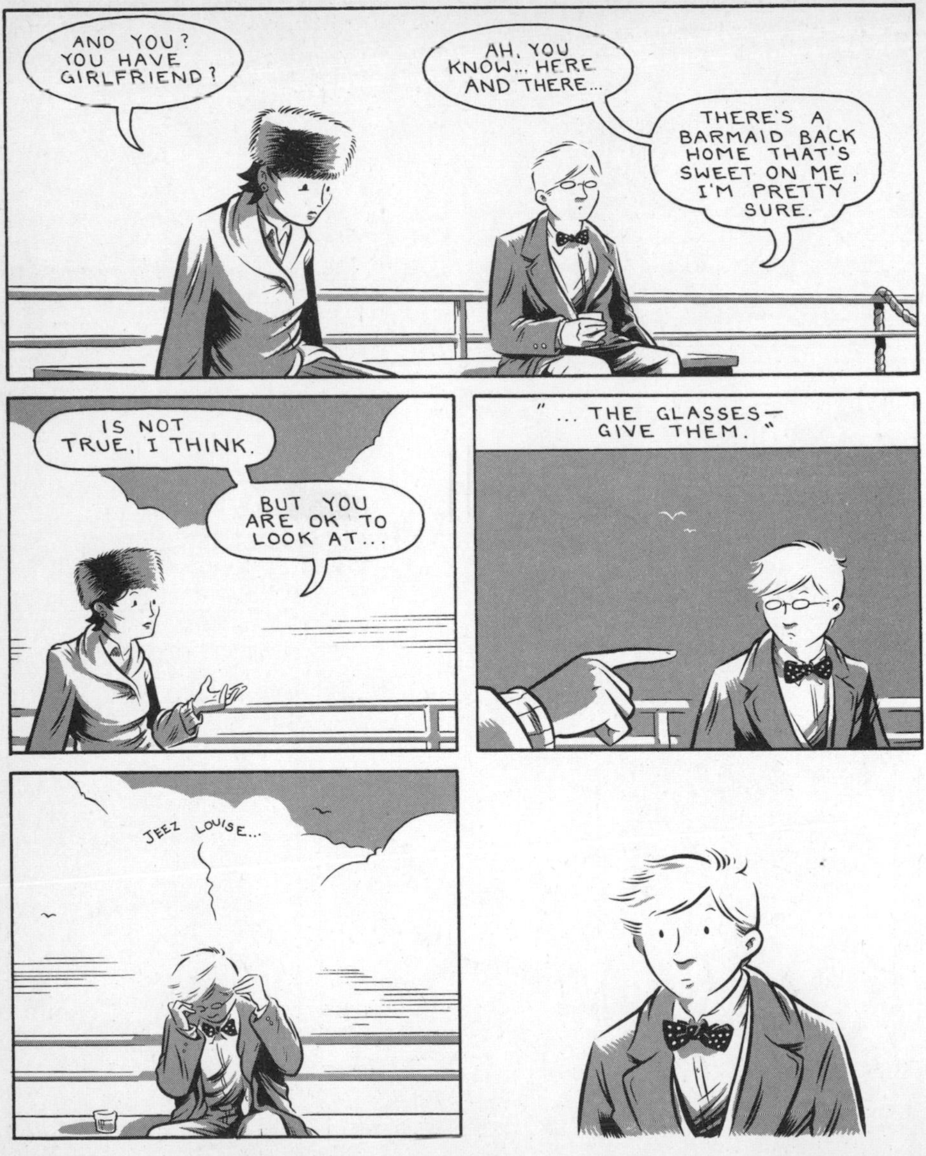
AND YOU? YOU HAVE GIRLFRIEND?
AH, YOU KNOW... HERE AND THERE...
THERE'S A BARMAID BACK HOME THAT'S SWEET ON ME, I'M PRETTY SURE.
IS NOT TRUE, I THINK.
BUT YOU ARE OK TO LOOK AT...
"... THE GLASSES— GIVE THEM."
JEEZ LOUISE...

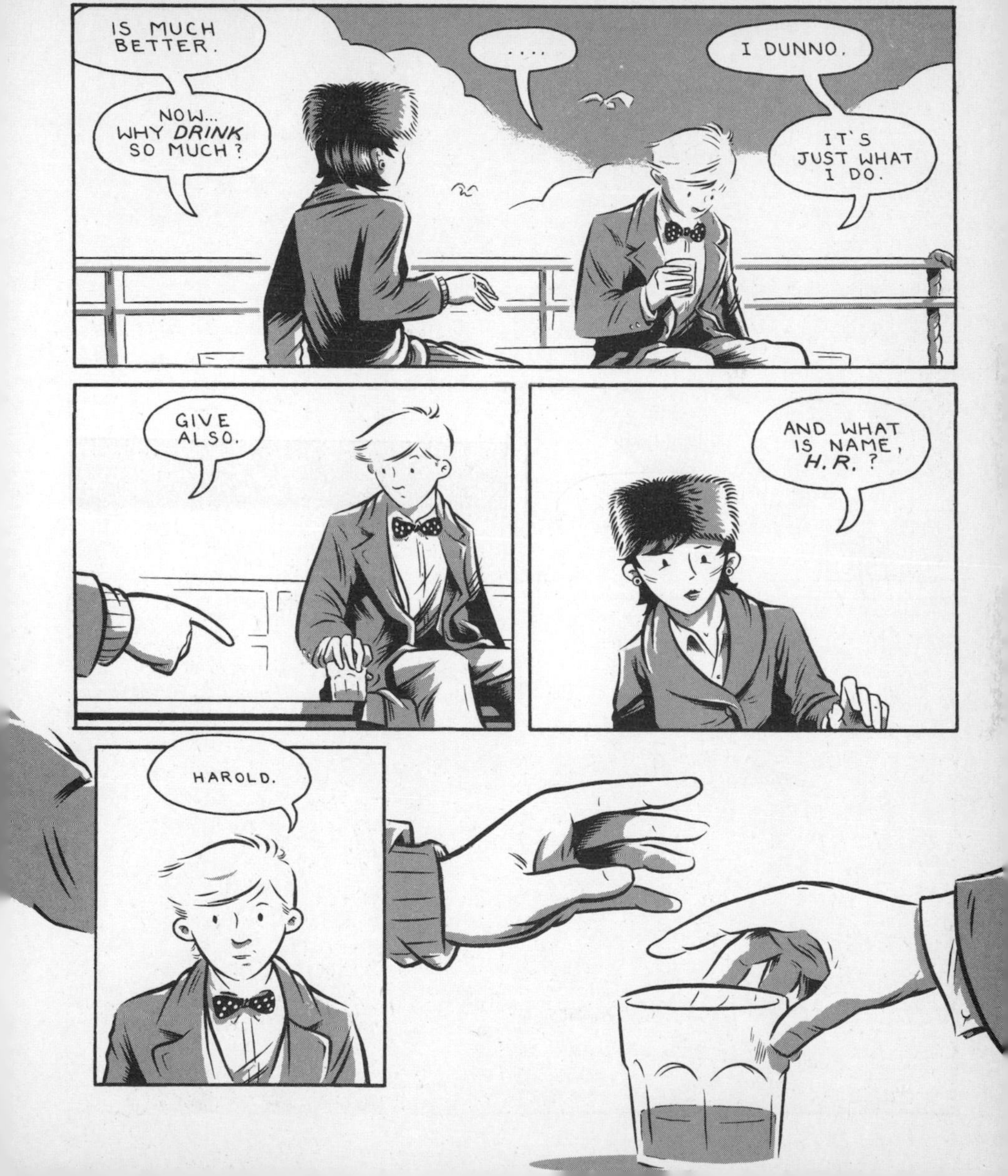
IS MUCH BETTER.
NOW... WHY DRINK SO MUCH?
....
I DUNNO.
IT'S JUST WHAT I DO.
GIVE ALSO.
AND WHAT IS NAME, H.R.?
HAROLD.

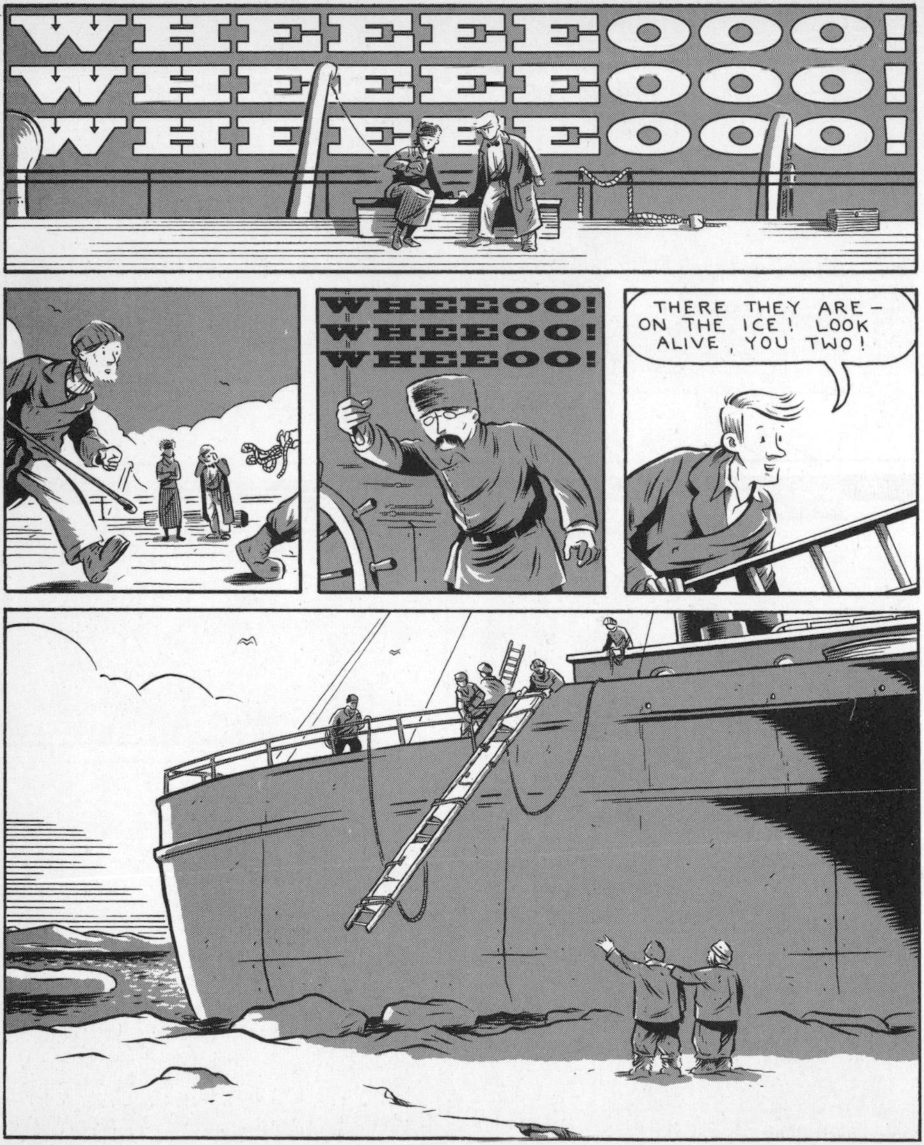
WHEEEEEOOO!
WHEEEEEOOO!
WHEEEEEOOO!
WHEEEOO!
WHEEEOO!
WHEEEOO!
THERE THEY ARE – ON THE ICE! LOOK ALIVE, YOU TWO!

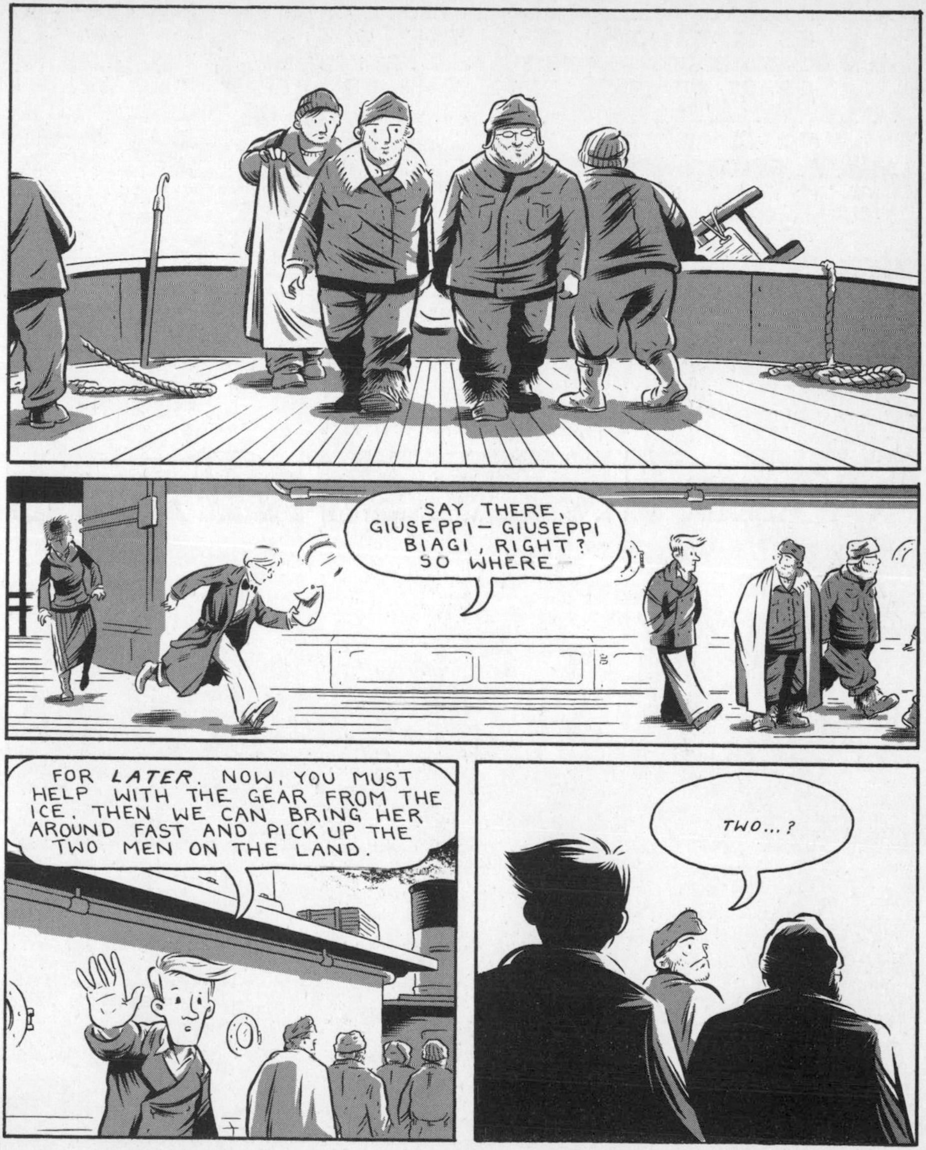
SAY THERE, GIUSEPPI– GIUSEPPI BIAGI, RIGHT? SO WHERE–
FOR *LATER*. NOW, YOU MUST HELP WITH THE GEAR FROM THE ICE. THEN WE CAN BRING HER AROUND FAST AND PICK UP THE TWO MEN ON THE LAND.
TWO...?

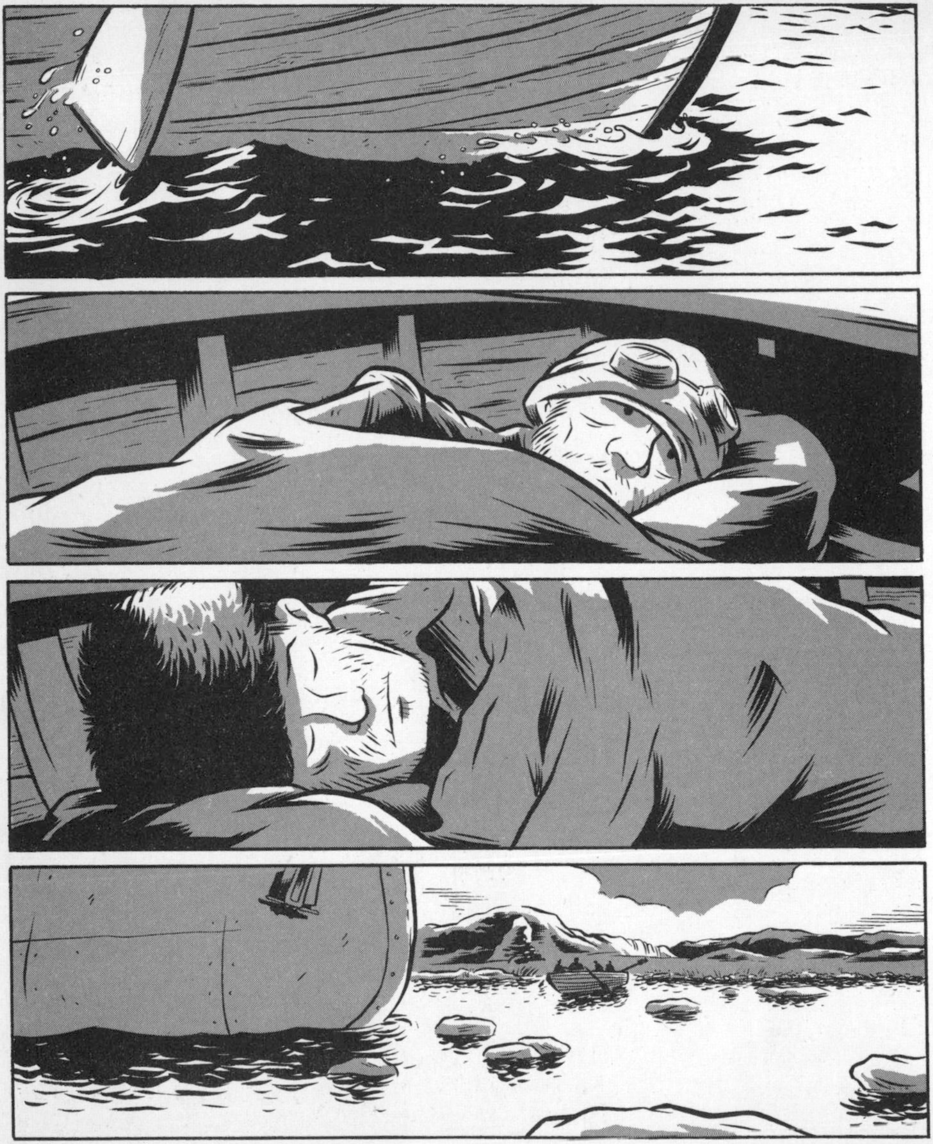

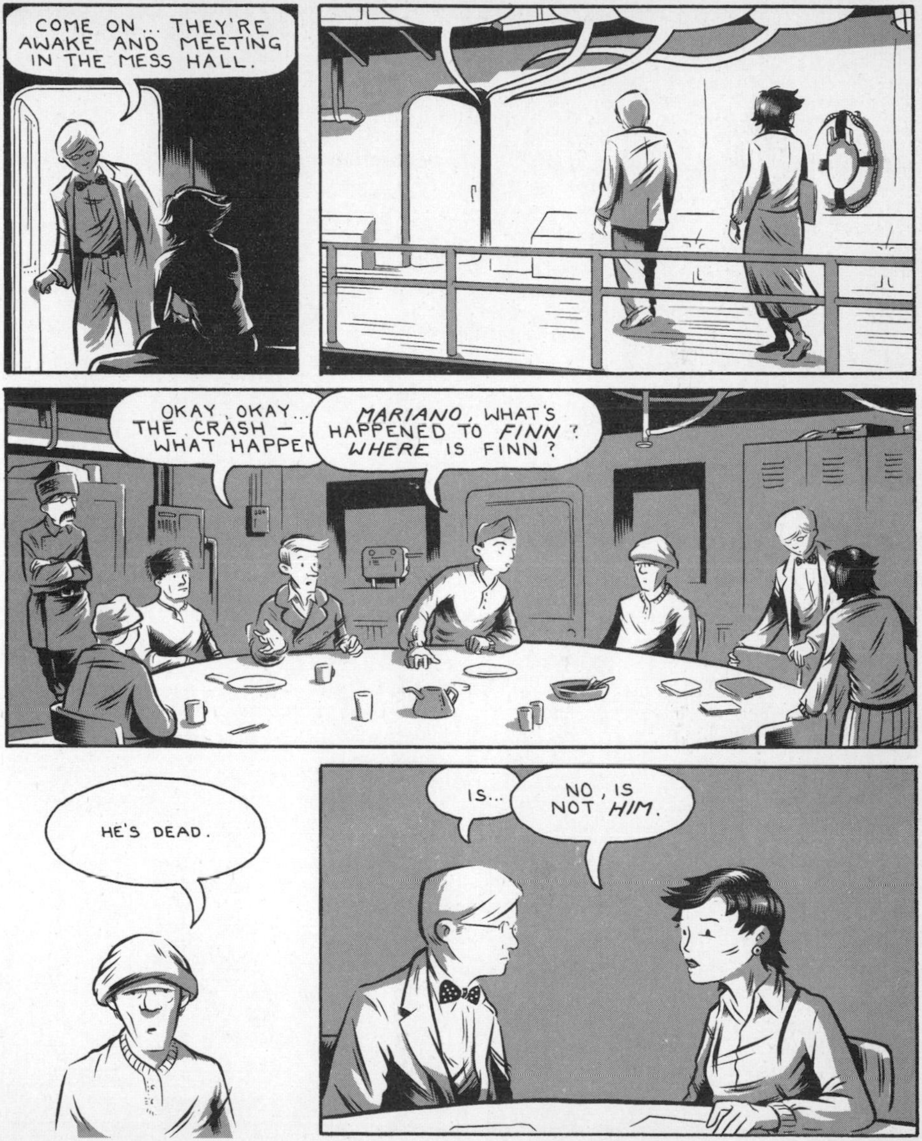
COME ON... THEY'RE AWAKE AND MEETING IN THE MESS HALL.
OKAY, OKAY... THE CRASH — WHAT HAPPEN
MARIANO, WHAT'S HAPPENED TO FINN? WHERE IS FINN?
HE'S DEAD.
IS...
NO, IS NOT HIM.

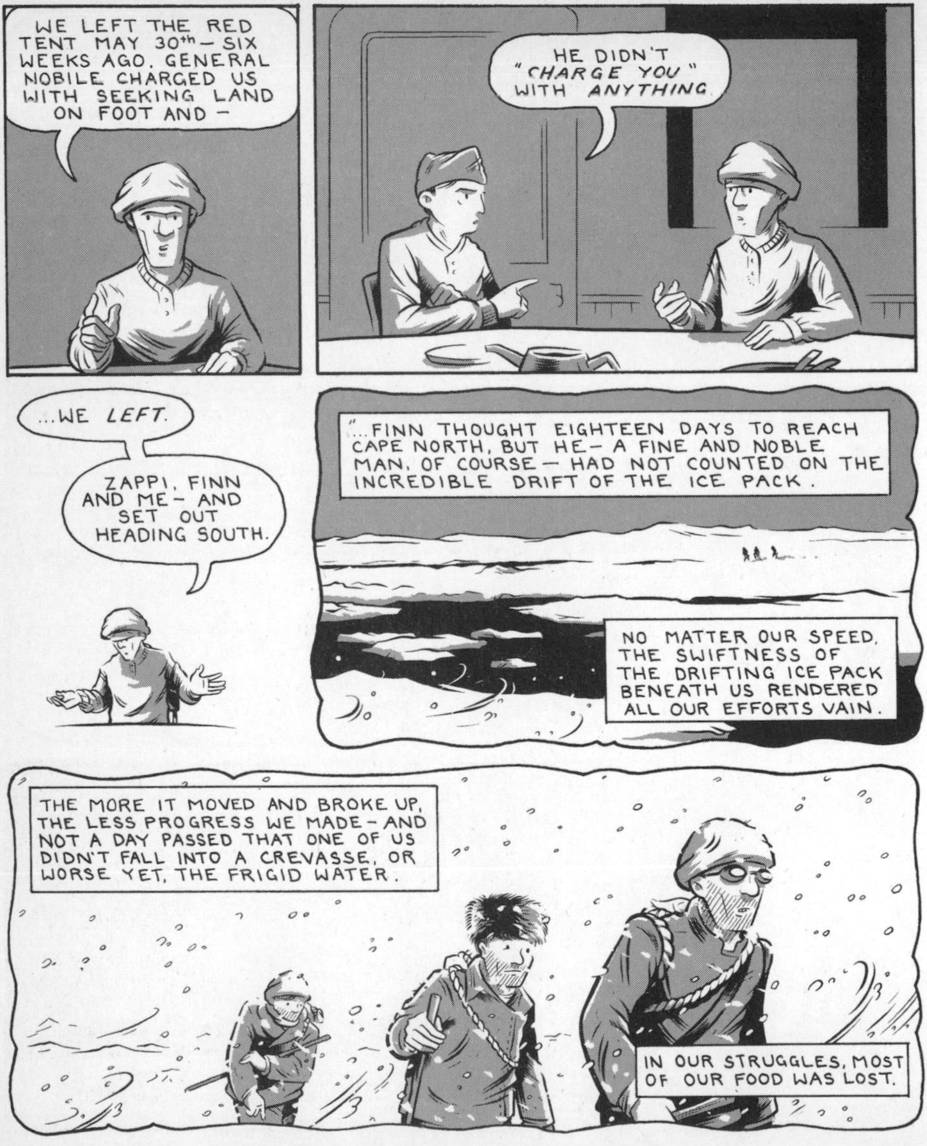
WE LEFT THE RED TENT MAY 30th — SIX WEEKS AGO. GENERAL NOBILE CHARGED US WITH SEEKING LAND ON FOOT AND —
HE DIDN'T "CHARGE YOU" WITH ANYTHING.
...WE LEFT.
ZAPPI, FINN AND ME — AND SET OUT HEADING SOUTH.
"...FINN THOUGHT EIGHTEEN DAYS TO REACH CAPE NORTH, BUT HE — A FINE AND NOBLE MAN, OF COURSE — HAD NOT COUNTED ON THE INCREDIBLE DRIFT OF THE ICE PACK.
NO MATTER OUR SPEED, THE SWIFTNESS OF THE DRIFTING ICE PACK BENEATH US RENDERED ALL OUR EFFORTS VAIN.
THE MORE IT MOVED AND BROKE UP, THE LESS PROGRESS WE MADE — AND NOT A DAY PASSED THAT ONE OF US DIDN'T FALL INTO A CREVASSE, OR WORSE YET, THE FRIGID WATER.
IN OUR STRUGGLES, MOST OF OUR FOOD WAS LOST.

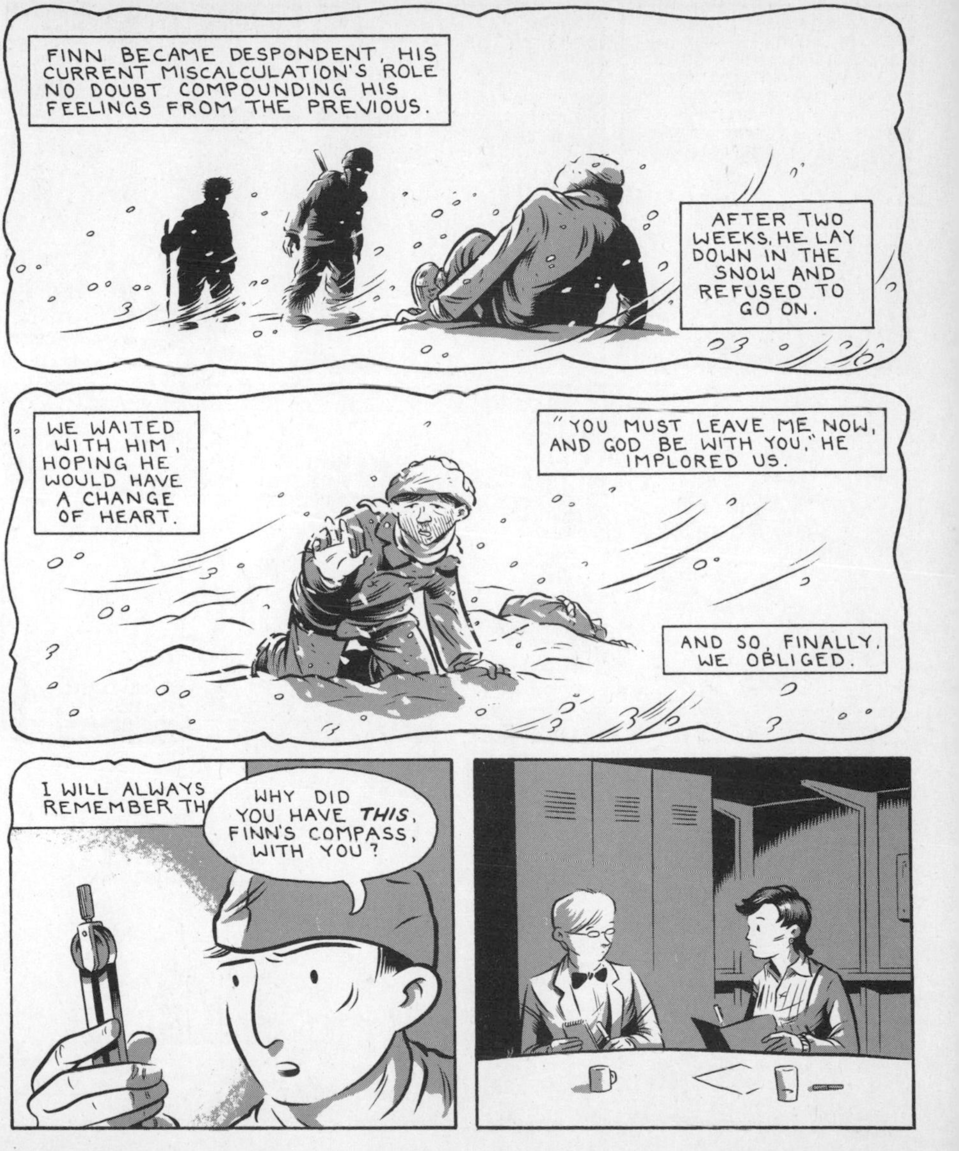
FINN BECAME DESPONDENT, HIS CURRENT MISCALCULATION'S ROLE NO DOUBT COMPOUNDING HIS FEELINGS FROM THE PREVIOUS.
AFTER TWO WEEKS, HE LAY DOWN IN THE SNOW AND REFUSED TO GO ON.
WE WAITED WITH HIM, HOPING HE WOULD HAVE A CHANGE OF HEART.
"YOU MUST LEAVE ME NOW, AND GOD BE WITH YOU," HE IMPLORED US.
AND SO, FINALLY, WE OBLIGED.
I WILL ALWAYS REMEMBER TH
WHY DID YOU HAVE THIS, FINN'S COMPASS, WITH YOU?

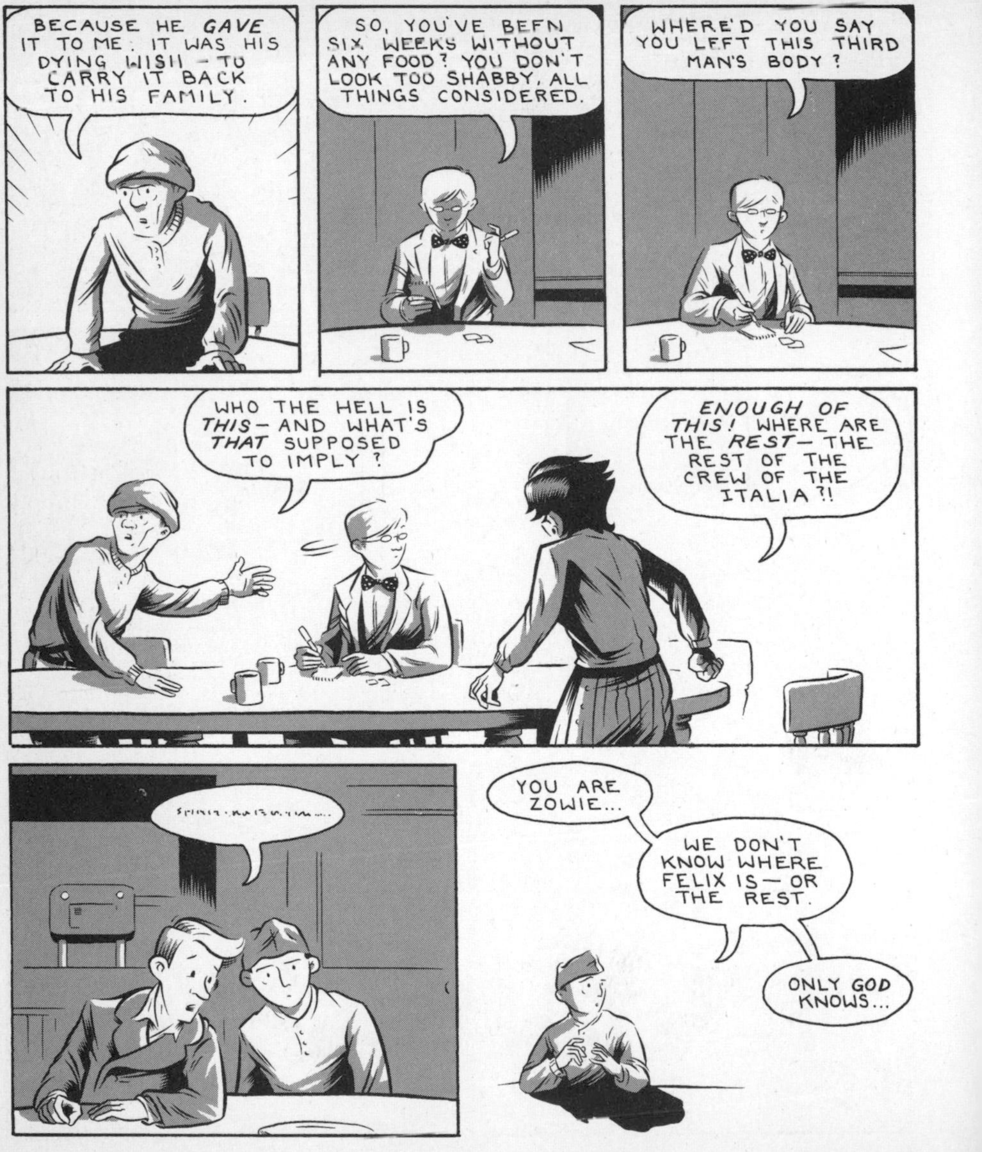
BECAUSE HE GAVE IT TO ME: IT WAS HIS DYING WISH — TO CARRY IT BACK TO HIS FAMILY.
SO, YOU'VE BEEN SIX WEEKS WITHOUT ANY FOOD? YOU DON'T LOOK TOO SHABBY, ALL THINGS CONSIDERED.
WHERE'D YOU SAY YOU LEFT THIS THIRD MAN'S BODY?
WHO THE HELL IS THIS — AND WHAT'S THAT SUPPOSED TO IMPLY?
ENOUGH OF THIS! WHERE ARE THE REST — THE REST OF THE CREW OF THE ITALIA?!
YOU ARE ZOWIE...
WE DON'T KNOW WHERE FELIX IS — OR THE REST.
ONLY GOD KNOWS...

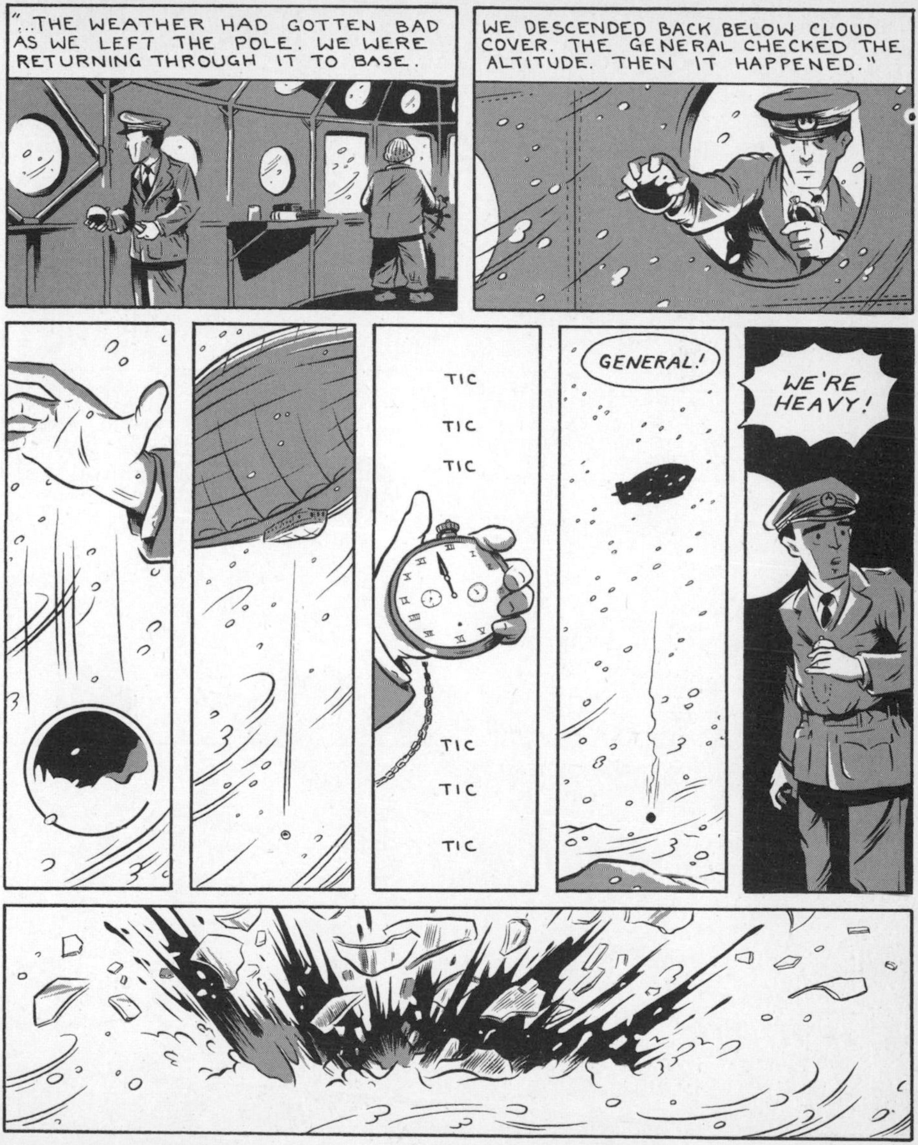
"...THE WEATHER HAD GOTTEN BAD AS WE LEFT THE POLE. WE WERE RETURNING THROUGH IT TO BASE.
WE DESCENDED BACK BELOW CLOUD COVER. THE GENERAL CHECKED THE ALTITUDE. THEN IT HAPPENED."
TIC
TIC
TIC
TIC
TIC
TIC
GENERAL!
WE'RE HEAVY!

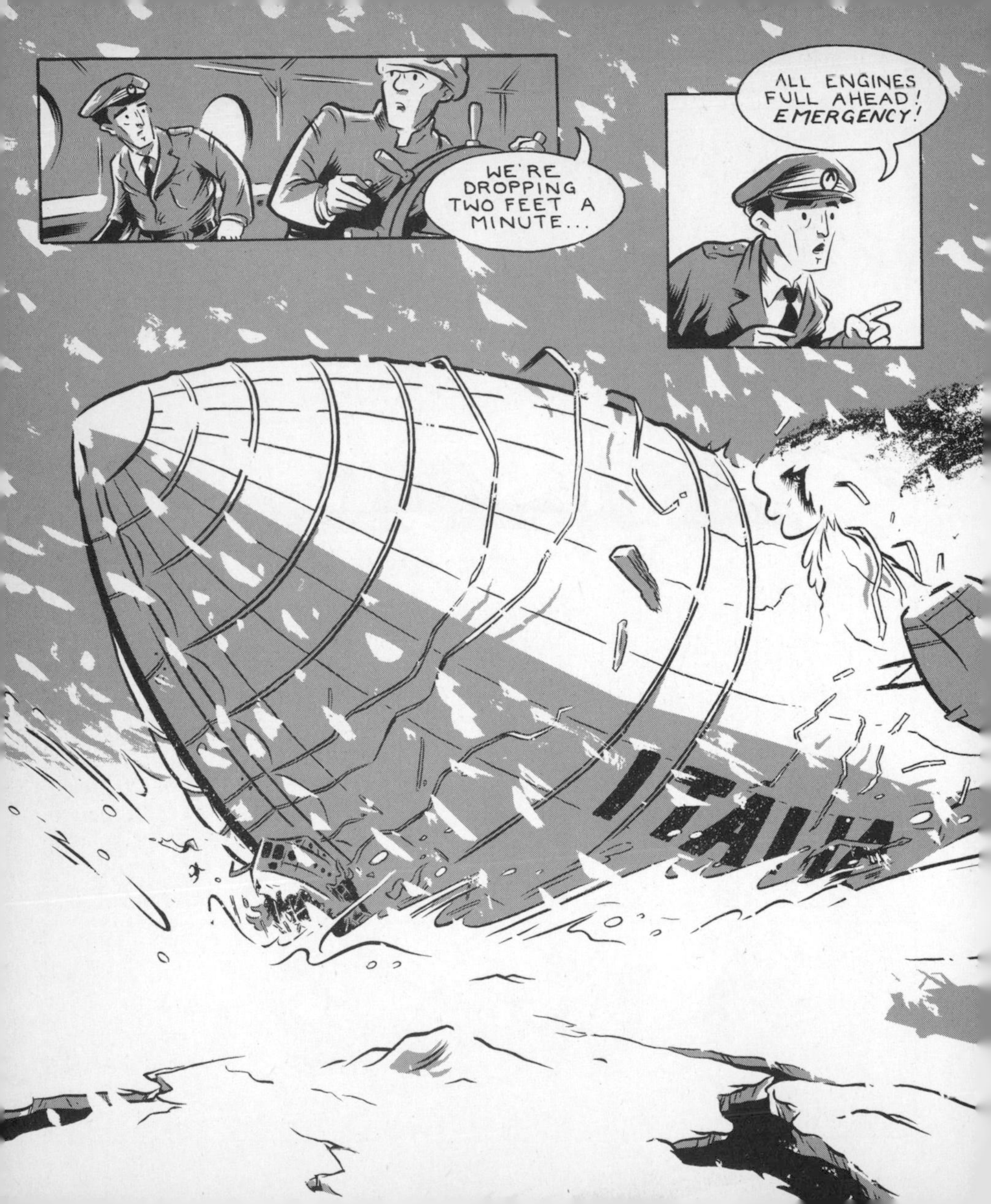
WE'RE DROPPING TWO FEET A MINUTE...
ALL ENGINES FULL AHEAD! EMERGENCY!
ITALIA

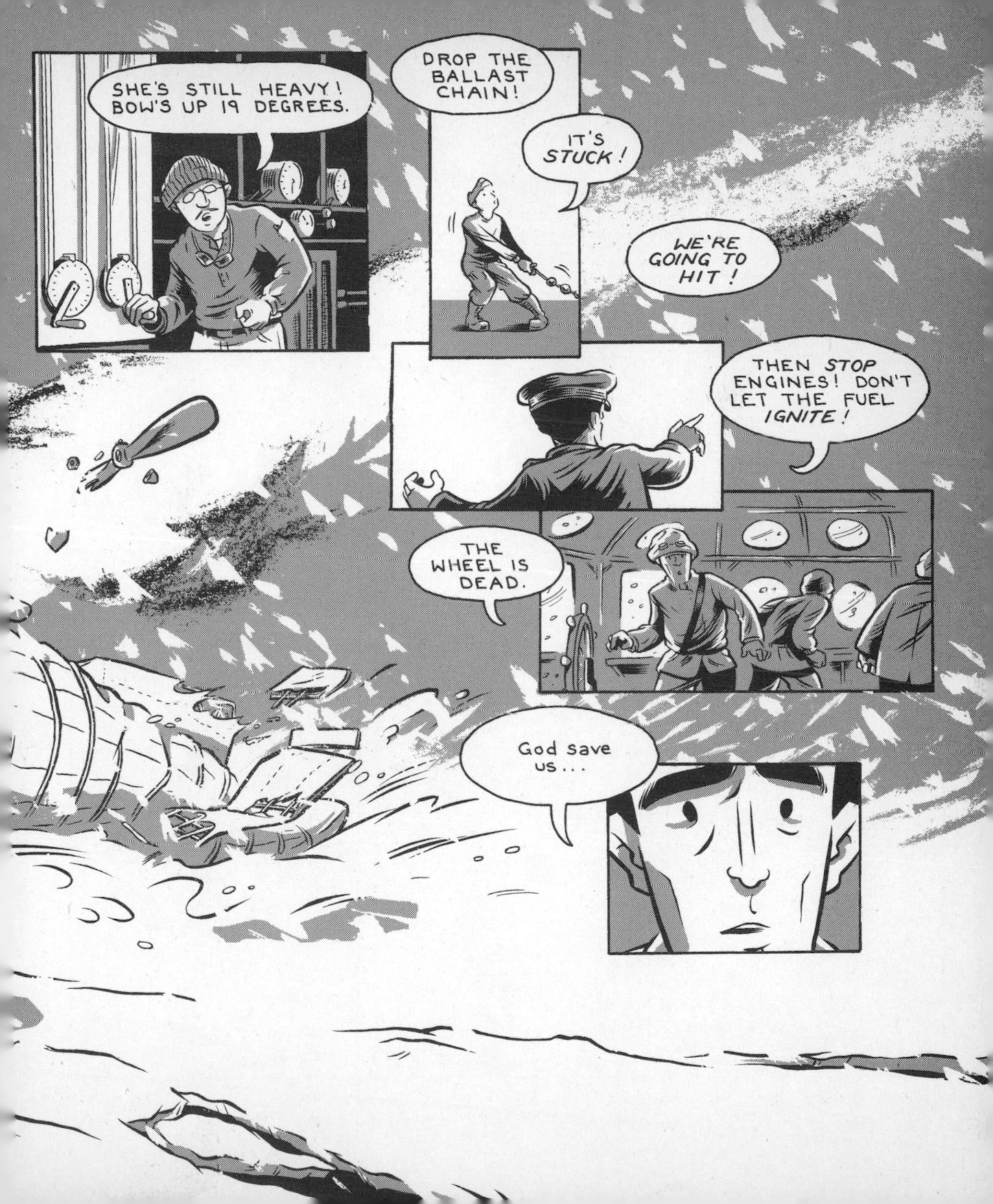
SHE'S STILL HEAVY! BOW'S UP 19 DEGREES.
DROP THE BALLAST CHAIN!
IT'S STUCK!
WE'RE GOING TO HIT!
THEN STOP ENGINES! DON'T LET THE FUEL IGNITE!
THE WHEEL IS DEAD.
God save us...

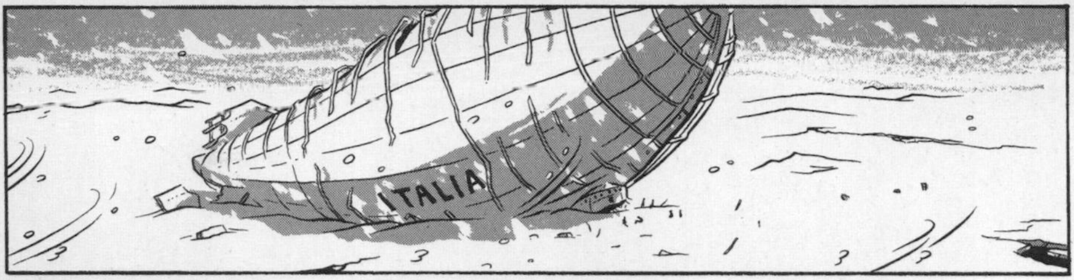
ITALIA

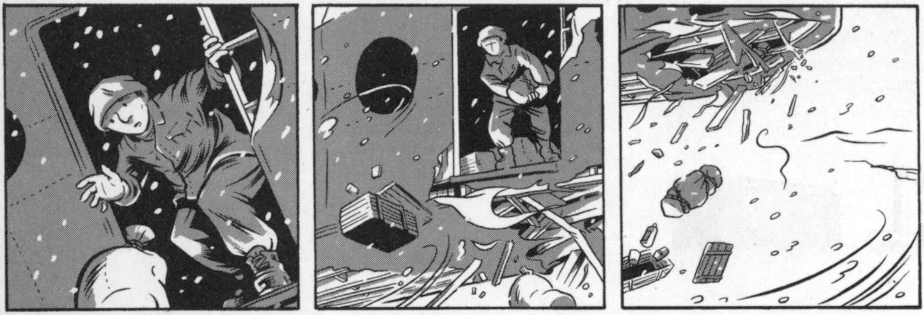

THE GONDOLA HAD SMASHED OPEN AND THE CHIEF ENGINEER, ETTORE, BEGAN THROWING SUPPLIES OUT ONTO THE ICE.

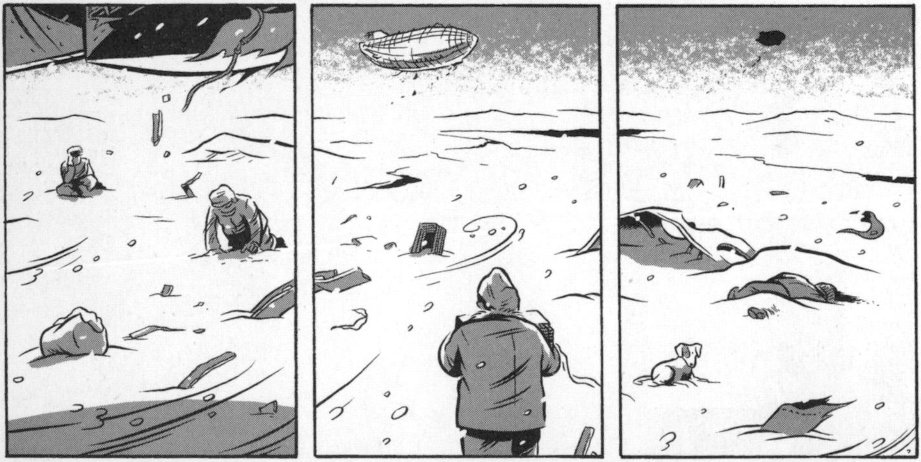

RELEASED OF THIS WEIGHT, THOUGH, THE ENVELOPE LIFTED FREE OF THE ICE AND DRIFTED AWAY BEFORE OUR EYES...

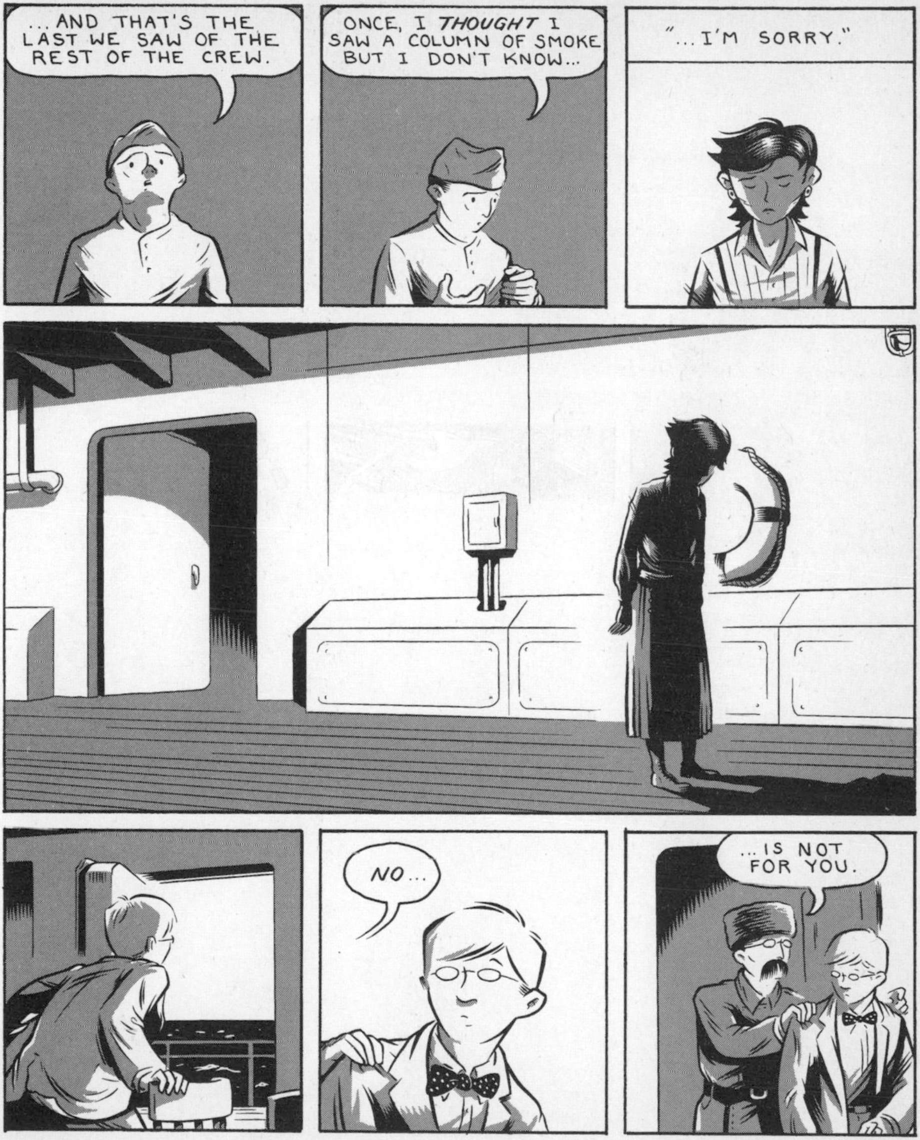
...AND THAT'S THE LAST WE SAW OF THE REST OF THE CREW.
ONCE, I *THOUGHT* I SAW A COLUMN OF SMOKE BUT I DON'T KNOW...
"...I'M SORRY."
NO...
...IS NOT FOR YOU.

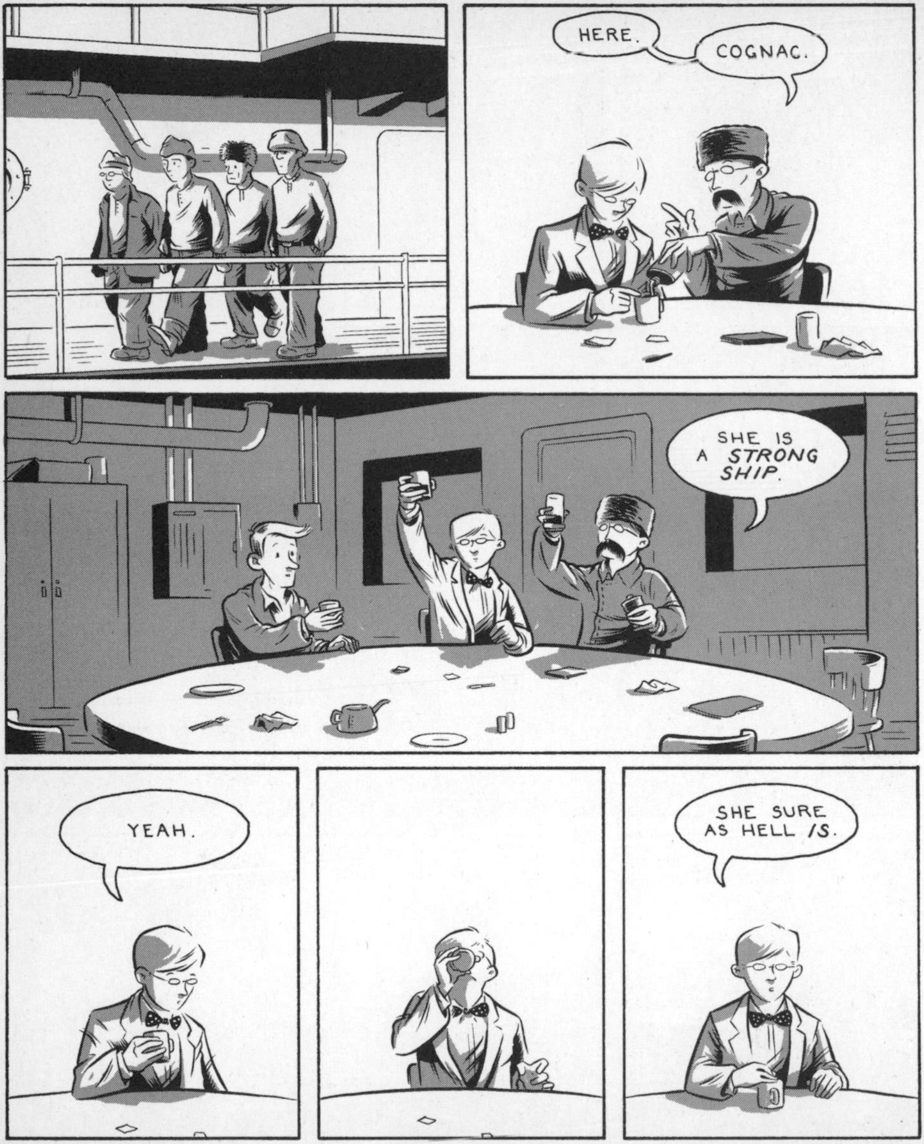
HERE.
COGNAC.
SHE IS A *STRONG* *SHIP*.
YEAH.
SHE SURE AS HELL *IS*.

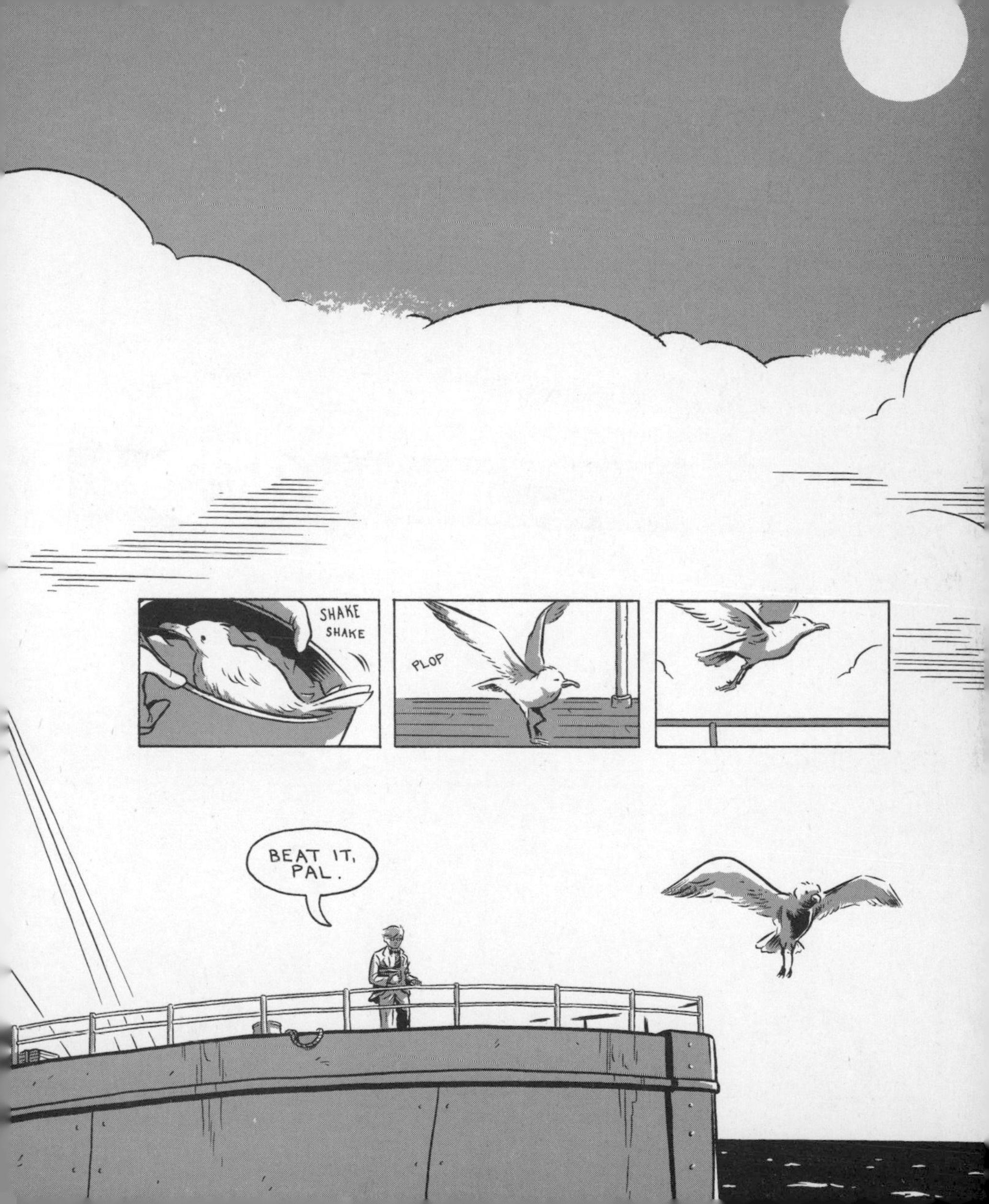
SHAKE
SHAKE
PLOP
BEAT IT, PAL.

Midnight Sun is a work of fiction. This much is fact, though: On May 25th, 1928, on her way back from the North Pole, the airship *Italia* crashed on the arctic ice pack, killing one crewman on impact, stranding nine and carrying off the remaining six. Nearly seven weeks later, eight of the men were rescued by the *Krassin*, a Russian icebreaker. The ninth had died trekking for help on foot.

Clearly, even in this small bit of basic information, *Midnight Sun* is at odds with the historical "stage" on which its characters operate. Inevitably then, one asks, "How much of *Midnight Sun* is true?" If by "true" one means "factual," the answer is: Not a whole lot.

It's a cliché certainly, but an accurate one in the case of the *Italia* disaster: Truth *is* stranger than fiction—and a complete, factual dramatization of the bizarre and fascinating events surrounding Nobile's second expedition to the Pole would extend well beyond the scope of a humble hundred-and-change page graphic novel. Even ignoring the political elements of the tale—how Nobile and his pursuits conflicted with the emerging Fascist government in Italy before and after the expedition—the crash and eventual rescue of the crew of the *Italia* ultimately involved five countries, twenty-two airplanes, eighteen sea vessels and over 1500 men. A number of would-be rescuers died in the attempt to reach Nobile and his men, among them the famous Norwegian explorer Roald Amundsen, whose demise would further a pre-existing friction between Norway and Italy regarding a previous arctic airship expedition mounted by Amundsen but piloted by Nobile.

No, *Midnight Sun* is a work of fiction, albeit one that takes as its starting point a real event from history. Of the book's two main characters, H.R. and Biagi, the former is entirely fictional and the latter shares only his name and occupation (radio operator) with his real-life counterpart. Further, a quick count of the real-life crew and the fictional crew from the book show a narrative trimming down of the cast of characters. Some crewmen are entirely absent, others merged together, and none—save only Nobile—bear any visual resemblance to their historical counterparts.

A laundry list of story alterations would too extensive for inclusion here, but I'll mention two of the most notable.

First, on communication: A good story requires the author to slowly dole out bits and pieces of information as the story unfolds, and thus I've generally diminished the quantity and substance of radio communications throughout *Midnight Sun*. Portable two-way radio was a fairly new technology at the time and often unreliable, but once radio contact was established, the location and number of the remaining men was known. Second, I have "merged" two significant events together—the story of the party on foot (which I have shown in the book) and the story of an attempted rescue by dog sled (which I have not). It was in fact the sled group who were first spotted from the *Krassin*, but left temporarily in the interest of first getting the crewmen off the disintegrating ice. The two surviving men traveling on foot were picked up a day before the men at the red tent.

Given both the high drama and the historical significance of the *Italia* disaster (not to mention its being front page news for nearly two months world-wide), it's surprising how little information is available for one seeking out the true story of the *Italia*. Many involved with the incident, surviving crewmen and rescuers alike, wrote books on the subject after the fact, but only a small subset of those were published in English, and none remain in print today. Fortunately though, there are two more-recent books on the event, both of which are readily available. One is *Disaster at the Pole: The Crash of the Airship Italia* by Wilbur Cross, which is currently in print, and the other is *Ice Crash* by Alexander McKee, which can be easily be found used online. I recommend that the truly curious read both books, as each author has a different take on the story, particularly some of the more controversial elements thereof.

My intention with *Midnight Sun* was simply to tell a good story, and where that goal butted up against the facts, the tale won out (disgruntled history buffs can send hate mail to the email address supplied below). I hope, though, that my work has preserved if not the *facts* behind the real-life events, then the *truth* behind them: that in our affairs— whether as mundane as a simple attraction between two people, or a life and death struggle for survival—it is fate with which we ultimately vie, and against which the human spirit must prevail, or else be prevailed upon. - *Ben Towle*

benzilla@benzilla.com
www.benzilla.com